Narrative Is Everything

Narrative Is Everything

The ABT Framework and Narrative Evolution

Randy Olson

Narrative Is Everything:
The ABT Framework and Narrative Evolution
Randy Olson

Cover and interior design by Dante Cervantes
Edited by Adina Yoffie

ISBN: 9781072232575

Library of Congress Control Number:2019907274

TABLE OF CONTENTS

	INTRODUCTION	1
1	BUSINESS - Branding is ABT	35
2	POLITICS - Messaging is ABT	59
3	ENTERTAINMENT - Story is ABT	123
4	SCIENCE - Scientific Method is ABT	177
5	RELIGION - The Double-Edged Sword	205
6	NARRATIVE SELECTION - The Future	215

APPENDIX 1 - Defining "Narrative" Versus "Story" 245

APPENDIX 2 - Story Circles Narrative Training   251

APPENDIX 3 - Examples of Narrative Analysis   273

ACKNOWLEDGEMENTS   335

A Note About This Book

This book is just the nuts and bolts. If you want the detailed academic version of the ABT Framework read my 2015 book Houston, We Have a Narrative. It's published by University of Chicago Press, which is … an academic press.

I wrote this book initially for our Story Circles Narrative Training program as kind of a manual, but then I decided to make it more widely available. It's still somewhat of a work in progress, so please don't hesitate to send me notes and thoughts—all input is appreciated.

- Randy Olson (rolson@usc.edu), May, 2019

Therefore

ABT—it's all about ABT—or so my friend asserts,
Author, consultant to corporations, keynoters,
This his mantra—ABT: And, But, Therefore—
Just as ii—V—1 in jazz,
A squared plus B squared equals C squared,
The Trinity. E equals MC squared.
Triune truths. Essence precedes existence.
But back to ABT:

And, we look out upon our world,
And, know it was once fecund, diverse, intact:
But, icebergs are melting, coral reefs whitening,
But, arable land vanishing, water for sale.
Therefore, fellow inhabitants, what shall we do?
Therefore, my dears, what on earth shall we do?

- Paul Cummins, 2018

INTRODUCTION

"We have nothing to fear but boredom itself."
- Not F.D.R.

This book is about a new approach to communication. It's useful on two levels.

At the practical level it introduces you to the ABT Framework—the one-sentence template involving the three words And, But, Therefore. If you're interested only in improving your communication skills, it will provide plenty of help.

At this point the ABT Framework is more than just a "neat trick." We've been running our Story Circles Narrative Training program (which is built around the ABT Framework) for five years, with a range of government agencies, including the National Park Service, the US Department of Agriculture, the US Fish and Wildlife Service, the National Institutes of Health and a number of universities. We're approaching 500 graduates, and we recently posted over 100 of their stories of how they are using the training in the real world. Which means there is a very practical aspect to what is in this book.

But on the larger, grander scale, the book is about a whole new approach to understanding how human culture changes over time. At the core is what I have termed "narrative selection." It combines the simplest elements of what neurophysiologists are learning about the brain with what Hollywood has learned over the past century about narrative structure.

For this pulling together of evolutionary theory and Hollywood knowledge, I ask you to keep in mind two things. First, I earned my PhD in evolutionary biology from Harvard University long ago, which gave me an evolutionary perspective on the world. Second, I left a tenured professorship of biology to spend 25 years in and around Hollywood, learning what I could about narrative.

My learning about evolutionary biology began in my late teens, before my brain had completed its development. The result is a view of life through the prism of "evolution by means of natural selection," about which Charles Darwin famously said, "There is grandeur."

Here's one simple example of what I mean about my view of the world: In our first semester of film school we had to take a wonderful class on the history of silent cinema. I was 38 years old, having just departed my science career. For my term paper I wrote an essay comparing the early oddball, one-and-done forms of silent movies to the early oddball, one-and-done forms of life seen in Cambrian fossils from over a half billion years ago.

I compared the bizarre silent movie *The Passion of Joan of Arc*, which had more close-ups of faces than any movie since, to the bizarre Cambrian fossil Hallucigenia, which had a form never seen since. (It looks like a cross between a hair braid and a picket fence; thus its name.)

TWO FORMS NEVER SEEN AGAIN. The excessive close-ups of faces in *The Passion of Joan of Arc* and the spiny Hallucigenia from the Cambrian period.

That was 25 years ago. The film professor loved it and gave me an "A"; he had never had his beloved silent films compared to ancient life forms. That's how I view the world: through the prism of evolution.

And so that's what I ask you to keep in mind as you read this book: It's a different approach to communication. I'm showing how the process of "narrative selection" has repeatedly produced the ABT narrative structure throughout our culture—from business to politics to entertainment to science to religion.

You can think of it this way: DNA is the universal element that natural selection has produced in living creatures. The ABT is the universal element that narrative selection has produced in human culture.

THEREFORE ... THE ABT IS THE NUCLEUS OF NARRATIVE

Let me tell you how the ABT works. In 2001, my longtime marine-biologist colleague and hero Dr. Jeremy Jackson contacted me about the challenges he faced with communication. He had just published a powerful scientific paper that had made the cover of the most important scientific publication in the US, Science magazine. He wanted help with communicating his findings to a broader, non-science audience.

His paper was about the collapse of ocean ecosystems. In it he explained how we are destroying the oceans through pollution and over-fishing. He said to me, "We have all the research we need and we know how to save the oceans, but what we don't have is action."

What this meant is that he had figured out his setup (the oceans), had figured out the problem (we're killing them) and now wanted to focus on implementing the solution (motivating people to stop bad practices). In the language I would eventually formulate, he knew his AND, he knew his BUT, he was now looking to implement his THEREFORE.

This is the ABT. It's the nucleus of narrative, and narrative is the heart of humanity.

The THEREFORE is what everybody wants these days. We know our world, we know the problems, what's needed is the THEREFORE—the actions that are actually going to fix the problems.

We want this in all facets of life. In business, we want the THEREFORE of how your product will solve the problems of our daily lives. In politics we want the THEREFORE of how your agenda is going to solve the problems in our society. In entertainment we want the THEREFORE of how your media is going to solve the problem of keeping us entertained. In science we want the THEREFORE of how your research is going to make our lives better. And in religion ... we want the THEREFORE of what it all means.

THEREFORE ... the title of this book—narrative is indeed everything. And, yes, I know this starts to sound like I think the ABT is a hammer and everything is a nail. All I can say to that is, "could be"; I'll let you decide at the end of our journey through the ABT Framework.

FROM NATURAL SELECTION TO NARRATIVE SELECTION

What I am presenting is the synthesis of my 40-year journey from scientist to filmmaker to "communicationeer" (can't quite find the right term for what I do now). In 1993, I left a tenured professorship of marine biology and moved to Hollywood in search of a possible golden chalice for broad communication. I found it with the ABT.

Which means it's time for an introduction. Ladies and gentlemen ...

INTRODUCING THE ABT NARRATIVE TEMPLATE

I call it the ABT Universal Narrative Template. I've been presenting it since 2012. I gave a TEDMED Talk about it in 2013 AND introduced it formally to the science world with my 2015 book Houston, We Have a Narrative (University of Chicago Press). BUT what was clear from the outset is that the ABT is present in all forms of communication.

THEREFORE it's time to show it's pretty much everywhere.

The ABT is this:

_____ AND _____ BUT _____ THEREFORE _____ .

You can use it to boil down the narrative structure of just about anything to a single sentence.

You may feel it's very familiar, AND that you even learned it in grade school, BUT in 2012, when I searched everything to do with "the ABT Template" on the internet, I found nothing, THEREFORE please consider the possibility that something so simple could have gone somewhat unnoticed, unexplored and undocumented.

Actually, the sad truth is that the philosophers of the 1800's did identify it. They were smart. But today's world has gotten cluttered with too much information, resulting in simple, structural devices being obscured and even seen as trivial because they are not cluttered and obscured themselves.

So why is the ABT important? Let's start with leadership.

NARRATIVE IS LEADERSHIP: WHY THE ABT "MATTERS"

In 2018, Forbes magazine reported on "Five Reasons Why Global Leadership Is in Crisis." They cited the 2015 "Survey of the Global Agenda" from the World Economic Forum that reported that 86% of respondents felt there is a leadership crisis in the world today.

The five causes they presented were: obsession with outcomes, linear thinking, arrogance, lack of self-awareness and lack of meaning. Nowhere in their mix is the simple problem of leaders who bore and confuse.

Notice I said "simple." And notice their elements are all fairly complicated. I'm a fan of simplicity, as you'll see throughout this book.

So the simple truth is that people follow leaders who can hold their attention. They don't follow leaders who are boring or confusing.

We're in the Information Era, and the world is awash in excess information. People are desperate for leaders who can make sense of the world. It's only logical that they would follow those who can hold their interest and not leave them lost.

And that's where the ABT enters. It's the central tool for narrative structure. Narrative structure is the central element of communication. And communication is the central element of leadership.

Ergo, ABT is leadership. That's perhaps the most important reason why the ABT is important.

HOW THE ABT BEGAN WITH CAVE PEOPLE (PROBABLY/MAYBE)

So where did the ABT start? Let's dig deep into your DNA and see if you can think back millennia. What was the first thing two cave people did as they approached each other on the plains of Africa? They communicated. Visually at first, by waving from a distance, then vocally when they got close.

What were the first significant things they said? We can never know, but my good friend and fellow ABT explorer Park Howell, host of *The Business of Story* podcast, has a wild guess.

He says they began with agreement. One cave man, let's call him Creb (drawing on the old *Clan of the Cave Bear* series), began signaling to the cave woman, Ayla. As Creb pointed to the distant hills and made the sign of a wildebeest, Ayla conveyed her understanding by saying, "Unh-hunh, unh-hunh, unh hunh." They agreed he had been hunting.

Creb conveyed a few more details until Ayla was starting to get bored. But then Creb put his fingers in front of his mouth, imitating a saber-toothed cat. Ayla responded with, "Uh oh."

Creb started to walk away, but Ayla grabbed him. She needed to know what happened with the saber-toothed cat. He was leaving her aroused, in suspense. Creb pantomimed picking up a big rock and konking the cat on the head.

Ayla smiled broadly and replied, "Ah ha!"

And there you have it — the first ABT sequence for the human race. Unh-hunh, unh-hunh (the "AND" setup), uh oh (BUT, the problem), ah ha (THEREFORE, the solution)! That's how communication began. At least according to my buddy Park Howell, expert brand storyteller BUT ... amateur anthropologist.

Maybe. Who knows? But what's certain is that communication is definitely that old. It's what all creatures do. Humans have just taken it to the highest heights (and deepest depths).

Cut to several thousand years later, and there's Carly Rae

Jepson up on stage singing to thousands of screaming teen fans. Guess what structure you can see in her most popular song?

She sings, "Hey, I just met you, AND this is crazy, BUT here's my number, SO (= THEREFORE) call me maybe." Her music video of that song, "Call Me Maybe," has over a billion views.

Yes, the ABT structure is how we communicate, at the broadest and most fundamental of levels. But ...

HERE'S THE PROBLEM: MORE INFORMATION, WORSE COMMUNICATION

The human race is vast, and today it has major problems with communication. I can show you specific examples from the world of science to support this notion. It's a sad fact that as we've gathered more information, we've gotten worse at communication.

Here's a specific and very important example: There's this gigantic global organization for the study of how the earth's climate is changing called the IPCC (Intergovernmental Panel on Climate Change). It's the best humanity knows how to do right now to deal with its biggest environmental crisis ever. But ... more than one study has shown that communication by the IPCC has gone from bad to worse.

A study published in Science in 2008 showed that the supposedly simple summaries of the IPCC reports could not even be understood by most science graduate students at M.I.T. Then another study in Nature in 2015 showed that the "ease of reading score" for the reports has gone straight downhill over the past two decades.

This worsening of communication happens everywhere. In the second chapter I will show you how the World Bank has gone from interesting to boring in its reports.

Unfortunately this is a natural human progression — to go from interesting to boring. It even happens in lots of marriages, right? Oh, wait, that might be something different.

Anyhow ...

OBFUSCATION NATION

In 1975, before leaving his medical career, legendary techno-thriller writer Dr. Michael Crichton (author of Jurassic Park) documented this problem for the medical world. He analyzed a few medical research papers and showed that they suffer from one common trait: "obfuscation."

This word refers to "the action of making something obscure, unclear or unintelligible." He showed it has been the case for medicine over the course of the past century. Doctors used to communicate with simple, plain, easily understood language. Today they obfuscate.

Same for scientists, same for lawyers, same for accountants, same for sports buffs, same for construction experts, same for forensic pathologists ... pretty much, same for everyone with knowledge.

SO, DO YOU HAVE A COMMUNICATION PROBLEM?

Let me get personal about this now. This book is about improving communication, which has to start with you. But that has to start with a few simple questions.

Do you, personally, feel you have a problem when it comes to communication? Do you think you could communicate more effectively? Do you think you could get better at telling stories?

If the answer to any of those questions is "yes," then this book is for you. But if it's "no" to all of them, then please go no further.

It's a lot like Alcoholics Anonymous, where they say you have to begin by admitting you have a drinking problem. Same thing here. You have to begin by admitting you're a less-than-perfect communicator and be ready to invest the time and energy for it to work. You'd be amazed how many people I encounter (especially academics) who consider themselves "natural communicators."

Nope. Sorry. Nobody is that great. Especially me. I've been at it for a long, long time, yet I still write first drafts that are exercises in the dull "And, And, And," structure we're going to explore in detail.

We all need to work on communication. Especially in a world of growing complexity. If you agree with this, then read on.

AND HERE'S THE SOLUTION: THE ABT FRAMEWORK

"THANK YOU, ABT": THE TEMPLATE IN ACTION

So how do we get back to the simple old days when everyone could understand each other better? The answer is the ABT Narrative Template.

Here's how the simple ABT template works at a birthday party:

I was at a birthday party for an old friend in a private room of an Italian restaurant in New York City. Someone clinked a fork against a glass, the room went silent, the speeches began.

We were all old buddies of the guest of honor. We took turns telling raucous tales that stretched back decades, but among the old timers there was one relative youngster: my 32-year-old business partner Jayde, seated beside me. She had known the birthday gentleman for only a few months. Worse, she'd had a couple glasses of wine.

She whispered to me, "I'm gonna say something!" I glared at her, then as she stood up, I looked at the floor, bracing for the worst.

She said, "This is such an amazing group of old friends, AND you're sharing the most incredible stories, BUT I have a tale to tell that shows how quickly this man has the ability to change a person's life, THEREFORE … let me tell you how he helped me out …"

Everyone was hooked and listened intently.

She told the brief and dramatic story of a health issue three months earlier. She had been in a panic, BUT … upon hearing of her problems he had connected her to a series of excellent doctors. More importantly, given my trained ear, I could hear her entire tale had tight ABT structure (i.e. "… AND I told him I was fine, BUT he insisted he call his doctor for me, THEREFORE I ended up going to see the doctor …")

Her story was funny and heartwarming as she told it in a concise and compelling way, prompting a solid round of applause at the end. As she sat back down, she said to me with a broad smile, "Thank you, ABT!"

The stakes had been high. Had she bored or confused the group at the start, someone would have interrupted her with something funny, and she would have had the floor taken away from her.

But she didn't.

IT'S LIKE THE ARROW IN THE FEDEX LOGO

The ABT Narrative Template is the simplest, most powerful tool to help you combat these communications problems. From the Carly Rae Jepson song to the front page of *The New York Times* every day (as I'll show in Chapter 3), the ABT is all around us.

Communications veteran and buddy of mine Aaron Huertas notes that, "The ABT is like the arrow in the FedEx logo — once you see it, you can never not see it when you look at the logo." When he first made that comparison to the ABT I had never seen the arrow in the FedEx logo. Now I can't pass a FedEx truck without thinking to myself, "Yep, there it is, the arrow right there in the logo, plain as day."

THE ABT IS LIKE THE FEDEX LOGO. Once you see it, you can never
not see it when you look at the logo.

Same for the ABT once you work with it. We hear this all the
time from graduates of our Story Circles Narrative Training
program, which is built around the ABT. It changes how you
view the world, quite possibly just as much as the idea of
natural selection changes how scientists view the world (as I
will suggest in the final chapter).

So let's start with a few basic ABT details.

IT'S THE ABT (NOT THE ABS)

A number of people have pointed out that "therefore" is a
clunky word that's rarely used in conversation. This is true.
The more conversational word is "so."

You can see it in the second paragraph of Martin Luther King,
Jr.'s landmark "I Have a Dream" speech, which we'll examine
in Chapter 2. The paragraph has perfect ABT structure, yet he
begins the last sentence with, "So we are gathered here today
..." — using "so" instead of "therefore."

This has prompted folks to suggest calling the template the ABS. Well, I hate to dismiss suggestions, but … for starters, that kinda sounds like IBS, Irritable Bowel Syndrome.

It's not a trivial point. The entire strength of the template is the simple, memorable acronym that sticks with you. People have a very, very easy time remembering ABT.

ABT "sticks," ABS doesn't. Why is that? A linguistics friend pointed out that words ending with a "t" have a hard edge to them.

If you ever saw *Rocky Horror Picture Show* (and memorized it as I did), you might remember when Dr. Frank N. Furter invites Brad and Janet to "stay for the nighT." He hits the "t" at the end of "night" hard, and then Riff Raff echoes the word and pronunciation. He does the same thing for the next line, saying, "Or maybe a biTe," with Columbia echoing "biTe" with the hard "t."

Also, when it comes to constructing content, "therefore" is a powerful word of consequence. It begs the next word when you say, "Thereforrrrre … ?"

"So" sounds more dismissive. Bottom line, ABT has stuck.

WHY "FRAMEWORK"?

As you will see, I have chosen the term, "ABT Framework" to convey pretty much everything to do with the ABT. You may wonder, Why this term? The answer is … because it sounds cool.

Seriously. That's about it. I use it to kind of mean everything to do with the ABT. I got it from my niece who is a superstar "information architect" in New York City. When I told her about the ABT a few years ago, she said, "You need a cool term for the entire concept," then offered that up. I said okay.

That was the depth of that thought process. As I've said, I have a fondness for simplicity. So let's dive into the basic nuts and bolts of the ABT.

IS THE ABT NEW?

Yes and no.

Yes, I formulated it in 2012, derived from "The Rule of Replacing," which I had heard from the co-creators of the animated series *South Park*. (They had gotten it from their writing teachers.) So you could say it's new.

But no, it's ancient, because (as I'll present in Chapter 3) those guys were pre-dated in the ABT dynamic by legendary screenwriting professor Frank Daniel. He talked in the 1980's about replacing "and"s with "but"s and "therefore"s. And his knowledge of narrative structure had to have been influenced by the great mythologist Joseph Campbell of the mid-1900's, who in turn must have learned much from the philosophers of the 1800's who developed "the triad" of "thesis, antithesis, synthesis." And they drew from the ancient Greeks, who first described the same structure, realizing that it underpinned their plays.

So you can see, it's both new and old. What's a shame is that the triad was a fundamental element in teaching just a few generations ago. But somehow it got kicked to the curb over the years.

In my first screenwriting course in 1989, the instructor made a side comment, "And this is basically the old thesis, antithesis, synthesis thing" — as if first, we all knew "the old triad" thing (none of us did), and second, "the old triad" just was too old-school to be worth teaching any more. And that is exactly how we get to Crichton's excess complexity problem, in which simplicity is deemed just plain uncool and a sign of cluelessness.

The truth is that simplicity is the ultimate in cool. There is the quote that's attributed to tons of famous people from Da Vinci to Steve Jobs (but like so many quotes these days, the internet reveals that nobody is sure who said it originally): "Simplicity is the ultimate sophistication." Whoever said it was simply correct.

So now let's talk about the three forces that underlie the ABT.

THE PROBLEM-SOLUTION ANIMAL

We are "problem-solution" animals. In 2010, Jonathan Gottschall published a nice little book titled *Storytelling Animal*, which helped ignite today's current storytelling stampede (both Linked-In and Twitter report that the most popular self-descriptor people use in their profiles is now "storyteller").

Gottschall argued that humans have been telling stories since we began communicating. I agree with that, but his book really should have been titled *Problem-Solution Animal*.

Think about it: What is the most primal thought process in the brain? Is there something more primal than telling stories? Yes.

Every animal begins every day with two existential challenges: How am I going to eat and how am I going to reproduce? There are lots of other secondary challenges, but without nutrition and reproduction everything ends.

These are both problems for which the animal must find solutions. This is true for flatworms, flat fish and flat-headed peccaries. They are all focused on problem-solving, all day long.

The process has three parts: setup, problem, solution. The flat fish thinks "I'm hungry" (setup), it starts trying to find some little shrimp it can catch (problem), then it catches one (solution). And then maybe later in the day it tells "the story" of this experience to its friends using the same three elements.

It is literally insane how consumed humans are with the problem-solution dynamic. Our brains are so hyper-programmed to solve problems that we end up creating massive enterprises to deal with the excess amount of problem-solving we are driven to do.

What do you think games are? They are like when a power grid has too much energy; some of it has to be siphoned off. Puzzle-solving, murder mysteries, reasoning, sports—it's all the endless, relentless desire of the brain to solve problems, whether the problems are life-sustaining or not. At some point the brain doesn't care; all it's thinking is, "Just give me a problem to solve—ANYTHING!"

So why wouldn't the brain develop the entire process of communication around this three-part structure? (This, by the way, is pretty much the lead-in for the final chapter of this book, which presents what I call "narrative selection.")

And then why wouldn't the three parts dominate pretty much

everything we do?

THE THREE FORCES OF NARRATIVE

When you search the three words of the ABT, you come to realize they are connector words. They are not verbs, not nouns, not adjectives — they are words that connect other text.

"And" connects pieces of information that are in agreement — like, "We went here AND we went there AND we went there ..."

"But" connects text that contradicts itself — "She was happy, BUT she was also sad ..."

"Therefore" connects text with its consequence — "He was sick, THEREFORE he stayed home from school."

Now you see the three fundamental forces of narrative at work.

They are:

AGREEMENT - the setup, what we can all agree upon

CONTRADICTION - the problem, what we're confronting

CONSEQUENCE - the actions being taken, or the solution itself

This is how we communicate, all day, every day. We talk about things we agree upon. We hit points of contradiction.

Then we resolve the contradiction with the consequence.

Furthermore, we work these three elements at different scales. This is what good storytelling is about: small-scale stories, medium-scale stories, and overarching stories, all overlain on each other to make a seemingly complicated whole story. You'll get to see this in Chapter 2 in Oprah Winfrey's wonderful Golden Globes speech that *The New York Times* called "a story of stories."

These three forces are so powerful and ubiquitous that I've taken to format-coding them (blue, red, green) as a way to analyze the narrative structure of texts. Also, for black and white text, I use plain, bold and italics for the three forces. To see the breadth of their application in our language in a wide range of material, check out the examples in Appendix 3.

Truly effective communication requires all three forces, used in the right measures and in the right sequences. This is what the ABT is—a little bit of agreement for the setup, the contradiction that states the problem, then the consequence as either the action towards solving the problem or the solution itself.

EXPANDING THE ABT INTO THE NARRATIVE SPECTRUM

Earlier I mentioned *Rocky Horror Picture Show*. One of my favorite lines is when Brad sings to Janet, "There's three ways that love can go. That's good, bad or medioooocre ..." (It took me years, in the pre-internet era, to figure out that second line.)

Same thing for communication. Sing along with me, "There's three ways that communication can go. That's interesting, boring or confuuuusing ..."

The element that determines which of those three outcomes you have is the central element: contradiction. People like to talk about how the media is "conflict-driven," which is true. But conflict is just one of many potential sources of contradiction, including suspense, mystery, inquiry — they are all possible driving forces for narrative. The key thing is that the overall category is contradiction.

There are lots of words that are used to establish contradiction (such as "despite," "however," "yet") but the most commonly used word is "but." You can find a number of websites that list the most commonly used words in the English language. "And" is always in the top 3. "But" is usually around 15 to 25. None of the other words of contradiction are even in the top 100. So that's why we choose to focus on "but" — the most common word for the most powerful part of narrative.

You need the contradiction for the narrative process to begin. If there's just a lot of facts with no contradiction, you end up with the AAA structure (And, And, And), which is non-narrative and boring.

It's the contradiction that activates the brain. There's now starting to be substantial neurophysiology research on how narrative activates the brain. I talked about this in detail in my science-oriented *Houston* book.

We can talk about a happy family (non-narrative so far), living in a happy town (still non-narrative and starting to get boring), and every day is happy for them (totally non-non-narrative and definitely boring), *but* then the father is found dead (yes! Now we have a story because we have contradiction; the narrative part of the brain is activated and we're in the narrative world with a "whodunnit" problem to solve).

So you need some contradiction, but ... on the other hand, if there's too many elements of contradiction ("but we didn't want to leave, but they said we had to, but nobody heard them, but we were busy watching television, but ...") you end up with confusion. Rather than call this particular structure the BBB, I opted to use some other words of contradiction (there's lots of them). I call it DHY for "Despite, However, Yet."

THE ABT WALK OF LIFE. We're born boring, we die confusing.

DHY ends up being the kind of speech you hear from academics who are very smart and like to challenge themselves by speaking on multiple planes. They speak parenthetically, they go on tangents, they do anything to make things complex, challenging, and, for most average people ... confusing.

They say, "Immigration is an important issue DESPITE the tendency of politicians to neglect it, HOWEVER some issues are so neglected they are never even talked about, YET when it comes to politicians, some can never stop talking ..." You can see this structure leads to randomness and confusion. Your brain locked onto immigration, but then we led you to politicians, and then to talking — like a treadmill of thoughts.

So if you want to be truly engaging, understandable, compelling — all of which add up to interesting — then your goal is the ABT. It has just the right mix of: agreement to set up the context, contradiction to pose a problem that activates the narrative part of the brain, and consequence to point to the solution to the problem.

These three structures come together in the Narrative Spectrum. It is the central tool for our Story Circles Narrative Training program.

THE NARRATIVE SPECTRUM

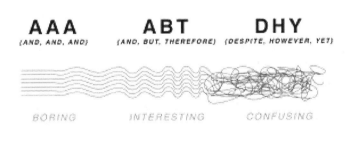

AAA *(AND, AND, AND)*   **ABT** *(AND, BUT, THEREFORE)*   **DHY** *(DESPITE, HOWEVER, YET)*

BORING   *INTERESTING*   *CONFUSING*

NON-NARRATIVE   NARRATIVE   OVERLY NARRATIVE

THE NARRATIVE SPECTRUM. Most content can be placed somewhere across the spectrum from an absence of narrative structure (AAA) to an excess (DHY). The target is in the middle (ABT).

AND HERE'S WHY IT'S IMPORTANT

COMMUNICATING BROADLY: THE INNER VS. OUTER GROUP

Once you begin to absorb the ABT structure, you start to see how it embraces the central dynamic for communicating within or between audiences. This is how it reaches its ultimate power: it's the tool that lets you reach the masses.

Communications experts usually say the most important rule of communication is, "Know your audience." That's what this is about. There are two basic audiences: those that need narrative structure and those that don't.

I've seen this divide with many organizations and institutions I've worked with. For example, I've given workshops at the Centers for Disease Control and Prevention (CDC) in Atlanta. The communications folks tell me that when there's an outbreak of a disease, it's actually pretty easy to communicate to the public because everyone is intensely interested.

Not only do they not need a story or the ABT; they don't even want one. They don't want a spokesperson who begins a press conference about the outbreak with, "Once upon a time there was ..." They don't even want to begin with, "This is a disease that has been studied for over a century." No, they just want to "cut right to the chase" with the information — like, "The cause of this disease is a virus for which there is no known cure."

But when CDC wants to interest the public in something less urgent — like getting ready for natural disasters when we don't know when or if they will happen — it turns out narrative structure helps a lot.

They found this out in 2011, when they tapped into the story power of zombie attacks to communicate about disaster preparation. They realized that the things you need in your house to survive a zombie attack are the same things necessary for surviving an earthquake, flood or fire. They launched a campaign called "Zombie Preparedness" that was hugely popular and effective. The core thinking was, "Natural disasters need preparation, AND it can be hard to interest the public in this, BUT it turns out that what you need to prepare for a natural disaster are the same basic items you would need to prepare for a zombie attack, which is much more attention-grabbing, THEREFORE ..." That little bit of ABT thinking reached a much bigger audience than would normally be interested in disaster-preparation kits.

Think of the two basic audiences as the Inner Group and the Outer Group. The Inner Group is already interested in what you have to say; the Outer Group isn't.

THE TWO AUDIENCES. The Inner Group already knows your language and the problems you work on. The Outer Group doesn't. Are you sure you know how small your Inner Group is?

For the Inner Group, all you have to do is give them the facts. They are already interested, which means they are willing to "bear the burden of communication." Give them the facts, and they'll arrange them into an effective structure.

So the AAA structure works fine if you're already interested in the content, but not so much if you aren't. If a disease occurs only in flat-headed peccaries, then you, as an audience member, might not have any interest in it and so will find the facts boring. If that's the case then you're in the Outer Group and will need a different approach.

This is where narrative structure comes into play, which means the ABT. You need something like, "Flat-headed peccaries suffer from a version of flu AND more than half of them die from it, BUT it was recently discovered they can't reproduce without it, THEREFORE ..." Pose a good question/problem, and a much larger audience will be interested. As Hollywood knows, everyone loves a good mystery. (btw, I just made that up about peccaries)

HOW UNIVERSAL IS THE ABT?

I've called the ABT "the Universal Narrative Template." So just how universal is the basic dynamic? To give you a feel for how widespread the triad structure is, let's draw an analogy using the terminology of genetics.

The collective information in our genes is called the GENOTYPE. The way it gets expressed in different environments is called the PHENOTYPE.

What this means is that you might have the information in your genes (genotype) that says you'll be tall, but your actual height (phenotype) might be short if you're raised on a poor diet, or tall if you're well-fed. Same initial information, different outcomes.

Now think of the three forces of narrative as being like the genotype, and then look at the various ways the forces get expressed in different subjects. I've come to realize much of this over the past few years as I've explained the ABT to various audiences.

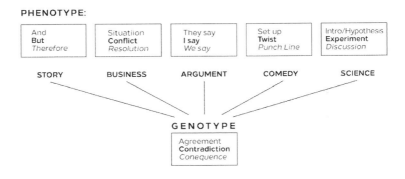

THE TRIAD STRUCTURE IS EVERYWHERE. The three forces of narrative underpin communication throughout society.

First, we have the world of storytelling, in which we see that the ABT structure of *And, But, Therefore* is ubiquitous, as we'll explore in Chapter 3.

Then there's the business world. A few years ago I presented the ABT at a workshop for Deloitte executives. One of them asked, "Is this the same thing as how we structure our case studies in the business world as 'situation, conflict, resolution'?" Yes, absolutely.

Then take a look at the basics of argumentation. My friend Gerald ("Jerry") Graff, senior statesman of the humanities world, is the co-author, with his wife, Cathy Birkenstein, of one of the best-selling textbooks of all time. The book is about the use of templates for argumentation. It has sold over 2 million copies and is used in college classes on comparative literature, rhetoric, and English in general.

The title is *They Say, I Say*. Those are the first two elements of the triad. It's the simplest, clearest, most effective way to present an argument. First you present what we can agree is the argument of your opponents, then you present how your argument contradicts it. And then you pull the two together with the synthesis, which is the "therefore."

Now think about comedy. The standard joke consists of a setup (Man walks into a bar), the twist (the bartender is a duck), and punchline (insert funny thing duck says here). Comedians live and die by the ABT, whether they realize it or not (we'll explore this in Chapter 3 and see that they adhere to the ABT dynamic better than anyone).

As for science: They discovered the triad structure long ago, as I talked about in detail in my *Houston* book. In the 1600's, scientists initially tried to communicate with the AAA structure; they wrote papers that were just streams of information. But by the 1800's their papers began to take on the ABT structure. Today almost all scientific journals follow some version of the IMRAD template which stands for Introduction (agreement), Methods, Results (contradiction), And Discussion (consequence). It's a pure expression of the three narrative forces.

THE ABT IS THE BRIDGE THAT CONNECTS EVERYTHING

In 1959, novelist/physicist C.P. Snow presented his "The Two Cultures" lecture, which became a landmark essay on the differences between the humanities and science. He was both a significant literary figure and a scientist. He had two groups of friends: literary folks and scientists. He said he had to speak two different languages for them. He talked as though the divide were hopeless, but he made no mention of this universal dynamic called narrative (the problem/solution dynamic) that dominates all cultures.

The basic three-force structure is everywhere, and if scientists and literary types want to know what their best shot at connecting with each other is, this is it. The ABT is the bridge that connects everything. It just needs to be recognized and used, not left in the past or obscured by too much complexity.

AND HERE'S WHAT THE ABT IS REALLY ABOUT: SIMPLICITY

SIMPLICITY YIELDS TO COMPLEXITY (ENDLESSLY)

I believe that complexity is the bane of humanity. Good things start out simple, but then there's always a sort of "mission creep," in which more and more is added on.

This sort of conundrum is well known in fields like computer programming, which has the term, "feature-itis," described on Wikipedia as "feature creep." It's the well-documented syndrome of the expansion of features added to a new product.

The world of software development is awash in examples, starting with Netscape (which Wikipedia uses as a case study). It became more "bloated" with each new updated version until it went extinct.

It's the same basic problem you go through endlessly with the desktop of your computer. You organize everything into a few simple folders, then you go back to work, and then a couple weeks later you wake up and realize that entropy is at work; it's all turned back into a complicated, cluttered mess, meaning you need to go at it again to bring things back to simplicity.

This, then, connects back with what Michael Crichton identified in 1975 as the central problem for communication in the medical world: obfuscation. It's the same deal. Obfuscation basically means excessive complexity.

So if we know that the solution to complexity is simplicity, why don't we just use this knowledge to fix things?

BUT … HERE'S THE BAD NEWS … SIMPLICITY IS HARD WORK

Lots of great and smart people over the ages have said things to the effect of, "I would have written a shorter letter if I had the time," or, "If you want me to talk for an hour I can do it now, but if you only want ten minutes it will take a few days."

The basic message of such quotes is, "Complexity is easy;

simplicity is hard."

It's easy to remove all constraints and end up with a large, complicated mess. Establishing firm structure and distilling things down into a simple form is endlessly difficult.

This is the challenge of editing in general: trying to say more with less. Whether it's print or film, it's all about taking the long-winded and making it concise while still keeping it compelling.

And this is where the ABT comes in. It's the tool for doing this. It's so short and simple it can feel like a miracle cure to communication. And, actually, it pretty much is. But there's one catch, which is, "Nothing has really changed since Longfellow."

What do I mean by that? Well, listen my friends, and you will hear, of the greatest thing since the midnight ride of Paul Revere.

WHAT LONGFELLOW KNEW: "IT WAS SO HARD FOR ME"

Henry Wadsworth Longfellow was a great American poet in the 1800's. He wrote the classic poem about the midnight ride of Paul Revere. One of his most enduring pieces of work was his epic poem, "Evangeline." He sent an early draft of it to a friend who wrote back that he loved it, especially "how easy it was to read."

Longfellow wrote back that the poem was "so easy for you to read, because it was so hard for me to write."

And there you have it—all the way back then—the secret

formula for communicating well. If you don't find communication to be hard, you're not doing it right. If you think you're a natural-born communicator who doesn't need to work on it, you probably aren't.

But ... there is hope (ah, the classic infomercial turn).

It's time for us to embark on an ABT journey of our own. I've been working with the ABT for seven years now, AND I've learned a lot about its strength, BUT most of what I've done has remained in the world of science, THEREFORE it is now time to try and prove to the broader public that ...

NARRATIVE IS EVERYTHING, using the ABT Framework as the central tool. I will try to show you how ubiquitous this simple structural pattern is throughout the worlds of business, politics, entertainment, science and religion.

I invite your critical thinking as you read the material. Some of the data and anecdotes taken by themselves may not be all that convincing, but I think that as you look at the entire "body of evidence," the breadth of narrative at work throughout our world will eventually filter through.

When I'm done making my case for the ubiquity of the ABT Framework, I offer up my belief that just as "natural selection" molds nature, "narrative selection" molds culture. It is the grand synthesis of my 40-year journey. It is admittedly audacious, yet if you can keep your mind from obfuscating the details around it, I think you'll see it's both logical and quite possibly true.

So here we go...

1) BUSINESS

1) BUSINESS - Branding is ABT

"What's the story, morning glory?" - Oasis

What I have to say about the ABT in business is best captured by the story I'll tell you in a bit about the sportswear company that had me meet with the five members of their global branding team. I had each of them write out what they thought was the one-sentence ABT of the company. When they read them aloud, each one was drastically different from the last. Which meant they were all telling different, not totally compatible stories for the company. That's not a very efficient way to promote a brand.

The key to success in business is efficiency. Henry Ford knew this and pioneered mass production. Efficiency requires everyone to be on the same page. Too often it's just assumed or hoped that everyone is. The ABT is the tool that strips back the veneer, revealing that, yikes—we've got five branding professionals here who have completely different and even incompatible ideas of what our company is about. That's not good.

Business is story. If you doubt this, listen to the *Business of Story* podcast hosted by my good friend Park Howell. He'll make a believer out of you on that point. So business is story, story is ABT, therefore the ABT lies at the heart of business.

1.1) ABT = EFFICIENCY

You're the C.E.O. of a company. You want efficiency all the way from human resources to the factory floor. You need everyone to be working towards common goals—not wasting time on bad directions, but instead focusing all effort in the right direction.

Knowing "the narrative" of your mission is central to achieving this. If you know the narrative, then you know what is essential to advance the mission. You also know what is a waste of time and resources. Knowing these two dimensions empowers you to make the important decisions and lead.

The ABT is your tool to articulate the narrative. It enables you to define, refine and condense down your narrative, ultimately to a single sentence. Which means the ABT becomes the essence of corporate leadership and branding, as we shall explore.

BRAND STRATEGY: HEAPS OF BRANDING BOOKS

There are heaps and heaps and heaps of books about the arcane and elusive art of "branding." Try typing "branding book" into Google and see what you get. I just did, and the first thing that came up was a banner with the covers of 51 books on branding.

There are, of course, endless facets to creating a brand, AND endless people willing to charge for their expertise to help you develop your brand, BUT …

I think you know what I'm going to say here. At the core, everything memorable is ABT. As Carly Rae Jepsen knows, it's the structural secret to being "catchy."

Think about one of the greatest television commercials of all time. A large audience of more-or-less zombies is seated in front of a gigantic screen listening to the Great Leader drone on and on, BUT ... a woman runs in, throws a hammer at the screen, and THEREFORE ... the rest was branding history for Apple computers.

The seated zombies and the boring leader were the "AND" — the frustrating world we agree exists. The heroine was the "BUT" — the contradiction that disrupted everything. The "THEREFORE" was the consequence — that if you put your faith in Apple, they will shatter the norm and one day be the world's most profitable company. Apple owes everything to Steve Jobs' innate feel for the ABT.

"MINE GOES TO ELEVEN"

"We're better than our competitors" is pretty much the age-old strategy for marketing, stated as simply as possible. Taken to its extreme you get Nigel Tufnel of the 1984 mockumentary Spinal Tap boasting about his amplifier being better than all the others because "it goes to eleven." It's that simple.

Branding, at its core, is just about conveying to everyone that you're better than everyone else. The way you do that is with the ABT:

There are lots of competing products, AND they will tell you they're great, BUT none of them does what our product does, THEREFORE ... buy our product.

Yes, there's lots more to branding. You want to be relatable and tap into emotion and be likable and all that stuff, but, at the core, more than anything else, you just want to say you're the best in a way that doesn't bore or confuse your customers. The ABT is how you do that.

"THEY SAY, I SAY": ARGUE YOU'RE THE BEST

I mentioned earlier the mega-best-selling textbook *They Say, I Say*, by Gerald Graff and his wife, Cathy Birkenstein. It's used in college humanities courses such as comparative literature and rhetoric. It's about the use of templates in argumentation and ought to be mandatory reading for everyone.

A brand, a message, a story, a scientific theory — they're all the same things at the core, which is an argument. Think of branding, then think of *They Say, I Say*. They're the same thing. Your "brand statement" is basically the argument that, "They (everyone else) say the way to make a product is like this, but I (we) say you do it like this." You're arguing for your brand.

So that's what you want to do: argue for your way of doing things. And if you can do it clearly, then you can begin to achieve the following …

BUSINESS LEADERSHIP: THE ABT CUTS THE WEEDS

Narrative is leadership. I hit this note already. People follow voices that are concise and compelling (i.e., ABT-structured). They don't follow voices that are boring (AAA) or confusing

(DHY).

There are, of course, a few exceptions. Did you ever see the movie *Being There*? Peter Sellars plays Chauncey Gardner, the clueless gardener who makes vague, elusive, confusing statements that result in everyone being so mystified they feel he must be extremely smart. They find their own messages in what he says as they eventually appoint him president.

That might happen in the movies, but not so much in real life.

One of my favorite books for the business world (which I'm sure has long since been dismissed; such is my dated business knowledge) was the 1980's best seller *In Search of Excellence*. Authors examined the business practices of the Fortune 500 corporations. They looked for recurring patterns in the most successful companies. One attribute they found was the tendency of successful companies to have a single individual — usually the founder or CEO — who gave rise to "the founding story" of what the company stood for. The founding stories were strongly ABT in their structure.

Which means the ABT is the tool for corporate strategy. Planners need to get together, identify the company's long-term goals, pinpoint the problem preventing them from achieving their goals, then articulate the THEREFORE — the set of actions being taken to address the problem.

Yeah, I know, there's lots more to corporate strategy. But I guarantee you a lot of that "lots more" leads to countless well-intentioned people getting lost in the weeds. The ABT is the antidote to the weeds. It's your best hope for avoiding getting lost in information overload, and it starts with something as simple as having the ability to explain your work clearly during a brief elevator ride, which is also known as …

THE "ONE-FLOOR ELEVATOR PITCH"

Ah, yes — the elevator pitch. Workhorse of the business world. The short, concise statement of your product, program or project that you're able to spin out in the brief moments an elevator takes to go between a few floors as you're standing beside the big cheese, who just asked what you do.

Everyone knows about it, but what most don't realize is that the ABT can give you what my buddy Park Howell (in another of his brilliant ABT contributions) calls "The One-Floor Elevator Pitch." That's the beauty of the ABT — one sentence that, if crafted well, can be delivered in just a few seconds.

Dan Pink's 2013 best-selling book *To Sell Is Human* has an entire chapter that goes through 6 structures for an elevator pitch. The closest he gets to the ABT is his version of "The Pixar Pitch." It's just an elaborate (i.e., more complicated) ABT structure that would take you several floors. One floor is better.

Most websites for crafting a winning elevator pitch recommend content-oriented attributes, such as the need to be "punchy" and "get to the point" and "grab the listener." But the sad fact is that if you present a bunch of supposedly grabby "And, And, And" material, it's still ultimately going to be boring. The ABT structure lays out the problem, takes us on a journey and pulls it all together. That's what makes for a good elevator pitch.

Like this:

BOSS (as he walks onto the elevator): Son, what are you working on?

EMPLOYEE (already in elevator): Well, people have been making widgets for a hundred years, AND we know that society demands a certain level of widget production, BUT we're running out of the raw materials needed to make them, THEREFORE I'm now designing a widget-recycling plant.

There's your concise and compelling ABT-structured elevator pitch. If you've got it down and don't stumble, you should be able to get that out in the ride up or down just one floor. And if you do it right, you can reach audiences way outside your inner circle, like this ...

THE POWER OF THE BRAND NAME

What's really important is to go back to those concentric circles. How big is that inner circle for you? If your brand has "name recognition," that circle may actually be very large — to the point of including everyone you want to reach.

If that's the case, you may not need any of this narrative stuff. When you get to that level you can afford to produce the pretentious Super Bowl commercials where you have a clip of a civil rights leader saying something visionary followed simply by your logo.

If you're a huge brand, everyone will quietly say, "Powerful." But if you're a no-name brand, everyone will think, "Well, that was a waste."

I always marveled as a kid when I watched *Late Night with Johnny Carson.* He would have major celebrities as guests who would talk in detail about walking their dogs or taking their clothes to the dry cleaner. I would think to myself, "There is not one person in the world who would want to hear me share those details, yet these guys get to share them with millions, and the audience can't get enough of it."

That's the power of the brand name. If you have it, everyone will listen, regardless of whether you're AAA or ABT or even DHY. Just watch any talk show. You'll see countless guests who are solidly AAA (boring — just listing one fact about their life after another) or DHY (maybe wildly enthusiastic but totally confusing — think Tom Cruise, Drew Barrymore or Kanye West).

BRAND BLINDNESS

So this becomes the delusion that happens to people who work with powerful brand names: They begin to think of themselves as brilliant communicators. I've seen it countless times with folks from NASA or the Smithsonian or *National Geographic*.

All they have to do at a cocktail party is mention where they work, and the room will go quiet with awe. And then it's just like they were on Johnny Carson — everyone's listening with rapt attention (until it turns out they're boring).

Such are the ways of the world. You need to be aware of these things. You need to know how much of your communication success is because you're a talented communicator versus how much is because you work for a powerful brand name. And you need to have a clear feel for how well you actually are communicating, rather than just assuming you're doing well. That's where the ABT can double as a tool to analyze your "brand consistency."

THE ABT AS "BRAND CONSISTENCY ANALYZER" (OR "GESTALT-BUSTER")

So here's that story of the sportswear company: I gave my talk, they wrote down their ABTs for their company, then we went around the group as they read them aloud.

Each one was completely different. The first person's ABT said the company is about sports celebrities who endorse their brand. The second said they represent "authenticity." The third was about edgy style and fashion, the fourth about youth and the fifth about rebellion.

The head honcho turned to me at the end and said, "We've got a problem, don't we?" I nodded. When your top five branding folks each have a different idea of what the brand is, that's bad, m'kay?

What this means is that it's important not to make assumptions that everyone is "on the same page" without any proof they are.

Do you know the German word "gestalt"? It basically refers to "the whole" of something. There's often a tendency for people to have a clear *gestalt* feeling for the overall subject we're talking about and just assume they know the individual parts that make it up. But do they really?

For this little experiment, the branding folks all had the same *gestalt* sense of the company: that it's cool, popular and successful. But when they got more analytical about the brand by using the ABT, it became clear they really didn't have the same take.

This will come up again in subsequent chapters. You hate to push people too much, but too often everyone wants to "go along to get along," and just believe they are all in alignment.

Sometimes that's good for the overall dynamic, but sometimes it can be better if you pull back the veneer and find out if they really are on the same page. The ABT is the tool for doing just that.

1.2) PRESENTATIONS: "BUILDING OUT" INSTEAD OF "CHOPPING DOWN"

Everyone gives presentations to groups, but the business world seems particularly consumed with them. So here is my simple recommendation for developing a presentation: *everything should start with your ABT.*

You begin conceptualizing a presentation by figuring out your ABT. It's the first thing you assemble. It's your "narrative road map." It tells you what to keep in, and it tells you what to cut out. It tells you what "advances the narrative" (keep it in) and what is "off the narrative" or essentially a sidebar (cut it out).

Once you've locked in your ABT, you then use it to "build out" your presentation. Be forewarned that a first draft of an ABT can take just a few seconds, but a good draft can take months.

I work with a lot of professionals who give ten-minute presentations. I have them begin with a two-minute, three-slide presentation, presenting only the *And*, the *But* and the

Therefore of what they have to say. Then they set to work adding more content that is essential to strengthening it. The result is a solid narrative core.

What I don't recommend is the typical approach of starting with a 28-minute amorphous mass of everything you think is relevant, then whittling down/paring down/chopping down to 10 minutes. When you come at it from that direction you end up removing essential narrative bits, resulting in a choppy flow that can eventually get confusing or boring. You want to start with the core narrative and never lose it.

For example, I might have someone start with exactly these three slides:

```
┌─────────────────────────────┐
│          Slide 1            │
│                             │
│   Lots of work has been done,│
│   AND some of it is good,   │
│                             │
│                             │
└─────────────────────────────┘

┌─────────────────────────────┐
│          Slide 2            │
│                             │
│      BUT the problem        │
│    is not being solved,     │
│                             │
└─────────────────────────────┘

┌─────────────────────────────┐
│          Slide 3            │
│                             │
│    THEREFORE we need a       │
│       new approach          │
│                             │
└─────────────────────────────┘
```

THE THREE CONVERSATIONAL ABT SLIDES TO START BUILDING A PRESENTATION. This provides the concise spine, now you begin adding the content to make it compelling.

That's an extremely common storyline for everything from healthcare to sports teams. You've created the concise version of your narrative. Now you want to make it also compelling by adding in only the pieces of information that are essential.

For example, you might have a next draft that says, "Lots of work has been done to improve the offense of the Cleveland Browns, and the addition of Baker Mayfield has helped a lot, but the team still isn't having winning seasons, THEREFORE they need to improve their defense."

As you add this material, the presentation gets longer, and you keep rehearsing it. Eventually you reach the ten-minute length and still have a tight narrative structure.

And now you're seeing the central challenge of the ABT: to be both CONCISE and COMPELLING. These are the two fundamental goals. The problem is they work in opposition to each other. You can explore this by getting to know the three basic forms of the ABT.

CONCISE VS. COMPELLING: THE THREE FORMS OF THE ABT

You want your ABT to be CONCISE (as short as possible), but at the same time you want it to also be COMPELLING (as narratively powerful as possible, which comes from the information you add to it). I recommend varying these two factors to create the three forms of the ABT in a sort of Goldilocks search ("this one's too big, this one's too small, this one's juuuuuust right.")

VERSION ONE: The Informational ABT

This is where you include everything that's compelling without worrying about being concise. The result is a ton of information, something like:

Surfing is a popular sport AND has a history going back hundreds of years with the Polynesians AND takes place everywhere from the Arctic to the Great Lakes AND is a professional sport that is being added to the next Olympics, BUT the commercial industry has been experiencing a sustained downturn that has lasted a decade and caused many of the product manufacturers, magazine and sportswear companies to go out of business, THEREFORE new approaches to marketing and promoting the sport are needed to regain surfing's previous popularity.

That's a lot of interesting information about surfing, but it's far too long and clunky to be the central spine of what you want to say. So the second move is to create the concise version.

VERSION TWO: The Conversational ABT

This is the version that goes to the other extreme. You want to create a super-short punchy statement that can roll off your tongue even if it has zero impact. You want a version that you could say in a circle at a cocktail party and not have anyone roll their eyes or get lost.

It ignores what's compelling, going only for the most concise statement possible. Like this:

We've got something that used to be one way, but it's been failing, therefore we're working on a new way.

That's an ABT that is definitely very concise, broad and common, but now it is so devoid of content as to be almost meaningless. Nevertheless, it does at least capture the core "story" in its very simplest form. You can see how general a story it is. It could be the story of a computer repair shop, or it could be the story of a travel agency. It's just the age-old story of the need for updating.

You could begin a presentation about your surfboard rental company by saying exactly that statement above. Let's say your audience members — one of whom works for a real-estate company — don't know you and have no idea what you're going to talk about. You open by saying, "I'm going to tell you the story of how we used to run our business, but we were failing, and so here's how we're now running our business better."

That real-estate person might still not know what you're going to talk about, and yet they may be thinking, "This sounds exactly like the story of my real-estate company right now; we also just finally improved how we're doing business."

That person — who might have zero interest in surfing — is actually now interested to hear the next words you say to see if you continue to tell a similar story. The person is narratively connected, which can be true of anyone, not only a surfer who is connected simply because of the content.

But still, this version is too devoid of compelling content, so you need something a little longer. Which means it's now time to find the sweet spot.

VERSION THREE: The Keeper ABT

The conversational ABT tells you the central narrative you want to convey, which then serves as your criterion for deciding what to keep in and what to cut out. As interesting as the history of surfing and the fact that it happens in the Artic might be, those are not key elements of your core narrative.

So I'd suggest something like this:

Surfing is a sport with a long history, and it generates $1.2 billion in trade worldwide, but the past decade has seen a decline in its popularity, therefore new ideas are needed to rebuild it.

The exact wording of the Keeper ABT is something to be wrestled with at great length. Remember that quote from Longfellow about it being easy for you because it was so hard for him? This is where you realize what Longfellow was talking about.

It's really easy to whip up a first draft of an ABT in less than a minute, but try involving several people in the process. It gets complicated quickly. Which is fine; that's the challenge of "finding the narrative."

If you think it's easy, you're probably mistaken. Just ask writers in Hollywood who are stuck in "development hell." That's the term used to refer to the endless rewriting of a story. Most of the time much of that rewriting is about trying to solve these basic ABT dynamics.

THE FIRE-DRILL RULE FOR YOUR PRESENTATION

Here's a very simple and effective little rule for working on the overall structure of a presentation. If a fire alarm were to go off in the middle of your talk, forcing everyone to go outside into the parking lot for ten minutes, when it's over, and they're let back in the building … how many would really want to come back for the second half of your talk?

Seriously. How many of them would say among themselves, "You know what, that was a great talk, but I think I got the general idea; I'm gonna head back to my office to answer emails."

In contrast, how many would say, "Dang, I've got all these emails I can see on my phone that really need to be answered, but I've just got to hear the end of this talk, so I'm going back to hear the rest"?

I guarantee you that if the presentation is about a murder, and we haven't yet been told who dunnit, pretty much everyone will be coming back. But in contrast, if it's a big "And, And, And" presentation with no overall ABT arc, the speaker is going to notice that the formerly full lecture hall is now half-full—and mostly with people who feel too guilty to abandon the speaker.

It's not impossible that your talk—even though it's about this year's revisions to the tax laws—could still have some degree of ABT structure that will indeed have an ending that will bring the audience back after the alarm. The only catch is the old Longfellow problem: for them to come back it will probably have to have been hard for you to create. Sorry, no getting around it: narrative is endlessly tough.

IMAGERY: EVERY PICTURE TELLS A STORY

In the advertising world imagery is everything, but how do you determine if the images you're using are sending the right messages? Just as you can test branding by having everyone craft what they think is the ABT of the company, you can do the same sort of test for imagery using the ABT.

One of our favorite things to do in workshops is to simply put a photo of an interesting painting on the screen and let audience members come up with an ABT for it. A great source is Norman Rockwell. His paintings were legendary for the stories they told.

It's fun, but try doing this with a group, and you'll start to see how variable the messaging of a given image can be. Take a look at this painting and write your own ABT for it.

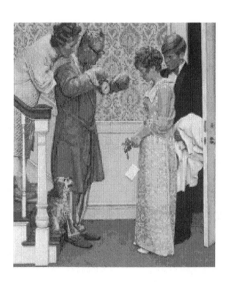

EVERY PICTURE TELLS AN ABT STORY. What is your ABT for this Norman Rockwell painting?

Here's what I just came up with: "Young Mary told her father that George was really good at fixing alarm clocks AND he was her date for the dance, BUT when they came home her father confronted them with the clock George was supposed to have fixed but didn't, THEREFORE he was not allowed to sleep with Mary that night."

Okay, I'm guessing you came up with something a little different, which means we have two ABTs for this painting so far. I'm sure lots more are possible.

If you want to use an image for your company's campaign, you might want to gather a group and have them come up with what they think the ABT is for the image. If their ABT's are all similar, you've probably got a good image for your brand. But if they are wildly different, you might want to rethink your choice of artwork.

1.3) SLOGANEERING: THE "THEREFORE" TEST

You gotta have a slogan. That's as age-old and fundamental as marketing itself. But what are the rules for coming up with a good slogan? As far as I can tell, there aren't any more specific rules for a slogan than there are for an elevator pitch. There are just vague notions of, "It needs to grab people" and, "It's gotta be punchy."

How do you define "grabby" and "punchy"? Those are holistic terms. What's needed is something more analytical.

Which means the ABT.

Now let's think about the three forces of narrative that underpin the ABT.

First off, agreement. Would you want your slogan to be a statement of agreement? Something like, "Coca-Cola is a liquid!" is something everyone can agree on, but it is not going to be very catchy, much less grabby or punchy.

Next is contradiction. Would you want your slogan to be a statement of contradiction? "Stress in your life can cause depression!" Yeah? And? Is that really a slogan you'd want to have under your product name? Yes, it might be a lead-in line for an advertisement, but it's not a slogan.

Now, would you want your slogan to be a statement of consequence (meaning action)? Let's try a few. "Think different." "Just do it." "I'm lovin' it." "Eat fresh." "State Farm is there." "We try harder."

Just look at the first two. They are two of the most successful ad campaigns ever. Both are statements of consequence, telling you which actions to take. And that's what you want for a slogan: a statement of consequence.

Which means here's a simple test for your slogan: Try saying it after the word "therefore." It should sound good.

"Therefore ... think different." "Therefore ... just do it." "Therefore ... I'm lovin' it."

You know what doesn't sound good? "Therefore ... Coca-Cola is a liquid."

This is not the entire set of advice on how to construct a

slogan, but for something like sloganeering that has zero concrete criteria associated with it, it's at least a little bit of an analytical device for you to use in finding a good slogan.

1.4) BOTTOM LINE: HOW TO USE THE ABT IN THE BUSINESS WORLD

So let's briefly review what this chapter presented: at least six different ways you can use the ABT Narrative Template in the business world. It should be the structural underpinning of 1) a **BRAND STATEMENT**. It can be used to assess 2) **BRAND CONSISTENCY (= GESTALT-BUSTING)**. It provides the narrative structure for 3) an **ELEVATOR PITCH** that will be "catchy." It should be the starting point for 4) a **PRESENTATION**. The last element of the ABT— "therefore"—should be used to test how powerful a statement of consequence 5) a **SLOGAN** is. Overall, every corporation should have a long-term 6) **CORPORATE STRATEGY** that can be boiled down into the ABT that underpins the company itself. It is basically "the story of the company."

There's also more business-relevant material to be found in the next chapter, where I go through the Narrative Index (NI) and the And Frequency (AF). It should become common practice to calculate these two indices for any text you've written. It takes less than a minute for both (just search for BUT and AND). Together they give you a decent assessment of whether you are drawing on the power of tight narrative, or if you've slipped into "The Land of And."

Lastly, anyone preparing for a presentation or press

conference should "figure out your ABT's." This means, write down the most common questions that you know are likely to be asked, then figure out what your ABT-structured answers will be. The last thing you want is to give answers that drift off into a mess of AAA or DHY.

2) POLITICS

2) POLITICS - Messaging is ABT

Just like with business, I have no major experience in the political world, so don't expect any content-related advice. But what I do know is form, meaning the ABT structure. If you're involved with politics you really should hear what I have to say in this chapter because I can't believe how ubiquitous the ABT structure is in everything from political speeches to campaign strategy to slogans to commercials. Every campaign speech writer, to say the least, should be familiar with what I say here. And keep in mind, all of this is new; there are no other books on the ABT.

HEAPS OF MESSAGING BOOKS

Politics is messaging, and messaging is narrative. That's what it's all about. You tell people your message (what you stand for and plan to do), and then they decide if they want to support you.

There's heaps and heaps and heaps of books on the arcane and elusive art of messaging (yep, same thing I said about branding at the start of the last chapter). But here's the problem with writing an entire book on political messaging: You have to fill at least, oh, let's say 133 pages for it to be seen as a real book. Then the reader feels obligated to read all 133 pages, even if a lot of it is just filler.

And that's what I find in the books I read about how to do politics. Most of them are filled with lots of hot air padding out a few core ideas.

So there's your "they say." Now for my "I say": I have only about 10 pages of substance to offer, but the good news is, there's no filler. I will keep things short and simple. In fact, let's dig once again into the need for simplicity by looking at the unfortunate tendency to over-complicate politics.

2.1) DON'T THINK OF A LAKOFF

In advance of the 2004 presidential election, a fascination arose in the Democratic Party with language and the belief that there might be magical words that could, almost by themselves, produce victory. It wasn't totally crazy thinking; there were nuggets of truth at the center of the idea. Labels like "tax relief" obviously change the public's perception of taxes from a fundamental need for society, to a burden that needs to be fought. But there are limits to the power of words, just as there are limits to the power of the ABT.

One voice leading this trend was pollster Frank Luntz who, in the 1990's, had established himself with the right-wing campaigns of Pat Buchanan, Ross Perot and Newt Gingrich. He developed an obsession with the power of individual words and their ability to shape perception. He would eventually write a bestselling book in 2007 called *Words That Work: It's Not What You Say, It's What People Hear*.

Parallel to the popularity of Luntz on the right, the Democrats began an infatuation with U.C. Berkeley cognitive linguist and philosophy professor George Lakoff. He ventured out of the ivory tower and began applying to the political world the principles of his academic books. In the 1980's he had written the non-political book *Metaphors We Live By*. A decade later, he translated that thinking to the political world with his 1996 book *Moral Politics: How Liberals and Conservatives Think.*

Then in 2004, he published his most broadly influential book *Don't Think of An Elephant.* He presented ideas from intellectuals and academics, including from the field of psychology. His central topic was the role of "framing" in argumentation.

Lakoff's work made for great conversation at dinner parties. I was involved in the issue of ocean conservation at the time and began to hear all the communications directors of the big NGO's in DC suddenly talking about "the need to frame the issue." It became a popular fad.

But there was a problem. Lakoff's ideas were so heavily laced with complexity that they probably did more to confuse Democrats than help them. John Kerry's 2004 presidential campaign was a major loss. By 2006, cognitive psychologist Steven Pinker publicly dismissed Lakoff's ideas as "a recipe for electoral failure." I agree with Pinker wholeheartedly.

The problem was good intentions (addressing framing) but a lack of practical specifics on how to implement those intentions. The fact is, the simple idea of establishing the "frame" (as in the "frame of reference") is important. The problem Lakoff and others ran into was that their approach was too vague and intuitive, not analytical.

The ABT is the analytical tool they lacked.

FRAMING: ABT TO THE RESCUE

The ABT provides the analytical starting point for the challenge of framing. Here's an example of how it allows you to boil down a problem. The issue of smoking can be addressed with two different frames of reference.

Frame 1—"Death": Smoking may be seen as cool, AND nicotine provides pleasure, BUT smoking causes cancer that will shorten your life, THEREFORE you should quit smoking.

Frame 2—"Health": Smoking may be seen as cool, AND nicotine provides pleasure, BUT smoking will cause your skin to dry out, your teeth to rot, your hair to fall out and leave you looking like a zombie, making your life miserable, THEREFORE you should quit smoking.

This is a shift of frame that was established long ago by the Centers for Disease Control and Prevention. Telling people smoking will shorten their life is not that effective in reducing smoking, but telling them it will make the life they live miserable is.

For intellectuals, this comparison seems so obvious as to be trivial. But for the less intellectual grassroots, hometown, smaller-scale campaigns and campaign workers, the ABT provides the more structured tool to work on the idea of framing. It provides an analytical way to approach the message, breaking it down into the three elements (context, problem, solution), guiding you to the frame that needs to be adjusted.

Some messages can be reframed by changing the A (context/setup), some can be reframed by changing the B (the problem, as with smoking), and some can be reframed by changing the T (the consequence/action to be taken).

Given the enormous amount of arm-waving that has traditionally accompanied the topic of framing, the ABT at least provides a systematic approach to the subject. It helps get beyond the gobbledygook that psychologists produce in their lengthy books when they get involved with communication, such as with the issue of gun control, as follows.

GUN CONTROL: BEWARE OF PSYCHOLOGISTS BEARING GIFTS

Americans are obsessed with the quick fix. Years ago, I was invited to speak at an NIH symposium on obesity prevention. The opening presentation said basically that today in America there are three main approaches to combatting obesity: pills, surgery or behavior change. You can get all the funding you want to study the first two—the quick fixes—pills and surgery. The last one is simpler and cheaper, but it involves hard work. Very few agencies or foundations want to fund it.

The problem is that nobody wants to do hard work. That was basically the message of the presentation. It's similar to the field of clinical psychology today, in which doctors prefer to quickly write prescriptions for pills than to spend hours talking to patients in therapy.

So the same thing happens with political messaging. There is this belief in the silver bullet of "the right language"; that somehow, if you land on exactly the right term, suddenly the gates of receptivity open up for you, and you don't have to do any hard work.

At a deeper level, there is the idea that we are "hardwired" for certain things. The thinking is that if we can somehow "decode" that hardwiring, then bingo — we're home free.

The only problem is a little group called "neuro-skeptics." They are a kind of neuro police, constantly pointing out how journalists like to take one obscure experiment conducted on the brains of rats and scale it up into a whole essay about how "we are hardwired for ...". Adam Gopnik gave a great review of this trend in his incisive 2013 *New Yorker* article, "Mindless," and the Neuroskeptic blog on the website of *Discover* Magazine is constantly on the job questioning unjustified conclusions.

And I love how Ed Yong at *The Atlantic* and John Oliver on his HBO show ripped apart celebrity scientist Paul Zak over his extrapolation of a tiny observation of rat behavior into a supposed principle that the brain chemical oxytocin is "the love drug." Our society is awash in such nonsense these days; thank goodness for the few neuroskeptics out there trying to fight the tide.

So the more you read from neuroskeptics, the more you begin to see how much overreach arises from the believers in the decoding dream.

A prime example of this can be seen with the issue of gun control. In 2007, the mass shooting at Virginia Tech produced an outcry for gun control legislation, but congress did nothing. It became clear that the National Rifle Association had a death grip on Congress, preventing all action.

In response to this, the psychologists went to work on the language, deciding that the word "control" did not sit well with the public, which generally wants messages of freedom. They devised alternative terms, tested them, and then many settled on "gun safety" as the way to talk about the issue.

But as was pointed out in *The Atlantic* in 2013, the term "gun safety" sounds more like a training course on ... gun safety. It doesn't directly address the issue, and it feels like caving into the aggressive voice of the NRA by being less confrontational.

As a result, the gun issue continued to stall in Congress, with no legislation passed for more than two decades. But that all changed in 2018 with the Parkland school shooting. Overnight a group of teenagers took control of the mass messaging. They didn't do any polling, they didn't consult any academics, they just acted from their gut feelings. They used the more direct, confrontational and traditional term "gun control" widely. And they succeeded in prompting passage of the first national gun legislation since the 1990's.

At the moment, the exact label for the issue is straddling both terms. You now see many politicians saying, "gun control and gun safety" — using the former term to connect all the way back to the original Gun Control Act of 1968 and the latter term to supposedly play to those who prefer it. But that's not good because, as we'll see in a bit with what Nicholas Kristof discusses, narrative is always at its strongest when it is singular. Having two terms for an issue just dilutes the effort. But, of course, psychologists don't care about that, as they are more fond of nuance than power when it comes to communication.

So now let's take a closer look at what lies at the core of political communication: narrative structure.

2.2) POLITICAL MESSAGING: THE QUALITATIVE AND QUANTITATIVE ANALYSIS OF NARRATIVE

Two things here.

First is the QUALITATIVE side of narrative structure in political communication. This means looking at the overall use of the ABT form, which means identifying the three fundamental forces of narrative (agreement, contradiction, consequence). To do this I'll point to the three forces at work in some famous speeches and political messages.

The second is the QUANTITATIVE side of narrative structure. Using the ABT Framework I will present the Narrative Index—a simple quantitative tool I've developed that reflects the "narrative strength" of any given content.

Overall, the biggest challenge to communication is always the need to keep things short and simple. It's the essence of effective communication, especially in today's information-glutted world. It all begins with just having a core message, which sadly sometimes politicians don't even have, as I shall now (painfully and regretfully) remind you.

THE SIMPLE AND SINGULAR MESSAGE: HILLARY HAD NONE, TRUMP HAD ONE

Hillary Clinton, as a politician, was basically "a scientist." I wrote a book in 2009 titled *Don't Be Such A Scientist*, in which I itemized the most prominent traits of scientists that make them so bad at communication. As Hillary Clinton emerged as a candidate for president, I began to convulse in front of my TV realizing she embodied all these problems.

She is, of course, incredibly bright and well-educated. She's often called a "policy wonk," which is exactly her problem. My book was about the challenges heavily educated people face with communication. It had four main chapters, each one starting with, "Don't be ..."

The "Don't be"'s of each chapter were, "so cerebral, "so literal minded," "such a poor storyteller," and, "so unlikable." She is all of them, with the last having been ruthlessly measured. Her unlikability rating was widely bemoaned in the final stretch of her presidential campaign (though it was always noted that Trump's was the worst ever).

Tragically, she ended up being a candidate for president without what I would call an "S&S Message," meaning "Simple & Singular." In August of 2016, she was on a news show where the host asked her for the one main issue of her campaign. She chuckled and said there wasn't any one main thing — as if that was for simpletons. Then she gave a list of some of the great things she was fighting for. And then she lost.

KEEP IT SIMPLE AND SINGULAR (S&S)

You have to have a message that is S&S. The academics and intellectuals may yearn for complexity, but there's not enough of them to get elected. There's the famous quote about how a young woman asked Adlai Stevenson to run for president in 1952. She said, "Every thinking person would be voting for you." He replied, "Madam, that is not enough. I need a majority." He ran anyway (twice) — and also lost.

The masses need a simple message, and that's what Clinton's opponent knew at a very deep level. As odious as he might be to most Americans, Donald Trump has a deep grasp of this need to be S&S. (Note: keep that word "odious" in mind; we'll come back to it.)

In my *Houston* book I coined the term "narrative intuition." I derived it from "story sense," the Hollywood term that screenwriters talk about. It's that state of knowing how to craft a story so well that you're no longer thinking it but rather feeling it, which is the same thing Malcolm Gladwell talked about in his great book *Blink: Thinking without Thinking*.

Narrative intuition means having a deep feeling for the problem-solution dynamics of any situation. It's what Donald Trump has.

Now let's be clear: Trump is *not* a storyteller—that's different. Ronald Reagan was a great storyteller. A story has a problem and solution at its core, plus a lot of other stuff, such as emotion and humor, and it is bookended with non-narrative material. Reagan had a grasp of, and love for, the entire package of a good story.

Trump is too impatient to be a good storyteller. He's a "cut to the chase" kind of guy, a "dealmaker," as his books will tell you. He is only interested in the problem and how we're (at least supposedly) going to solve it. That is what narrative structure is about. In Appendix 1 I give my detailed definitions for the words "narrative" versus "story."

He enters a room, skips the pleasantries, and goes right to the problem at hand. Then he moves on to seeking a solution. You can see that when he does dabble a tiny bit in pleasantries his mind is clearly thinking, "Can we get this part over with and get to what I'm here for?" He has no interest in the human side of the process. And most powerful of all (in communication dynamics) — he offers up ridiculously simple solutions ("a wall," "a tax cut," "a ban"), whether effective or not.

He had, and continues to have, a simple message that is not only concise, it's straight out of the ABT structure. His ABT message is: "We were once a great AND mighty nation, BUT we've slipped in the world, THEREFORE we need to *make America great again.*" The last four words are, of course, his slogan, which, if you read the section in the last chapter on slogans, you can see rolls right off the word "therefore."

Love him or hate him, you need to realize he came out of the gates with that slogan and hasn't changed a word of it in four years. That's what happens when you crack the nut of narrative — nobody feels the need to rearrange what you have to say.

And how am I so certain that a message needs to be simple and singular? Let me cite two tremendously simple, powerful and popular articles that I have used for years in my workshops.

2.3) TWO ESSENTIAL ARTICLES FOR MESSAGING

For years I have cited two very simple, broad articles in my workshops. On a word-for-word basis, I can't imagine any two short articles being more valuable for messaging in today's information-saturated world than these.

NICHOLAS KRISTOF: THE SINGULAR NARRATIVE

Nicholas Kristof is the three-time Pulitzer-Prize-winning columnist from *The New York Times*. In 2009, he published a stunningly simple and powerful essay in (of all the unlikely places) *Outside Magazine.*

The title is, "Nicholas Kristof's Advice for Saving the World." The subtitle is, "What Would Happen If Aid Organizations and Other Philanthropists Embraced the Dark Arts of Marketing Spin and Psychological Persuasion Used on Madison Avenue? We'd Save Millions More Lives."

Kristof and his wife worked on a health issue in Africa for many years. Over the years they watched many public-health education campaigns come and go. Most were failures; a few succeeded. Out of what they saw he crafted the article, delving into what worked.

There are many gems of wisdom in his article, but the one that addresses the need for a simple, singular message is one of the best parts. He says you need to keep the message about just one thing. Not even two things. Just one.

He says, "Storytelling needs to focus on an individual, not a group." He illustrates this point by citing a classic experiment in which people are asked to donate to help fight hunger in Africa. They are asked to help one little girl named Rokia. Now, wouldn't you think that if they were presented with the suffering of two little girls, they would be twice as motivated? But then what about five, or ten, or a thousand?

Of course it goes in the opposite direction. Narrative is at its strongest with the one, singular subject. He quotes the age-old adage, "The death of one person is a tragedy; the death of

72

a million is a statistic."

This is such an infinitely powerful and central property of narrative. It's so fundamentally important that it was the focus of an entire bestselling book in 2013, called *The One Thing: The Surprisingly Simple Truth Behind Extraordinary Results*, by Gary Keller and Jay Papasan. And I will talk about it in depth in the fourth chapter, when I explore the communication handicap of the science world.

DAVE GOLD: TRUMP HAD A CHRISTMAS TREE, HILLARY HAD A BOX OF ORNAMENTS

The other super-important article comes from Dave Gold, a long-time strategist for the Democratic Party. Just three months after Hillary Clinton's defeat he published a simple, concise and powerful article in *Politico* called, "Data-Driven Campaigns Are Killing the Democratic Party."

He delved into the fundamental problem of the Democrats failing to grasp narrative dynamics. He talked about the importance of finding the singular narrative at the core of a campaign, and he mentioned a great metaphor he had learned from one of his professors long ago.

The idea is to think of the central theme of a good campaign as "the Christmas tree" upon which all the issues of the campaign, the "ornaments," are hung. This Christmas tree metaphor is incredibly powerful and dovetails with Kristof's emphasis on the singular narrative.

Trump had an obvious Christmas tree: Make America Great Again. He was able to hang every issue on that tree. He said we need to reduce immigration to make America great again, we need to have a tax cut to make America great again and we need to ban Muslims to make America great again. On and on, with everything supporting the one overarching theme of making America great again. The approach was mind-numbingly simple to Democrats, but it worked for Trump with his followers, and it continues to work.

Hillary had no Christmas tree—only a box of ornaments. She is not remembered for any clear message. At all.

In a few pages I will present the Dobzhansky Template for finding the one-word theme at the center of a narrative. It is essentially the same thing as the Christmas tree. If you can figure out that central theme, you will have conquered the hardest part of the challenge of narrative.

And if you think you can just ignore it … well, look what happened with that election.

2.4) TRUMP, "THE ODIOUS TOAD," AND HIS SINGULAR INSULT NAMES

One of the clearest demonstrations of the extent to which Donald Trump lives and breathes the power of the singular narrative is his endless set of insult names for his opponents. There are the obvious ones from his election—Low-Energy Jeb, Lyin' Ted, Little Marco and, of course, Crooked Hillary. But when you look at the Wikipedia page for his nicknames, you see the list has over one hundred entries.

These names are powerful in a world of too much

information. They cut through the noise and are as cutting as the use of stereotypes. Why the Democratic Party fails to draw the connection to stereotypes, which are widely shunned by Americans, I cannot figure out. I don't understand why they don't call out the nicknames for being the stereotypes they clearly are.

They are damaging, and they stick. They roll off the tongue, and they send S&S messages — like "the failing *New York Times*."

When I grew up there was the little rhyme we were all taught: "Sticks and stones can break my bones, but words can never hurt me." That cute little line of thinking came from the pre-Information Era. It is no longer true. Words have the potential to be extremely damaging, as Trump knows.

What is most baffling is that not only do the Democrats try to laugh away the names (like Elizabeth Warren, who was eventually damaged by "Pocahontas"), they have failed to even attempt to create a singular name for him. Lots have been offered up, but because of a lack of leadership, none have stuck. So he continues to run communications circles around them as he amuses the masses, which makes the technique even more powerful.

I find the entire technique so reprehensible and demeaning that it just doesn't feel right to let him off without a nickname. THEREFORE ... from this point forward in this book, I shall refer to him as "The Odious Toad," and more simply (since the label needs to be S&S), as The Toad (and with apologies to a famous and wonderful tropical ecologist who humorously goes by that name).

This will hopefully enable Democrats to see that while I am pointing out the strengths of his communication style, I am not any sort of fan of him as a human being. And here, just to drive the point home—here's a photo of him, orange skin and all.

LADIES AND GENTLEMEN, THE PRESIDENT OF THE UNITED STATES, MR. ODIOUS TOAD. He has singular insult names for his opponents. Why don't they have a single insult name for him?

NESTED ABT'S: OPRAH TOLD "A STORY OF STORIES"

Let's take a more specific look at Dave Gold's Christmas tree as put to use by Oprah Winfrey in a powerful speech. The ultimate form of messaging is to deliver a narratively structured message at multiple levels. This means, for example, you give a speech that has an overarching ABT structure, but then within the body of it, you deliver smaller-scale ABTs. If you manage this, you end up with a structure of "nested ABT's."

This is exactly what Oprah Winfrey did in February 2018 with her Golden Globes speech, which was instantly hailed as a classic. I didn't see it that night, but the next morning I awoke to an email from a friend asking, "Does this fit your ABT structure?" All it took was a glance at the transcript to see that it did.

First, she had the same overarching ABT as Martin Luther King, Jr.'s legendary "I Have a Dream" speech, which we'll get to soon. His message was basically, "We were made a promise of civil rights, AND we've made progress, BUT the promise has yet to be completely fulfilled, THEREFORE we are here today to continue the mission."

Oprah laid out the same message as her Christmas tree, but she also presented, within the overarching structure, a series of smaller ABT's. You can see the structure in the format-coded version of it in Appendix 3.

The net result was an analysis of the speech in *The New York Times* that called it "a story made of stories." I read that phrase and kicked myself, thinking, "Argh, that's what I should have called that structure in my *Houston* book, instead of going with my nerdy 'Nested ABT's.'"

Oh, well, that's why they're *The New York Times*, and I'm just a former scientist.

2.5) MY NIGHT AT TULANE WITH JAMES CARVILLE

Going back to the Hillary versus The Toad comparison, I have a long story to tell (that I'll keep short) about how I found my way to the great and wonderful political strategist James Carville in 2016. He's the brilliant communicator who masterminded Bill Clinton's 1992 presidential campaign and coined the phrase, "It's the economy, stupid."

The phrase was a variation on the age-old KISS (Keep It Simple Stupid) message. Based on that alone you can see why he was the right guy for me to pursue.

In 2015, I began to see this fundamental divide in the communications dynamics of Hillary versus The Toad. When I realized this sharp contrast, given today's information-glutted world, I knew she was in for trouble.

I tried in vain to get the attention of her campaign and to publish a major editorial about this, but I hit brick walls everywhere I turned. There were lots (and continue to be lots) of people who think they know "the secret to The Toad's technique." I was stuck looking like one of those "experts." The result was nobody—and I mean noooo-body—understood or took an interest in what I was saying about the ABT dynamic. Except one guy.

In the spring of 2016, as a last-ditch effort, I searched three words—"Hillary Clinton boring." The first thing that came up was an article titled "James Carville Acknowledges Hillary Clinton is Boring."

I wrote a letter to Mr. Carville that included the scores for my newly devised "Narrative Index" (I'll explain it in a bit). Hillary scored 14, while The Toad got more than double, at 29. A friend of a friend managed to get the letter to Mr. Carville via folks at Tulane University, where he taught a political science class.

Mr. Carville called me up the day he read it (it was so reflective of who he is—not to have an assistant contact me but instead to just pick up the phone himself) and left a message saying he was intrigued with "how you got your scores here."

I called him back. He was hilarious, wonderful, and told me a bunch of great stories as I explained my observations. He got it. He wasn't the least bit dubious about how simple the ABT is (by contrast, the editors of 538.com said, "We're intrigued but skeptical that it's this simple"), he simply went to work.

KNOCKING ON BRICK DOORS

Mr. Carville tried in vain for several months to get Hillary's campaign staff to listen to me. They never did (nor did they listen to lots of other people with good but unsolicited advice—as is the dynamic with most political campaigns).

The rest is history, as she, the smart policy wonk, lost to the simple-minded toad. And, yes, the Russians probably did play a part, but regardless, there was no denying she lacked a clear message, as countless articles were written about this (and continue to be written for the Democratic Party as well).

It was hugely frustrating, but the one consolation prize I got was that Mr. Carville brought me to New Orleans to speak to his legendary Tulane University political science class of 50 students. They met one night a week in the high-ceilinged, ornate living room of the stately home he shares with his wife, Republican strategist Mary Matalin. It was one of the most fun nights of my life.

So the reason I'm telling you this is because of how he started the evening. He asked if anyone present knew who Edward

Everett was. The room was packed with bright students, but no hands went up. I didn't know either. He explained.

Edward Everett was the U.S. Secretary of State in the mid-1800's and, more importantly, was the main speaker on November 19, 1863, at the dedication of the military cemetery at Gettysburg, Pennsylvania.

He spoke for over two hours that day.   Then Abraham Lincoln took the stage and spoke for just two minutes. He asked the students to guess which one was remembered for his "Gettysburg Address."

Effective communication is that simple, stupid.

NARRATIVE IS LEADERSHIP: YOU BORE, THEY SNORE, YOU CONFUSE, YOU LOSE

The title of this book is, *Narrative is Everything*. Nested within that theme is my sub-theme, "Narrative is leadership." Now it's time to dig deep on this point.

People follow leaders who are interesting.   People do not follow leaders who are confusing or boring. This is especially true in today's short-attention-span world—you bore, they snore, you confuse, you lose.

So how do you avoid being boring or confusing? You have a clear ABT.

In fact, this dynamic is so simple that everyone teaching "leadership training" (something that's as common as books about messaging) should begin by teaching communication, and that should begin by teaching the ABT.

Abe Lincoln would endorse this approach. It's at the core of how you lead, and you can see it at work in those who succeed in leading. Which takes us back to The Toad.

The polls show that, at least within his party, The Odious Toad is a powerful leader. As he will eagerly point out, no one in recent memory has managed to consolidate the Republican party as he has; the polls show over 90% approval among Republicans. He communicates loudly, he communicates simply, and the one thing he has never been called is boring, other than by some bitter opponents.

His non-boringness is demonstrated by the staggering amount of media attention he constantly receives. Even filmmaker/Trump hater Michael Moore concedes this in his 2018 movie *Fahrenheit 11/9*.

As for confusing, yes, he can be confusing at times in the short term. But over the long term he has not been confusing at all. He came out of the gate in 2015 with a clear, single message of "Make America Great Again," and he has not wavered from it since.

The left has ridiculed The Toad for his simple message, while the right has fallen in line. He has demonstrated plenty of small-scale confusion, with his constant hirings and firings, but, overall, he's had one single message and stuck to it.

Now let's look at another Narrative Tool that's relevant here.

2.6) ANOTHER NARRATIVE TOOL: THE DOBZHANSKY TEMPLATE

We've talked about the need for a message to be simple and singular. What could be shorter than a single word? That's what I was thinking as I developed this narrative tool, and now it also applies to The Toad and his insult names as he boils complicated people down to single words.

For starters, I know you'll want a different, simpler name for this. Sorry, it's already stuck. And I love hearing students butcher it with names like, "The Bob Hansky Template."

The name comes from one of the most famous geneticists of all time, Theodosius Dobzhansky. I talk about it in detail in my Houston book if you're interested, but, for now, let's just talk about what the template is:

Nothing in _____ makes sense, except in the light of _____.

It's just a simple fill-in-the-blanks sentence to help you come up with the one- word theme that might be at the core of what you're talking about. I say "might" because it's not always possible to boil everything down to one word, but you never know until you try.

So let's go right to the guy who knew how to lock onto a simple, singular theme from the start (although I'm sure he's not so analytical as to actually have used something like this template). Right out of the gate, The Odious Toad had one word at the core of his presidential campaign. His theme statement, using the Dobzhansky, was that:

Nothing makes sense in <u>America today</u>, except in the light of … <u>greatness</u>.

Just about every speech he's given has been an exercise in messaging around that one word: making America GREAT again.

Is having a single word as your message an elegant thing to do? Not always. Does it work? In today's world of excess noise, it not only works, it's essential. The mass audience can't pick up on a nuanced message. They work best when there's mostly just one thing.

A couple of years ago I followed a Twitter argument between two very highly educated climate activists. At one point one of them shot back at the other, "I'd like to think people can keep two thoughts present in their minds at the same time."

Sorry, but no. Again, it's called the singular narrative. In Chapter 3 I'll tell of its origins in the age-old "classical design" of stories, and then in Chapter 7 I'll draw parallels with natural selection to explain why it occurs.

And by the way, gazing back on that 2013 bestselling book *The One Thing: The Surprisingly Simple Truth Behind Extraordinary Results*, by Keller and Papasan. That's what it's about—the importance of the singular narrative. (Though here's a critical note about that book: Remember at the start of this chapter, when I said I'd hate to write a 133-page book when I only had 10 pages of substantive content? Yep, I'm talking about books like that one—though the 10 pages of genuine content it has are definitely important.)

To this very point, on the morning after The Toad was elected, I appeared as the guest on the podcast *The Business of Story*, hosted by my friend Park Howell. On the episode, I ran through the depth of The Toad's grasp of these simple narrative dynamics and the inability of the Democrats to grasp it (btw, that episode ended up being the most popular of his first 200 episodes).

There is much to be learned. We can learn what does work in today's Information Society by studying The Toad, whether he repulses you or not. And we can learn what doesn't work in the Information Society from people who can't seem to grasp the idea of simplicity, meaning today's Democrats, as I shall now sadly relate.

CASE STUDY OF THE DOBZHANSKY TEMPLATE: THE DEMOCRATS AND THE KAVANAUGH HEARING

A couple of years after appearing on *The Business of Story*, I returned to talk about the mess that the Democratic senators had made of the hearing for Supreme Court nominee Brett Kavanaugh. What happened was a scattershot three-hour hearing at which each senator was given five minutes to ask questions.

The Democrats, instead of presenting a clear, simple, singular narrative, produced a chaotic "And, And, And" performance. And lost. Once again.

But let me give you the quick ABT Framework strategy that could have been used that day.

For starters, wouldn't it have been nice if the senators had gotten together that morning in a conference room and said, "Okay, what's our Dobzhansky?"

Mazie Hirono was on NPR that morning, and she hit on the

one word that would have been able to offer a perfect theme: temperament. She basically said she had no interest in sexual misconduct allegations of 35 years ago. What she was interested in was events in more recent years that simply showed he did not have the proper temperament for a Supreme Court judge.

Had that initial meeting of the senators happened, and had the group agreed with her to lock onto that one word — TEMPERAMENT — things could have come together into a narratively structured strategy.

Their "narrative coach" could have said, "Okay, Feinstein, you start the session by explaining to the American public what temperament is, why it is essential in a judge, and what reflects a lack of it. Then, Whitehouse, when you read the entries from his yearbook, explain how that material reflects on his TEMPERAMENT. Senator Harris, when you compare his process to Gorsuch, explain how Gorsuch had the right TEMPERAMENT to be a Supreme Court judge, which made his confirmation easy, but Kavanaugh does not. Blumenthal, instead of rambling through four topics, pick one that no one else has covered and relate it to TEMPERAMENT.
Then Harris, you're last, so give us an ending to our story by pulling everything together, saying that we feel all of what we've heard today underscores our belief that Judge Kavanaugh LACKS THE TEMPERAMENT to be on the Supreme Court."

And then the coach adds one more thing: "Klobuchar, if we should get lucky enough to see him lose his cool and snap back at you, asking if you have ever blacked out from drinking (which he did in a shocking moment of complete loss of composure), you need to jump on that moment and point out to the American public that THIS is what we're talking about — right here, in the frickin' hearing!"

Had all that happened the hearing would have been a story with a clear beginning, middle and end. Every news correspondent would have structured their story around THE MESSAGE, which would have been that Kavanaugh lacks THE TEMPERAMENT of a Supreme Court justice.

That is how messaging works.

It was all there, waiting to be narratively structured, but it didn't happen, because ... because why? A lack of awareness of the ABT Framework is what I would say.

Mazie Hirono was so close. She was the closest thing to a hero that day. Maybe next time.

So this narrative structure stuff really is important, and, furthermore, it can even be quantified, as we shall now explore.

2.7) WHAT IF WE COULD QUANTIFY HOW WELL YOU ARE TAPPING INTO THE POWER OF NARRATIVE?

Over the past decade a gigantic consensus emerged around the idea that the human being is a "storytelling animal," which was the title of Jonathan Gottschall's popular 2012 book. He stated it eloquently with that title, but unfortunately in recent years he's been joined by a stampede of prophets proclaiming this, over and over again, until all you can say is,

"Okay, we get it, storytelling is still— 4000 years after the first recorded story of Gilgamesh—at the center of how we communicate."

So now, let's move to the next level and ask if there might be some way to quantify how good of a job someone is doing tapping into this "power of story." The answer is yes.

INTRODUCING "THE NARRATIVE INDEX"

The logic behind the Narrative Index is (like everything in this book) simple. It's so simple I was very skeptical of it when I first devised it, but now I've accumulated six years of observations and analyzed thousands of speeches, books, essays, debate performances and other texts.

It is not a precise index, but it is definitely accurate. (Scientists are always keen to point out how something can be *accurate*, but not *precise*, or vice versa.)

As I mentioned briefly in the first chapter, I adapted the ABT from "The Rule of Replacing" that I heard from the co-creators of the animated series *South Park*. Their basic observation for editing a script is, "Every time you replace an AND with a BUT or a THEREFORE, the storytelling gets better."

I got to thinking in the summer of 2015 that if you took a given text and removed some ANDs and replaced them with BUTs (let's skip the THEREFOREs for now), you would end up with a simple metric. It would be the BUTs-to-ANDs ratio, which you could calculate before and after altering the text.

If you did this, the "after" value would be greater than the "before" value. And as we've said, we know that the "after" material is stronger storytelling—meaning greater narrative strength.

So this then becomes our index. The greater the Narrative Index value (the higher the BUT-to-AND ratio), the greater the story strength of the material. Also, to make it a whole number instead of a fraction, we multiply it by 100.

Which means the Narrative Index is this:

NARRATIVE INDEX = (BUTs/ANDs) X 100

Once I figured this out, I set to work analyzing political speeches and debates. Here's the first set of texts I analyzed. It ends up being the prototypical demonstration of the Narrative Index.

THE LINCOLN-DOUGLAS DEBATES OF 1858

In the summer of 1858, incumbent Illinois Senator Stephen Douglas engaged in a series of seven debates with challenger Abraham Lincoln. I'll spare you all the flowery descriptions of how hot it was that summer and how the nation was inching towards civil war. I'm like The Toad at times. Let's just talk about what matters here: the communication dynamics.

The debates were transcribed and can be found online. The texts for each man's performance average around 10,000 words, which makes for solid sample sizes (I'm generally leery of texts that are fewer than 1,000 words long.)

For each performance the patterns jump out immediately. Look at the graph here:

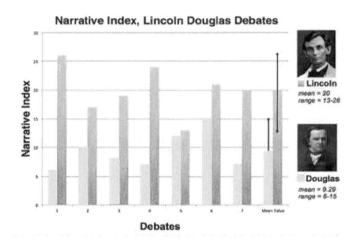

NARRATIVE INDEX SCORES FOR THE 1858 LINCOLN-DOUGLAS DEBATES. Lincoln's scores were greater for every debate than Douglas. The bars on the mean values represent 95% confidence intervals.

Prior to 1854 this country was divided into two great political parties, known as the Whig and Democratic parties. Both were national and patriotic, advocating principles that were universal in their application. An old line Whig could proclaim his principles in Louisiana and Massachusetts alike. Whig principles had no boundary sectional line, they were not limited by the Ohio river, nor by the Potomac, nor by the line of the free and slave States, but applied and were proclaimed wherever the Constitution ruled or the American flag waved over the American soil. (Hear him, and three cheers.) So it was, and so it is with the great Democratic party, which, from the days of Jefferson until this period, has proven itself to be the historic party of this nation. While the Whig and Democratic parties differed in regard to a bank, the tariff, distribution, the specie circular and the sub-treasury, they agreed on the great slavery question which now agitates the Union. I say that the Whig party and the Democratic party agreed on this slavery question, while they differed on those matters of expediency to which I have referred. The Whig party and the Democratic party jointly adopted the Compromise measures of 1850 as the basis of a proper and just solution of this slavery question in all its forms. Clay was the great leader, with Webster on his right and Cass on his left, and sustained by the patriots in the Whig and Democratic ranks, who had devised and enacted the Compromise measures of 1850.

In 1851, the Whig party and the Democratic party united in Illinois in adopting resolutions indorsing and approving the principles of the Compromise measures of 1850, as the proper adjustment of that question. In 1852, when the Whig party assembled in Convention at Baltimore for the purpose of nominating a candidate for the Presidency, the first thing it did was to declare the Compromise measures of 1850, in substance and in principle, a suitable adjustment of that question. (Here the speaker was interrupted by loud and long continued applause.) My friends, silence will be more acceptable to me in the discussion of these questions than applause. I desire to address myself to your judgment, your understanding, and your conscience, and not to your passions or your enthusiasm. When the Democratic Convention assembled in Baltimore in the same year, for the purpose of nominating a Democratic candidate for the Presidency, it also adopted the compromise measures of 1850 as the basis of Democratic action. Thus you see that up to 1853-'54, the Whig party and the Democratic party both stood on the same platform with regard to the slavery question. That platform was the right of the people of each State and each Territory to decide their local and domestic institutions for themselves, subject only to the federal constitution.

Stephen Douglas

SAMPLE OF TEXT FROM STEPHEN DOUGLAS. This shows the frequency of the word "and" and the rarity of "but," as his words flowed like a "rushing, unbroken stream."

MR. LINCOLN-Well, then, let us talk about Popular Sovereignty! [Laughter.] What is Popular Sovereignty? [Cries of "A humbug," "a humbug."] Is it the right of the people to have Slavery or not have it, as they see fit, in the territories? I will state-and I have an able man to watch me-my understanding is that Popular Sovereignty, as now applied to the question of slavery, does allow the people of a Territory to have slavery if they want to, but does not allow them *not* to have it if they *do not* want it. [Applause and laughter.] I do not mean that if this vast concourse of people were in a Territory of the United States, any one of them would be obliged to have a slave if he did not want one; but I do say that, as I understand the Dred Scott decision, if any one man wants slaves, all the rest have no way of keeping that one man from holding them.

When I made my speech at Springfield, of which the Judge complains, and from which he quotes, I really was not thinking of the things which he ascribes to me at all. I had no thought in the world that I was doing anything to bring about a war between the free and slave States. I had no thought in the world that I was doing anything to bring about a political and social equality of the black and white races. It never occurred to me that I was doing anything or favoring anything to reduce to a dead uniformity all the local institutions of the various States. But I must say, in all fairness to him, if he thinks I am doing something which leads to these bad results, it is none the better that I did not mean it. It is just as fatal to the country, if I have any influence in producing it, whether I intend it or not. But can it be true, that placing this institution upon the original basis-the basis upon which our fathers placed it-can have any tendency to set the Northern and the Southern States at war with one another, or that it can have any tendency to make the people of Vermont raise sugarcane, because they raise it in Louisiana, or that it can compel the people of Illinois to cut pine logs on the Grand Prairie, where they will not grow, because they cut pine logs in Maine, where they do grow? [Laughter.] The Judge says this is a new principle started in regard to this question. Does the Judge claim that he is working on the plan of the founders of Government? I think he says in some of his speeches-indeed, I have one here now-that he saw evidence of a policy to allow slavery to be south of a certain line, while north of it it should be excluded, and he saw an indisposition on the part of the country to stand upon that policy, and therefore he set about studying the subject upon *original principles*, and upon *original principles* he got up the Nebraska bill! I am fighting it upon these "original principles"-fighting it in the Jeffersonian, Washingtonian, and Madisonian fashion. [Laughter and applause.]

Abraham Lincoln

SAMPLE OF TEXT FROM LINCOLN. This shows how much more often he used the word "but" as he crafted ABT structured statements.

Abe Lincoln had more story strength than Stephen Douglas for each debate. That's the simple pattern the Narrative Index reveals. Abe's Narrative Index for every debate was greater, and his average was more than double his opponent's.

Furthermore, there's even in-person corroboration of this difference from newspaper reporters who were there and described the debates. One of them said, "Lincoln's words did not flow in a rushing, unbroken stream like Douglas."

That makes sense. When you're communicating via the AAA structure, all you're doing is spewing out disconnected statements of this AND this AND this AND this … you don't need to slow down and think because there's no real structure to what you're assembling. You can spew words like "a rushing, unbroken stream."

But when you're tapping into the power of the ABT, the elements are connected, and that takes time to work out. As a result, Abe spoke more slowly and thoughtfully. And that's the deal with narrative structure. Remember what Longfellow said: "It was easy for you to read because it was so hard for me to write."

The hard part for Longfellow was all the *time* he had to put in to make the pieces fit together. Same deal as Lincoln. Crafting narrative structure is hard and takes time.

So were the debates worth it for Abe? Did he win the 1858 election? No. But there was widespread agreement that he won the debates. By the last few, Douglas was losing steam, people were getting bored with him and everyone could sense a great voice emerging with Lincoln.

Now let's take a closer look at four of the best communicating politicians/activists in American history and see how completely they embodied the ABT Framework.

THE HEROES: ABRAHAM, MARTIN AND JOHN (AND BARBARA)

The ABT is a thing of beauty, just like the iconic 1968 song, "Abraham, Martin and John" written by Richard Holler and first performed soulfully by Dion DiMucci (for those of us who remember hearing it on the radio back then, it still pulls the heartstrings). The ABT reaches its apogee with these three great men, plus a woman who is a little less famous but was just as great a communicator, making it clear it's not just a male thing. Or a white thing.

All four of them have had what I termed in my *Houston* book "narrative intuition." This means the ability to shape the narrative structure of material, not by analytically using a bunch of tools and templates, but simply by having a feel for it.

ABRAHAM: GETTYSBURG ADDRESS

It was only two hundred and seventy-some words (there's small-scale debate over the exact text). It had only three paragraphs. But it was pure ABT structure, and therefore has persisted and remained popular.

Yes, it has some wonderful CONTENT, such as eloquent prose like "four score and seven years ago," instead of just "eighty-seven years ago." But focusing on that aspect is like focusing on the color of paint on a Mercedes. Nice paint, but it's a Mercedes! It's the form of the car that matters most, just as it's the form of the speech that matters most over the long term. Boring or confusing speeches do not persist. This is the essence of narrative selection.

The first paragraph sets up the narrative. (We've built a great country.) The second paragraph states the problem. ("We are now engaged in a great civil war.") The third and final paragraph states the actions that need to be taken ("It is for us the living, rather, to be dedicated here to the unfinished work.")

You can rave all you want about the prose (as Ken Burns did

in an hour-long documentary about the speech that made no mention of its narrative structure), but had Lincoln presented the elements in reverse order (making it a TBA), it would have been, "We're here today to remain dedicated to unfinished work. What is this work? We're now engaged in a great civil war. And why is it important? We've built a great country that we don't want to lose." That sequence would have worked okay—especially for intellectuals who enjoy reassembling the pieces into proper narrative form—but it wouldn't have lasted any more than stories that go, "End, Middle, Beginning." There's a reason why *The Curious Case of Benjamin Button* (a guy whose life follows that backwards timeline) is not on the AFI Top 100 list.

You don't start with the therefore; you build to it. Abe knew this. How did he know it? Because he had deep "narrative intuition." You can see it in all of his speeches and debate performances. And here's someone who knew it even better. Much better.

MARTIN: "I HAVE A DREAM" SPEECH

How do you think Martin Luther King, Jr., started the most important and memorable speech of his life? He started it with an ABT.

It was his "I Have a Dream" speech, delivered on the steps of the Lincoln memorial on August 28, 1963, to over a quarter-million civil rights activists on the Mall in Washington, D.C. He opened with one paragraph of pleasantries, then got down to the business at hand with his second paragraph, which has pure ABT structure.

Take a look at what he said, format-coded to show the structure:

Five score years ago, a great American, in whose symbolic shadow we stand today, signed the Emancipation Proclamation. This momentous decree came as a great beacon light of hope to millions of Negro slaves who had been seared in the flames of withering injustice. It came as a joyous daybreak to end the long night of their captivity.

But one hundred years later, the Negro still is not free. One hundred years later, the life of the Negro is still sadly crippled by the manacles of segregation and the chains of discrimination. One hundred years later, the Negro lives on a lonely island of poverty in the midst of a vast ocean of material prosperity.

One hundred years later, the Negro is still languishing in the corners of American society and finds himself an exile in his own land.

So we have come here today to dramatize a shameful condition.

Could it be any more obvious? It has the word "but," then the last sentence begins with, "so," which is the more conversational form of "therefore."

It's a fascinating speech. The Narrative Index value for it is only 14, but it's a different kind of speech in its overall structure.

The first two-thirds of the speech is mostly "setup" of the situation: his people were written a check that has failed to be cashed. Then comes the presentation of "the problem" ("But we refuse to believe that the bank of justice is bankrupt.")

Once he establishes all that, he then spends the entire last 37%

of the speech— more than the last third—delivering only one thing: statements of consequence. Try running The Therefore Test (which I presented in the last chapter) on it. Put the word THEREFORE at the start of every sentence in the last third. It works, over and over again:

> THEREFORE I say to you today …
> THEREFORE I have a dream …
> THEREFORE this is our hope …
> THEREFORE this will be the day …
> THEREFORE let freedom ring …

If you want to know how to inspire a crowd, just look at this. It's like with each line he is imploring his followers with the NIKE slogan: "Therefore, just do it!"

Martin Luther King, Jr., had a mind for sloganeering. One reflection of this is that all of his most famous and effective speeches had titles: "I Have a Dream," "Our God is Marching on," "The Other America," "Don't Sleep through the Revolution," "I've Been to the Mountaintop." He never knew the ABT structure analytically, but he embodied it intuitively.

Hillary Clinton's speeches didn't have titles.

JOHN: INAUGURAL ADDRESS

Of the many great and inspiring speeches John F. Kennedy delivered in his short presidency, the best was his 1961 inaugural address. *TIME* Magazine has it as one of the ten greatest speeches in American history. It culminates with the iconic line, "Ask not what your country can do for you—ask what you can do for your country"—the line that defined a generation of young idealists. You can feel the THEREFORE power of it.

The first thing to note about the speech is that Kennedy was said to have worked intensely on it for two months. That's the old Longfellow spirit; it's been easy for everyone to listen to that speech over the ages because it was so hard for him to write.

The second thing is the Narrative Index is 34 (13 BUTs, 38 ANDs). Very, very few political speeches have ever scored over 30.

Actually, here's something I love: The only inaugural address to ever score higher was Richard Nixon's first, in 1969. He rang the bell with a whopping 44 (17 BUTs, 39 ANDs).

Think about what was going on in Nixon's head and heart. He was narrowly defeated by Kennedy in 1960. By 1968 he was finally there. He could hardly contain himself—like Dr. Strangelove trying to control his mechanical arm.

Nixon was probably the most ambitious professional politician (notice I say professional—No Toads Allowed) to ever achieve the presidency. He was set to show the nation "how it's done." And look at this ominous ABT line that he opened with:

Each moment in history is a fleeting time, precious AND unique. BUT some stand out as moments of beginning, in which courses are set that shape decades or centuries.

How priceless is that? He was warning everybody to brace themselves because Tricky Dick's the boss now! His next line should have been, "Therefore, I'll see you at the Watergate in a few years."

Back to JFK. His speech was brilliant in many ways. Just look at the contradiction he opens with. He begins by saying, "We observe today not a victory of party, but a celebration of freedom."

That, right there, is the power of narrative, boiled down into 13 words. He sets up the status quo—he's saying most inaugural speeches are just part of a victory party—then he turns it on its head by saying that this one is going to be a celebration of freedom. That is how you jar the masses out of their complacency with a speech.

Then look how he ends the speech. He starts with, "And so ..." That's the same as "Therefore." That's how deep his ABT intuition was.

And, of course, he follows that structural cue with his grand synthesis, "And so, ask not what your country can do for you, ask what you can do for your country." Notice what's at the center of that tremendous plea to the public: contradiction. You could replace the second "ask" with "but."

This stuff is not coincidence. Not one bit. Wherever you find truly great oration like this material that persists over the ages—you will see the ABT at work.

BARBARA: 1976 DNC SPEECH

Most lists of the top ten speeches in American history include the barn burner of a speech given in 1976 by legendary lawyer, educator and politician of the Civil Rights Movement, Barbara Jordan. She was African-American, a U.S. Representative from Texas, a fierce debater, and she truly made the most of her finest public moment.

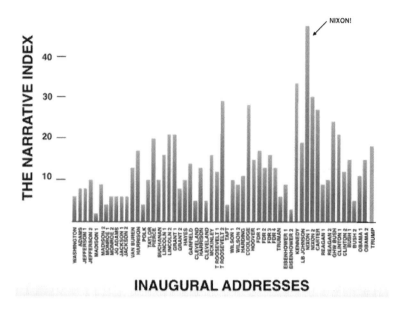

NARRATIVE INDEX SCORES FOR PRESIDENTIAL INAUGURAL ADDRESSES. Look at Nixon with the 44. Whoa.

In 1976, Barbara Jordan gave one of the opening keynote addresses at the Democratic National Convention at Madison Square Garden. Her speech was packed with energy and excitement. It scores a powerful 39 for the Narrative Index.

Just look how she started it: with a perfect ABT.

One hundred and forty-four years ago, members of the Democratic Party first met in convention to select a Presidential candidate. Since that time, Democrats have continued to convene once every four years and draft a party platform and nominate a Presidential candidate. And our meeting this week is a continuation of that tradition.

But there is something different about tonight. There is something special about tonight. What is different? What is

Special? *I, Barbara Jordan, am a keynote speaker.*

Adding to the strength of the material is that she draws on the element of time in the setup. This is an important note. There is nothing more powerful in the world of narrative than the past. If you want to know how to begin a narrative in the most powerful way, start with the past. This is what our brains are programmed to open up to. And notice that all three of the trio (Abraham, Martin, and John) opened their greatest speeches with references to the past.

She could have begun with something that did not draw on time, something like, "Keynote addresses are a great opportunity to start a discussion, but there is something different about tonight …"

That would have been okay, but nowhere near as powerful as harkening back to the distant past. It reaches into people's hearts, as she did with her speech.

And just look at how she closed it:

We cannot improve on the system of government handed down to us by the founders of the Republic, there is no way to improve upon that. **But what we can do is to find new ways to implement that system and realize our destiny.** *Now, I began this speech by commenting to you on the uniqueness of a Barbara Jordan making the keynote address.*

She says our government system is fine, but we need to find new ways to implement it, therefore: me! An African-American leader.

And also notice her statement brings the entire speech "full circle." This is straight out of the "monomyth" circular structure for stories first described by mythologist Joseph Campbell. She was the embodiment of what I mean by "narrative intuition."

DULLSVILLE: BUSH AND EISENHOWER

Okay, we've heard from the "smart-as-a-whip"s; now let's hear from the "dull-as-a-drip"s.

As I said before, the Narrative Index is not precise. I can't tell you if Abraham Lincoln was better than John F. Kennedy. They both almost always score in the upper teens or low 20's for their speeches. But here's what I can tell you with confidence: the Narrative Index shows us they were both much better with narrative than Presidents Dwight D. Eisenhower or George W. Bush (though don't think it's a Democrat-vs.-Republican thing — Nixon had consistently high scores).

Of the 15 speeches I've analyzed by good old "Ike" Eisenhower, all but one fall into the range between 5 and 13. And this is what I mean when I say the Narrative Index is accurate. It shows that the previous group was interesting, but Ike was kinda boring.

The same is true for George W. Bush. Talk about dull. His seven State of the Union addresses show incredible consistency: all of them scored between 2 and 5.

You might think it's just because Bush didn't like the word "but," but … let's just take a look at the first paragraph of his 2003 State of the Union Address (Narrative Index = 2).

BUSH: Every year, by law and by custom, we meet here to

consider the state of the Union. This year, we gather in this chamber deeply aware of decisive days that lie ahead. You and I serve our country in a time of great consequence. During this session of Congress, we have the duty to reform domestic programs vital to our country. We have the opportunity to save millions of lives abroad from a terrible disease. We will work for a prosperity that is broadly shared, and we will answer every danger and every enemy that threatens the American people. In all these days of promise and days of reckoning, we can be confident. In a whirlwind of change and hope and peril, our faith is sure; our resolve is firm; and our Union is strong.

He never gets to a statement of contradiction. It's just a listing of facts and observations, not really leading to much of anything, nor drawing on history.

And let me hammer further home the Narrative Index scores. I found a book of the collected speeches of George W. Bush, 2001-2008. The speeches total 194,157 words, a huge sample size. The Narrative Index is 5.9, the And Frequency is 4.0. That's bad. The former score is down there in the range of equipment manuals (seriously, I found five of them on the internet, the average score was 4.3 — you don't use a lot of "buts" when you're giving instructions for running equipment). The latter is up there with World Bank reports.

Now take a look at the opening for fellow Republican Richard Nixon's State of the Union Address for 1972 (Narrative Index = 23):

NIXON: Twenty-five years ago I sat here as a freshman Congressman—along with Speaker Albert—and listened for the first time to the President address the state of the Union. I shall never forget that moment. The Senate, the diplomatic corps, the Supreme Court, the Cabinet entered the chamber, and then the President of the United States. As all of you are aware, I had some differences with President Truman. He had some with me.

But I remember that on that day—the day he addressed that joint session of the newly elected Republican 80th Congress, he spoke not as a partisan, but as President of all the people—calling upon the Congress to put aside partisan considerations in the national interest.

He went on to make his THEREFORE point of the need to be bipartisan. Nixon was a wild man in the end, but he had pretty good narrative intuition (although I remember Dan Ackroyd on Saturday Night Live ridiculing Nixon's autobiography for being so monumentally boring).

THE TOAD VERSUS HILLARY

So as I said at the start, it was the 2016 match-up of The Toad versus Hillary Clinton that led me to the Narrative Index. The contrast was just so glaring. By the time they had been selected by their parties as the nominees, The Toad had an average of 29 for his combined speeches and debate performances, while Hillary averaged 14 for the same material. Several of his debate performances reached up to the mid-30's; her highest was 23.

Here's one of the first fundamental patterns I noticed early for the Narrative Index: the difference between speeches and debate performances. There's a difference in narrative content between when we speak (one-way communication) versus when we answer questions (two-way communication). This becomes obvious when you look at their scores.

SPEECHES (MORE AAA), DEBATES (MORE ABT)

As I began compiling scores for The Toad and Hillary, a difference became obvious. The scores for their debate performances were substantially higher than the scores for their speeches.

Take a look at this table. The Toad's debate performances scored nearly eight points higher than his speeches. Hillary's debate performances scored just over four points higher than her speeches.

	SPEECHES	DEBATE
TRUMP	18.6 (18, 7-41)	26.5 (11, 21-37)
CLINTON	13.4 (25, 6-25)	17.7 (11, 10-23)

NARRATIVE INDEX SCORES FOR TRUMP vs CLINTON. Values in parentheses are number of texts and the range of scores.

Why might this be?

I think it reflects how hard it is to draw deeply on the narrative part of the brain. In writing a speech you have to push yourself to dig into this structure, but in a debate, the speaker does the job for you by asking questions, putting you on the spot, which activates the narrative part of your brain, whether you want it to or not.

Another interesting observation is what happened to the scores of The Toad's speeches after he secured the Republican nomination. Previously he had ridiculed candidates for using a teleprompter. He boasted about how he didn't believe in them as his speeches spewed the bile that lifted him above his competitors.

But right about the time he won the nomination of his party, he started talking about being pressured to be "more presidential," and as a result he shifted to using the teleprompter. His scores immediately plummeted. Pre-teleprompter he averaged 27, once he started using it his average dropped to 12.

He also began using speechwriters, most notably Stephen Miller. The speeches became more diplomatic. And guess what I learned about diplomats a few years ago?

DIPLOMATS DON'T SAY "BUT"

I don't know that this is a hard-and-fast rule, but … a couple of years ago I ran one of our Story Circles Narrative Training Demo Days (explained in Appendix 2) with a group of 15 diplomats from the U.S. State Department. They informed me early on that they were trained to not use the word "but."

It makes sense. Diplomacy is about reducing conflict. Conflict is one of many forms of contradiction. The most common word of contradiction is "but." Therefore, if you want to be a good diplomat and avoid conflict, you'll want to avoid the word "but."

This explains what I've seen with The Toad's speeches since he secured the nomination. He mostly worked towards being "more presidential," and, concurrently, his Narrative Index scores dropped.

But ... you can take the boy out of the country, but you can't take the country out of the boy. Every so often he goes off script, and when he does, you can see it in the Narrative Index scores.

Like his speech at the traditional Al Smith dinner, where he was as smooth and diplomatic as Rodney Dangerfield at the dinner scene in *Caddyshack* (the Al Smith speech scored a 38). Or his speech at the Gridiron Club (scored a 44). And a bunch of feisty speeches out in the countryside, where he knows he's speaking directly to his base.

When he does those speeches he's almost certainly writing them entirely by himself, or just talking off the top of his head. Just like the Joker in Batman—saying to himself as he prepares, "What till they get a load of me."

THE BRAIN IS LAZY, BUT DEBATING ACTIVATES IT

Political campaigns are built largely around debates. As I said, political candidates score higher on the Narrative Index when they are debating than when they give speeches. I'm assuming the interrogative nature of debates prompts stronger narrative dynamics.

Keep in mind what social psychologist Paul Slovic says, citing Nobel Laureate Daniel Kahneman: "the brain is lazy." What this means is that the default state of the brain is "And, And, And."

This is the problem of social media. I constantly hear people saying, "Oh, it's the kids of today who are so good with communication—they're doing their social media stuff all day long."

Yeah, not so fast. Most of what gets tweeted and Facebooked and Instagrammed is non-narrative stream-of-consciousness AAA material. It takes time and energy to craft ABT-structured material.

It's really easy to tweet, "Today I went here and did this and saw this person and ate this food." It's very easy to have the words come out like the "flowing, rushing stream" of Stephen Douglas debating in 1858.

It takes time to craft something ABT-structured, like, "Today I needed to go here AND do this, BUT when I ran into this person I changed my mind, THEREFORE I ended up doing this."

Social media, for the most part, isn't about taking time or crafting anything meaningful; it's about rapid, short communication. It's quick, which makes it easy and fun.

DEBATING: JERRY GRAFF AND "THEY SAY, I SAY"

So AAA is the default form. But the ABT is different—it activates the brain in the same way as a line of questioning does.

Think about it. If I tell you to just say whatever you want, it's not going to be challenging. But if I start firing questions at you that I want answers for, you can feel the narrative part of your brain activating.

This is what Jerry Graff cued in on decades ago, that the most powerful form of learning is debating because it's all about contradiction, which activates a lot of the brain. He wrote a first book, *Beyond the Culture Wars: How Teaching the Conflicts Can Revitalize American Education* (1992), in which he "argued" (how fitting, given his expertise) that students learn best by studying "the conflicts," meaning, two sides of an issue.

Now here's the amazing thing with Jerry, which I've already mentioned: His short book (co-authored with his wife, Cathy Birkenstein) on the use of templates in argumentation, called *They Say, I Say*, has sold over two million copies as a textbook. It's one of the most popular textbooks of recent years. Most years it outsells *Strunk & White's Manual of Style*.

The book is broadly popular with students, and yet it's not that widely talked about in the higher levels of the humanities. Why? Probably because of the element of simplicity. Academics just aren't that keen on simplicity. In fact, they love to say, "Well, it's not that simple."

Of course, another element could also be his book *Clueless in Academe*. Not sure that title is the secret to endearing yourself to the higher levels of academe. Regardless, I'm a huge fan of Jerry's work and his wisdom over the ages. And his main point is that we learn best through argumentation, which I would explain as, we learn best when the narrative part of the brain is activated, which is what argumentation does.

WHEN TALK TURNS TO QUESTIONS

The same pattern of higher scores for debates than speeches held true for the other presidential candidates. And actually, a year after the election I noticed this difference again with a friend of mine who gave a small talk about her plans for a new yoga program.

I was in the audience and did what has become my standard nerdy narrative thing, which is to count BUTs on my left hand, ANDs on my right hand as I listen to someone speak.

Yeah, I know, how obnoxious. But also kinda fun.

Her talk was fairly boring and total AAA structure. She said, "I'm organizing a new program AND it's going to offer these classes AND it's going to be taught by these instructors AND it's going to start on this date AND ..." Her Narrative Index score was low — under 10.

It was just all the details of the program she was developing, which was fine if you were part of the INNER GROUP for this topic. But if not, it would have been nice if she had used the ABT structure to make the point, "Most programs offer this AND this, BUT they fail to offer this, THEREFORE I'm organizing this new program ..."

But ... what was fascinating was what happened after her talk. As soon as people started asking her questions, everything she had to say flipped. Suddenly she had solid ABT structure, producing a Narrative Index in the 20's. Over and over she would say, "That's a great question AND I thought about doing that AND even tried it out, BUT ... it didn't work, THEREFORE ..." It was impressive. She was compelling, and you could feel the audience being drawn in more during the Q&A than during her speech.

I told her about this later. She had no idea she had done it. The AAA is the default way we communicate, and it is what happens when you put little time into a talk, as she had. But when grilled, the narrative part of the brain fires up, and the ABT emerges.

MODERATORS TEND TO "BUT" IN

One interesting side note that is actually not surprising: moderators tend to have a Narrative Index that's about double that of the debaters. Just look at the scores for the moderators of the nine 2016 Democratic debates: 34, 46, 56, 38, 29, 25, 50, 24, 50.

The low was 25, the high was 56, and the average was 39. The candidates ranged from 6 to 24. Think this through and you'll realize it makes sense.

The job of the moderator is, first off, to "advance the narrative." How do you do that? You ask questions that challenge the candidates. The key word in achieving that is "but." As in, "The other candidates have said x AND y, BUT you've said z, THEREFORE you're in disagreement with them, why is this?"

That's what moderators are expected to do—find the contradictions and focus on them. If they're doing their job right, their scores should be high.

Which then gives you somewhat of a quantitative criterion to evaluate moderators. Just take a bunch of their transcripts and find their average Narrative Index score. If it's low, it doesn't necessarily mean they are bad, but it definitely means something. Which then gives you a starting point for digging deeper.

This is really good advice for training moderators and interviewers. Your job is all about the BUTs. That's how you activate the brain of your subject: by hitting them with tight, ABT-structured inquiry.

This is also the kind of pattern that needs a considerable

amount of text to be meaningful (doesn't work for short texts). Which brings me to this.

THE SAMPLE SIZE NEEDED FOR THE NARRATIVE INDEX

I've developed the general rule that I don't really trust the Narrative Index much for small sample sizes, which I define as roughly 1,000 words. Below that, things are a little fickle.

Abraham Lincoln's Gettysburg Address scores a 40 on the Narrative Index, which might sound impressive, but that's just the result of 2 BUTs and 5 ANDs. That's pretty flimsy, and I wouldn't want to throw a lot of confidence behind that score. The entire speech was less than 300 words.

But … on the other hand, the Gettysburg Address of Edward Everett, which I said earlier ran for more than two hours, was a total of 13,665 words. It had 56 BUTs and 470 ANDs, which produces the lowly score of 12. Meaning that he was not only long-winded, but his wind was also weak. Ugh.

With that large a sample size of words, you can feel pretty confident in the score. It reflects that the speech had little narrative structure and was probably pretty painful for the audience. (Though of course keep in mind that they didn't have any cell phones or email to be worried about back then, so they were probably thrilled just to see some lips flapping.)

Also, just to add a note on this: Everett's speech is actually a fascinating reflection of a longer-attention-span era. He opens with a preamble about the treatment of dead soldiers in ancient Athens that is itself three times longer than Lincoln's entire speech. This means he took three Gettysburg Addresses just to get to the subject he was there to talk about:

the recent battle.   Truly different times.

THE TWO WORDS OF STRUCTURE: "AND" AND "BUT"

So we've talked a lot about "but"; now let's shine a little light on "and."

"The Science of But and And" is coming. Someday soon, I promise you, someone will publish an entire book about the word "but," which will be followed by someone else publishing a book about the word "and." If a human doesn't do it, an Artificial Intelligence bot will, after machine learning latches on to the ABT dynamic.

There is so much to be said about both words. "But" is at the core of narrative.   "And" is the most common word of agreement. A former telemarketing guy told me about the training they received in "The 'And' Technique" — if you call someone, and they get angry, use the word "and" to defuse them.   Just tell them a series of simple statements, all connected with the word "and." They will start to calm down.

One interesting side tidbit — an expert on "sentiment analysis" (which Wikipedia defines as the analysis of "affective states and subjective information") chuckled at my interest in the words "but" and "and."   He said those are the sort of "garbage words" they ignore in a text because in their world they have no meaning. We agreed that "one man's trash is another man's treasure," meaning, their trash, my treasure.

They are the two most important words structuring how we communicate all day, every day. We lay out elements of agreement with "and," then we change direction (contradiction) with "but." Why wouldn't they emerge as extremely important elements of communication? (And, of course, lots of people blabber on and on with those two words until someone finally tries to cue them to get to their point by simply saying the powerful word of consequence, "Therrrrrrreforrrrrrrrre???")

And so therefore, let's now talk about "and."

2.8) "AND" ... A RUCKUS AT THE WORLD BANK

This is a fascinating recent story that slots right in with all that I've said so far about narrative structure.

All else equal, the heavy use of "and" is symptomatic of boring communication. This was the hypothesis behind a study published in 2015 from the Stanford Literary Lab, a project that focuses on the quantitative analysis of text.

Franco Moretti and Dominique Pestre authored a study in which they analyzed the legendarily boring annual reports of the World Bank. As an institution, it is said to have its own language, which the authors referred to as "Bankspeak."

What they did was very simple. They just counted the instances of the word "and," then calculated it as a percentage of the total words in each document. Take a look at what they found.

IN A WELL-EDITED TEXT, THE WORD "AND" IS 2.5% OF THE TOTAL WORDS

Let's begin by defining what I call the AF, or And Frequency. It's just the percentage of the total number of words that are the word "and."

Moretti and Pestre established a basic reference point of 2.6% for well-edited material. An assistant and I found roughly the same thing when we analyzed ten articles each from The New York Times and The New Yorker. Both averages were right around 2.5%. In the Stanford report they call the value the "average frequency in academic prose" (also you'll see it a bunch more in Chapter 3 when we look at books).

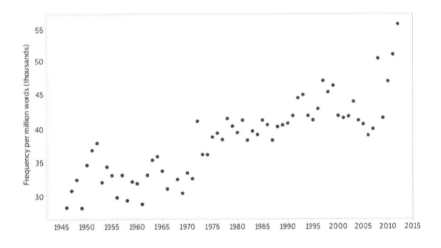

THE AND FREQUENCY (AF) FOR ANNUAL WORLD BANK REPORTS. Notice that in the beginning, 1945, the scores were near the ideal edit value of 2.5.

Then they began calculating the AF for the legendarily boring annual reports for the World Bank from 1945 to 2012. Back in 1945, they were actually readable, and the scores hovered around that well-edited value, as you can see in the above graph from their study.

But ... as the years rolled by, things changed. Decade after decade, the values crept upward, until in recent years the values are routinely over 5, meaning more than double the use of "and" from the good old well-edited days.

SIMPLICITY GETS THE LAST LAUGH

In the spring of 2017, the chief economist of the World Bank at the time, Paul Romer, read the Stanford Literary Lab report and issued an internal memo. He cited the value of 2.6% — the lowest the reports hit back in the old days — and said it was time to put things back into shape. He said that from then on, no reports would go out unless they had an AF of 2.6% or less.

Well ... that didn't sit right with the old guard at the World Bank (and I'm told there are a LOT of old guard there). They rose up and had Romer booted off the committee.

A wave of articles came out about it, including one in *The Economist* titled "Flap at the World Bank." I tried to interview Romer, but he wouldn't answer my emails, so I contacted the information officer at the World Bank. He wrote back a couple of days later saying, "Dr. Romer does not wish to discuss this incident any further." There were apparently serious bad feelings surrounding it.

But here's the wonderful punch line to the whole story.

Romer ... well, he got the last laugh. He left the World Bank at the start of 2018, returned to Columbia University, and in mid-2018 guess what he was awarded ... the Nobel Prize in Economics.

Booyah! Take that, Old Guard. Score one for the forces of simplicity and clarity.

THE AF (AND FREQUENCY)

So add the AF to your narrative tool box. It goes well with the Narrative Index and is even simpler to calculate.

The AF and the Narrative Index generally correlate inversely— a boring text has a low narrative index and a high AF, yet the AF still tells you a little bit more about editing. Here's a few values plucked to show the range.

LESS THAN 2.0

NOVA (3)	1.7
Nixon 1st Inaugural	1.8

OVER 2.0

Vanity Fair (10 articles)	2.2
Dave Chappelle (3)	2.2
Martin Luther King, Jr. (6)	2.4
New Yorker (10 articles)	2.4
The Odious Toad (14)	2.6
PBS Frontline (3)	2.8

OVER 3.0

EPA Climate Report	3.4
Design to Win Report	3.7
Hillary Clinton (9)	3.9

OVER 4.0

California Climate Reports (3)	5.6

REPRESENTATIVE VALUES OF AND FREQUENCIES. The And Frequency is simply the percent of total words in a text that are the word "and." In parenthesis is number of texts if more than one.

On the low end we see a tightly edited script for a NOVA documentary on PBS and Richard Nixon's "I'm the King of the World," his first inaugural address. Ten articles each from Vanity Fair and The New Yorker score in the low 2's. The same for comedian Dave Chappelle in a stand-up special. The Toad is also down in this tight narrative range with a dozen of his speeches.

Then we start to get a little more verbose with Tom Freidman's book The Earth is Flat, an EPA climate report, the "Design to Win" climate master plan for the major environmental organizations, and Hillary Clinton.

And lastly three climate reports for the state of California. These are documents that are just statement after statement, similar to the dreaded World Bank reports.

The bottom line is that if you've got a completed document, just try searching the word "and" and figuring out what your AF is. If it's over 3.5 you should be concerned. If it's over 5.0 you are officially boring — no two ways about it.

THE THEREFORE TEST FOR POLITICAL SLOGANS

We've made it through the AND and BUT for politics; the only thing left is the THEREFORE.

For starters, is there any more important word to voters? Isn't this what's on their minds as they listen to a campaign speech? Aren't they, deep inside, wondering, "Therefore? Therefore, how are you going to make my life better if I vote for you?" And so wouldn't it make sense that the test of a good slogan is how it sounds coming off the word "therefore," as I argued in the last chapter?

For the 2018 election campaign season, I did a segment on the Young Turks Network in which I took a dozen of the slogans of congressional candidates and subjected them to "The Therefore Test." As I sit here trying to remember them, the only two I can recall off the top of my head were the two best. All the rest didn't stay with me (once again, narrative selection in action).

The two best were for the two sides of what was probably the most fiercely fought campaign: youthful upstart Beto O'Rourke versus jaded veteran Ted Cruz. O'Rourke's slogan was great: "THEREFORE ... Texas Deserves Better." But Cruz was pretty much just as good,:"THEREFORE ... Tough As Texas."

Both of them roll off the word THEREFORE. And for contrast, I just looked at the blog post I wrote about the slogans. Here's one of the bad ones, from Phil Bredesen, who ran for U.S. Senate in Tennessee with the slogan, "THEREFORE ... working to get things done for Tennessee."

Pretty dull, pretty clunky, and he pretty much lost. There were of course many factors beyond just having a bad slogan, but it's a central part of campaigning.

In general, the top five attributes I would recommend for a slogan are that it is: 1) Consequential (rolls of the word THEREFORE), 2) Singular (just one slogan), 3) Contradictory (contradicts something else: "Better than ..." "Tougher than ..."), 4) Aspirational (reaching for something good), 5) Concise (as always, keep it short).

2.9 SO WHY AREN'T POLITICIANS USING THE ABT YET? EVER SEE MONEYBALL?

I hate that we are increasingly becoming a "metrics-driven world." I love Dave Gold's *Politico* article that I cited earlier, which rails against such metrics myopia. And yet, what can we do with all the patterns revealed by the metric of the Narrative Index? Are you really supposed to just ignore that knowledge?

The situation is very much like the book (which I didn't read) and the movie (which I loved), *Moneyball*. It was the story of a profession — baseball — that was deeply mired in the age-old tradition of "gut instinct." Player scouts based much of their decision-making on their overall gut feelings about players.

But Brad Pitt, as the coach of the Oakland Athletics, came up with a different way to approach the sport. He brought in Jonah Hill, the numbers nerd who was able to make simple, counter-"intuitive" (meaning the opposite of driven-by-gut-feeling) predictions which, if followed faithfully, would pay off.

It seemed like a simple innovation, but the problem was that Brad and Jonah were up against traditional baseball culture. Which is the same situation for a lot of politics, as so many campaigns are driven more by gut instinct than by any sort of analytical approach to messaging/narrative. And most are not interested in changing that.

Over the past five years, I've tried to get the attention of nine political campaigns. I've tried to interest them in the power of the ABT as a tool for pretty much all of their communication and messaging, but I've ended up like Jonah Hill: seen as irrelevant.

My buddy Jayde Lovell (who gave the dinner speech back in the Introduction) has a great expression from Australia that is very pertinent to all this:

You don't want to be the person who is so busy digging a hole with a spoon that you don't have the time to pick up a shovel.

This was what happened with James Carville trying to get the Clinton campaign to listen to me. The young fellow who did try to listen to what I was saying for a few months eventually told me that everyone on the campaign was so massively, flat-out busy, that even if the ABT were some sort of miracle cure, they just didn't have the time to listen and experiment.

So that's been the deal with the ABT. It's spreading slowly. There is suspicion about it being "too simple," plus most people see only limited value until they hit that magic moment when—like the arrow in the FedEx truck—they see it everywhere. Then things start to change. It's just going to take time.

HOW CAN POLITICIANS USE THE ABT FRAMEWORK?

This has been the longest chapter of this book because the ABT is such a central part of politics. I've presented a number of narrative tools:

- The ABT Narrative Template
- The Dobzhansky One-Word Template
- The Narrative Index (BUT to AND ratio)

- The AND Frequency (AF, total % of words that are AND)

There's a large number of ways the ABT can be used in the world of politics.

A political campaign ought to have the ABT structure at the core of **1) THE CENTRAL MESSAGE.** Then by using **2) THE DOBZHANSKY TEMPLATE,** you can find the theme of the campaign. The actual **3) FRAMING** of the campaign should be studied and adjusted using the ABT. The ABT dynamic gives rise to **4) THE NARRATIVE INDEX (NI)** which should be applied to every speech, policy statement, editorial and all other texts to avoid being boring (AAA). At the same time, **5) THE AND FREQUENCY (AF)** should also be applied to the same materials to make sure they're close to the baseline value of 2.5%, which reflects tight editing. Ideally, the ABT should be used at multiple scales to assure messaging throughout a text by creating **6) NESTED ABT'S** — especially for speeches in which you should aspire to present "a story of stories," as Oprah did. And once a campaign is ready, the final touch should be to apply **7) THE THEREFORE TEST** to the slogan to make sure you've got a strong, active, concise, motivating statement of consequence that will make voters think, "Therefore, let's just do it and vote for this candidate!"

Two important final notes:

First, as I mentioned at the end of the last chapter, no one should do a press conference where they are going to be asked questions without "Doing your ABTs" in advance. They should think about all the predictable and expected questions, figure out the ABT-structured answers, then rehearse these answers. You don't want to get caught going on and on with an And, And, And answer or confusing the crowd with a DHY.

Second, politicians need comedians for their speechwriting. They need them, not to write jokes, but because the good ones have deep narrative intuition. I make this point in depth in the next chapter in section 3.1. It's one of the most practical pieces of advice I could offer any politician. It's not about comedy, it's about narrative.

3) ENTERTAINMENT

3) ENTERTAINMENT - Story is ABT

THE ABT IS A TOOL FOR THE INFORMATION SOCIETY

For this chapter I do have a few credentials. I completed my Master's degree in cinema at the University of Southern California in the mid-1990's, having started at age 38. I followed that with 20 years of filmmaking in and around Hollywood. I directed a documentary feature that aired on Showtime and made a series of short environmental films that featured a range of wonderful comic actors including Jack Black, Melissa McCarthy, Dustin Hoffman and lots of others.

Just this past year I co-produced a documentary on surfing (my favorite sport), which is proving to be a huge hit at film festivals (over 25 festivals so far), has secured major distribution and should be on Netflix, Amazon or Hulu this fall. The young filmmaker Brent Storm made a great film, in large part because of our use of the ABT, as he will gladly tell you.

I also spent a few years taking acting classes in Hollywood, and at one point I had three agents at ICM, one of the biggest talent agencies, representing my screenplays. Most importantly, I took Frank Daniel's famous Script Analysis class at USC the year before he passed away. I'll talk about him in a bit.

Entertainment is a big topic, so I'm going to touch on just a few aspects— specifically movies/TV, books, music/poetry, and journalism.

And, yes, I'm calling journalism "entertainment." It makes sense these days given how it has devolved. You can thank the ABT dynamic and the Information Era for much of the transition.

In fact, let me start this chapter with a Dobzhansky statement. Here's is my basic belief that underpins all I say:

Nothing in our society today makes sense, except in the light of the Information Explosion.

I said this line towards the end of my 2006 documentary feature film *Flock of Dodos: The Evolution-Intelligent Design Circus.* It's my deep belief that just about all discussions of communication need to be framed in the context of the fact that we have become The Information Society.
If you're not thinking in terms of how "information overload" has changed our culture, then you're out of synch with today.

The Information Explosion explains the emergence and importance of the ABT. In simple terms, and as best as I can tell, the concept of the importance of the three words (And, But, Therefore) emerged in 1986 in a speech by Frank Daniel (whom I'll describe in this chapter). I haven't been able to find any mentions before that.

But the knowledge seems to have lain dormant for at least two decades.

It wasn't until the *South Park* co-creators put it to use in the real world, and then talked about the Rule of Replacing in a documentary, that the knowledge began to find a useful place in the world. Now, in part from our Story Circles Narrative Training program (Appendix 2), the ABT is starting to be put to use in a wide range of settings.

So ABT is a tool for the Information Society. It just took a couple of decades for its time to come.

3.1) MOVIES/TELEVISION

At the heart of entertainment is the timeless magic of storytelling, which is pure ABT. In today's world, storytelling reaches its pinnacle in the century-old art of moviemaking.

For the movie business, storytelling begins with the writing of the screenplay. So let's ask, "Are there are many books on screenwriting for the movie business?"

Well, let me put it this way: When I searched "screenwriting books," a whole stack came up, the last of which was titled *Not Just Another Book on the Craft of Screenwriting*. That kind of says it all.

But are they really that different from each other? There's a great 2014 short book from veteran BBC producer John Yorke addressing this question. It's called *Into the Woods*. At the end he presents a table with the most popular books on screenwriting and how they recommend structuring a screenplay. Turns out they all conform to the same overall three-act structure established centuries ago. Which means they're all giving the same basic advice.

And there's something else in Yorke's book—he mentions fractals. The subject of fractals became popular in the late 1980's but is not quite as talked-about these days. Let's see how it relates to storytelling.

ABT: THE FRACTAL ELEMENT OF STORYTELLING

A fractal is defined as, "irregular curves or shapes for which any suitably chosen part is similar in shape to a given larger or smaller part when magnified or reduced to the same size." The iconic fractal is an ice crystal, which repeats the same form at different scales. From a distance, you see one form. But then you zoom in, and you see the same form repeated over and over again as you continue to zoom in. Or out.

The concept is not as popular today as it once was. As you can see from this Google Ngram, its popularity peaked in the mid-1990's.

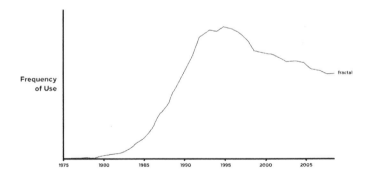

GOOGLE NGRAM SEARCH FOR THE WORD "FRACTAL." Frequency of appearance of the word "fractal" in published books from 1975 to 2005 searched by Google Ngram.

Fractals were popularized by the 1987 bestselling book *Chaos: Making a New Science,* by James Gleick. One of the key properties of fractals is that, "Out of simplicity can arise complexity." By assembling units that have a simple structure at the fine scale, a complex structure can be created at a larger scale.

In the last few years a number of people have started to realize stories have a fractal nature. Yorke mentioned that stories have this repeating structure at various scales, but, as far as I can see, neither he nor anyone else has offered up an actual structure for the replicating unit.

Until now.

Here it is...

```
      ABT          ABT ABT       ABT ABT ABT
    ABT ABT        ABT  ABT         ABT
   ABT   ABT       ABT   ABT        ABT
  ABT ABT ABT      ABT ABT          ABT
  ABT      ABT     ABT  ABT         ABT
 ABT        ABT    ABT   ABT        ABT
                   ABT ABT          ABT
```

The ABT is the simple, repeating structure that can be overlain on itself, from the overarching structure of an entire story down to the smallest scenes and moments. Which takes us back to Oprah's "story of stories" speech that I mentioned in the last chapter. She had what I termed in my Houston book "Nested ABTs." It's the same thing here as fractal structure: ABTs on top of ABTs.

You can see the nested ABT structure in episodic television

shows. For example, one of the best-written series ever, *Breaking Bad*, had tight story structure at all different scales. The show itself had an over-arching ABT: "Walter White is a struggling AND depressed chemistry teacher, BUT is diagnosed with terminal cancer and wants to leave enough money for his family, THEREFORE he turns to drug-making."

Then within each season there is an ABT. And within each episode there's an ABT. And within each sequence of the episode there's an ABT. And within each scene of the sequence there's an ABT. There are also individual character arcs, which means the ABT of the character. ABT is everywhere in good storytelling.

For example, with *Breaking Bad*, at the level of an individual scene, Walter comes home AND Skylar is cooking dinner, BUT then she asks him why he has two cell phones, which causes him to get angry and THEREFORE storm out of the house.

Of course, not all of the seasons and episodes and scenes are so simple as to have a single, clear ABT. But overall, most of them do and the show is simply driven by the endless sequences of ANDs (setups), BUTs (problems), THEREFOREs (actions leading to the next sequences).

Bottom line: The ABT is the driving force of narrative.

ISN'T THE ABT JUST THE SAME OLD DRAMATIC STRUCTURE STUFF WE LEARNED IN JUNIOR HIGH?

Yes. It's the same old thing. Only different, as I said in the Introduction.

It is indeed the same as what you learned of the old elements:

exposition, rising tension, climax, culmination, resolution, denouement and a bunch of other terms used over the ages. There's one very significant difference:

It's simple.

And replicating.

And quantifiable.

Actually, that's a lot of differences, and I'm just getting started. So okay, maybe it's not exactly the same.

THE ABT COMES FROM THE WORLD OF MOVIES AND TELEVISION BUT ... IT ISN'T USED MUCH IN HOLLYWOOD (YET)

I'm probably making it sound like Hollywood writers sit around all day long talking about their ABT's. They don't. Not yet.

The ABT *dynamic* is ubiquitous in Hollywood. But the ABT terminology is not yet in wide use. However ... it will be eventually. It has to be. It's the central element of the entire profession.

Before the early 1950's, no scientists talked about the double helix. Geneticists talked about inheritance, and cell biologists could see chromosomes, but nobody knew yet that the structure of what they were seeing was in the form of a double helix. Today the double helix is as routine as biology itself.

It will be the same thing for the ABT. It was less than a decade ago that the co-creators of *South Park*, Matt Stone and Trey Parker, first spoke publicly about the three key words (And, But, Therefore), with their "Rule of Replacing." These things take time, as I've seen with the slow spread of the ABT since I began speaking about it in 2012.

But make no mistake — if hugely successful writers like Stone and Parker are using it, that's about as big of a validation as can be expected. And here specifically is them talking about it in a presentation to a film class at NYU. Trey Parker discusses the sequence of "beats" (individual story moments) of a scene, saying:

... between every beat that you've written down is either the word therefore or but — it should be: "this happens, and therefore this happens, but ... this happens, therefore this happens" — you get a show that feels like, okay, this to that to this to that, but this — here's the complication — to that.

The point I'm making here is that the *And, But, Therefore* dynamic isn't my little invention. Nor did it arise with the *South Park* guys. It can be tracked back (at least) to Frank Daniel, who was a legendary screenwriting instructor. He founded the screenwriting program at Columbia University, was the artistic director of the Sundance Institute for a decade, and then became head of the screenwriting program at U.S.C.

I was fortunate enough to take his Script Analysis course at USC in 1995, a year before he died. He was a tremendous instructor with a great analytical mind, able to see the structure within a good story just as Joseph Campbell did in the world of mythology.

I've done a lot of work trying to figure out where the ABT thinking came from. This seems to be the first clear formulation of it. It's from a speech by Frank Daniel in 1986 (spotted by my friend Marty Kaplan of the USC Annenberg School for Communication and Journalism), in which he said:

Monotony is a problem in first drafts. There are several reasons for it. One usually is the fact that the scenes follow in the forbidden pattern: and then, and then, and then.

In such a case immediately you have monotony. In a dramatic story the pattern usually for the connecting scenes is: "and then," "but," "therefore," "but," and towards the culmination "meanwhile." If you don't have this "but" and "therefore" connection between the parts, the story becomes linear, monotonous. Diaries and chronicles are written that way, but not scripts.

There's your problem in simple language. Do you really want to read diaries and chronicles? Not much. You want stories.

A diary is the real world, which on average is just too boring for most brains because it is the unshaped "And, And, And" form. Keep this point in mind; it's very important. Let me say it   here   writ   large:

THE   REAL   WORLD   IS   MOSTLY   AND,   AND,   AND

The real world mostly needs to be reshaped into the narrative world that will hold our interest.

Which leads us back to the Narrative Index. I believe it is the driving force for television based on something I call "The Narrative Imperative," which is derived from the Narrative Index. Let me show you a few numbers to back this up.

TELEVISION: "THE NARRATIVE IMPERATIVE," QUANTIFIED

I believe there exists what could be termed "The Narrative Imperative" for television. This is the idea that you must have a certain amount of "narrative strength" in order to hold the eyeballs of viewers. If your narrative strength is below a certain threshold, you'll end up on PBS, C-Span or public-access television.

Think of the comparison of the PBS News Hour (more AAA) to the CBS Evening News (total ABT). The humble voice of truth playing to the long-attention-span crowd versus the loud, graphics-driven voice of excitement for the lemmings of today. That's your fundamental divide.

The Narrative Imperative is quantified using the Narrative Index (the BUT/AND ratio). Here are two data sets to support this idea.

1   TV DOCUMENTARIES

I'm not quite sure how you would measure the BUT/AND ratio for a dramatic show. It seems like a lot of the "But's" would be more visual and not obvious in the script. For example, a man comes home, takes off his jacket, sits on the couch, the camera pans around until it reveals another man hiding in the shadows of the room. That's a pretty big moment of contradiction, but there's no "but" in the script. Documentaries, on the other hand, if they are heavily driven by narration, as most documentary series on television are, should have a greater number of narrative twists and turns punctuated by the word "but."

Here's a sample of Narrative Index scores for some television documentary series. For each one I randomly picked five episodes of scripts I could find on the internet.

They all average above 15. Furthermore, of the 25 episodes chosen, only two scored under 15.

DOCUMENTARY SERIES	AVERAGE NARRATIVE INDEX
American Experience	21.6
Frontline	17.8
NOVA	27.8
Cosmos	32.6
48 Hours	16.6

This is what I define as "The Narrative Imperative." It's the hypothesis that television demands a certain minimum level of narrative tension, which I suggest is a Narrative Index of at least 15.

Yes, you could produce an "And, And, And" documentary series whose episodes all scored under 10, but I bet it would have a hard time making it to air on commercial television.

2   THE TRUMP CAMPAIGN AND MSNBC: "EYEBALL GLUE"

A second line of evidence for the Narrative Imperative comes from the presidential campaign of The Odious Toad. As I said in the last chapter, it was during his campaign for president that I began to calculate the Narrative Index. While I was starting to notice the narrative strength of his speeches and debate performances, something else was happening.

MSNBC, the traditionally left-leaning cable news network, started interrupting their scheduled programming to provide live coverage of speeches and campaign rallies by candidate Toad.   This sort of large-scale free media exposure was previously unheard of for a political candidate, and it certainly did not occur for his opponent, Hillary Clinton. What was happening?

Political pundits said it was because of the aggressiveness and even hatred The Toad spewed at his rallies. But there have been political candidates like David Duke who have stood for terrible things yet never drawn such media coverage.

Lots of explanations were offered. Who knows which is most correct. All I know is that the Narrative Index gives you cold, hard numbers that could explain at least part of the preferential treatment.

Look at the average Narrative Index scores for The Toad's speeches each year since announcing his candidacy for president.

YEAR	NARRATIVE INDEX (# of speeches)
2015	27.9 (7)
2016 pre-nomination	16.5 (4)
2016 post-nomination	12.9 (15)
2017	11.9 (7)
2018	24.3 (6)
2019	29.6 (5)

In 2015, at the start of his campaign, he was shooting from the hip, giving speeches without a script or teleprompter. His Narrative Index was sky-high. He gave a rabid speech to his rabid fans in New Hampshire in December 2015 that scored a 41 on the Narrative Index. Almost nobody ever scores above

40; Richard Nixon did it once, comedian Michelle Wolf did it once, and that's all I've found so far out of a few thousand texts.

So it's only a hypothesis, but it's what I would guess was the most significant factor behind all the free air time on television. He was punching away, basically ABT-ing so ferociously that he was scoring record-high Narrative Index scores.

The content of what he was saying was horrible and hateful, but the form was concise, punchy and ABT-structured. He was basically saying things to the effect of, "We love the Mexicans AND they are welcome to visit, BUT too many are illegals, THEREFORE we're going to build a wall," and "Taxes are essential AND we need them, BUT the current tax code is unfair, THEREFORE I'm going to get the best people to revise it," and "Muslims are okay AND we can live with some of them, BUT too many are terrorists, THEREFORE I'm calling for a ban on them entering the country."

Over and over again he identified problems then offered concise (albeit largely unrealistic and even dishonest) solutions. His average Narrative Index was 26. In having such simple solutions, he was able to steamroll through far more ABT problem-solution scenarios than his opponents (average Narrative Index scores for their debate performances in parentheses): Marco Rubio (18), Jeb Bush (13) and Ted Cruz (12). Also, keep in mind that debates generally score higher than speeches.

And so The Toad spoke with a high Narrative Index that shot well above the Narrative Imperative of 15 as he drew huge audiences. Some were drawn in through their agreement with what he said. Others tuned in because of their outrage at how simplistic and offensive (to them) his solutions were. Many disliked him, but no one called him uninteresting.

By the end of 2015, this "ABT Eyeball Glue" element evident in The Toad, prompted the cable networks to interrupt their normal programming to cover his speeches and rallies. The Toad's inauguration speech was eventually revealed to have been written by both Stephen Miller and Steve Bannon. The former was milquetoast, the latter bombastic. Together they combined for a speech with the mid-range value of 18.

After he was elected, he continued giving dull speeches for his first couple of years, but as he became more comfortable in the office, his higher Narrative Index began to return. He also resumed giving some speeches without a teleprompter, especially in smaller cities where he was warmly embraced by his "base" and felt inspired to go free-form.

In February 2019, he gave a Rose Garden speech with a Narrative Index of 30. However, in the Q&A, his answers jumped up to 36 — showing the dynamic I described in the last chapter, in which inquiry prompts a greater use of ABT structure.

There are endless examples with The Toad. In December 2018, his awkward, restrained speech at the U.N. scored a mere 6, but just a few days later he gave an embattled interview to two reporters from The Washington Post that scored a 33. When he is fighting, his Narrative Index shoots up, as would be expected.

So that's what you get with an aggressive politician. And keep in mind another famous adage that is usually traced back to the Nazi propaganda minister Joseph Goebbels — that a lie repeated enough becomes the truth. Well, that's certainly true for the masses. But a lie repeated by someone with a low Narrative Index just eventually becomes a boring lie and vanishes.

Without narrative structure, you eventually die. I call it "narrative selection." It's the subject of the last chapter of this book, and it is especially true if you're a comedian, as we shall now explore.

NARRATIVE STRUCTURE: COMEDY IS KING

So we've established a hypothetical Narrative Imperative. Now let's talk about the people for whom narrative structure is most imperative.

Who lives and dies with each performance? Who sometimes says, "I died last night on stage," and, at other times, brags, "I killed last night!"

Comedians. They know narrative, probably better than anyone else. It's their life's blood, and it is reflected in their Narrative Index scores.

If politicians bore or confuse, they lose, then move on to their next campaign. If comedians bore or confuse, they don't have a career at all. If they fail to use narrative power effectively, they end up standing in front of a very small audience, basically doing "performance art."

Here's the scores for a range of comedians, analyzing their standup-comedy performances. The numbers in parentheses are how many scripts I analyzed for each one. The nice thing is that almost all performances are at least 5,000 words, with many over 10,000, making for solid sample sizes.

The first thing you see is that the elite, "edgy" comedians are way up there (though keep in mind the old, "Who writes your stuff?" line for all of these folks). Bill Maher almost always scores above 30. Michelle Wolf's scorched-earth performance at the 2017 White House Correspondents Dinner, where she insulted pretty much everyone across the spectrum, scored a blistering 47. Just about every statement she made was followed by a "but" — as in, "I did have a lot of jokes about Cabinet members, but … I had to scrap all of those because everyone has been fired" (one of her jokes).

The superstars are all over 25: Kevin Hart, Chris Rock, Sarah Silverman, Dave Chappelle. The comedians below 15 (the Narrative Imperative) have much smaller audiences or are not even comedians. Kevin Smith is a filmmaker, Henry Rollins is more of a musician and actor than a comedian and Ron White reminds me of unfunny fraternity bros I have known.

The one great exception that proves the rule is the legendary "Philadelphia Incident" from 2006 involving Bill Burr, who tore into the audience for an eleven- minute, insult-packed rant. Notice that Burr generally scores a 20 for all other performances. But that night in Philadelphia the audience had booed the previous comedian, his good friend. He responded with a spontaneous performance that was little more than an "And, And, And" barrage of statement after statement of insults. There were only two BUT's. He wasn't crafting a narrative, he was just unloading in a manner so overwhelming, the offending audience finally gave in with a standing ovation at the end. Clearly the audience was all in his inner circle, so he didn't even need narrative.

ABOVE 30

Bill Maher (3)	42
Michelle Wolf (2)	37
Kevin Hart (3)	35
Chris Rock (6)	34
Bill Maher, HBO Real Time (62)	33

ABOVE 20

Sara Silverman (3)	26
Dave Chappelle (3)	26
Ricky Gervais (2)	26
Amy Schumer (3)	24
George Carlin (3)	24
Daniel Tosh (3)	24
Bill Burr (3)	20
Eddie Izzard (4)	20

BELOW 20

Jim Jeffries (5)	18
Chris Tucker (1)	13
Ron White (2)	12
Kevin Smith (1)	11
Henry Rollins (1)	10

Bill Burr, "Philadelphia Incident" 7

NARRATIVE INDEX VALUES FOR COMEDIANS. Taken from scripts for stand-up comedy performances. The value in parentheses is number of scripts. (Most of the transcripts came from the website "Scraps from the Loft.")

POLITICIANS NEED COMEDIANS

This is a piece of advice I have for politicians that I mentioned briefly at the end of the previous chapter.

Politicians should add comic writers to their speechwriting teams, NOT to write jokes, but because they have narrative intuition. Good comic writers understand the need to have strong narrative structure, and they know how to create it.

The bane of politicians is their endless lists of campaign promises. Yes, everyone wants to hear what you're going to do, but if it's just a laundry list, they're going to get bored. You can do much better if you tap into the power of narrative.

A prime example of the narrative strength of good comedy writers I've been following for several years is Bill Maher and his HBO show *Real Time*. He ends every episode with his "New Rules" segment, which concludes with a roughly five-minute monologue. Most of the monologues are around 1,000 words, which is small for a sample size, but I averaged 62 of them, which I think provides a fairly reliable estimate of the narrative strength of the material.

More importantly, be a nerd like me and see for yourself. Watch his next episode. I can almost guarantee you the ratio will be at least a 20, usually something like 5 BUTs, 25 ANDs. Sometimes it will shoot up over 50 because the sample size is so small—something like 6 BUTs, 12 ANDs. Regardless, you can feel the structure at work: statement, statement, statement, then a "turn" using the word "but." Comedians know narrative structure.

In fact, one of the greatest ever was Al Franken, who even in his saddest hour of his final resignation speech managed to score a 22. The Democrats not only shot themselves in the foot with him, they shot off an entire leg of communications savvy when they forced him out of the Senate.

MOVIES: BLOCKBUSTER (ABT) VS ARTSY (AAA/DHY)

Movies are the ultimate weapon of mass entertainment, and thus their creators have an intimate knowledge of the ABT dynamic. A basic sense of the ABT is present throughout the work of those who analyze how movies work.

Robert McKee is the long-time reigning guru of the "how to" for writing the screenplays from which movies arise. His workshops and books on Hollywood screenwriting were made legendary in part by the 2002 movie *Adaptation*, in which he was portrayed by actor Brian Cox. In McKee's foundational 1997 book, *Story*, he presented what has come to be known as "McKee's Triangle."

Here's what fascinates me. McKee's triangle (which I'll present in a minute) explains so much of human culture over the ages, and yet … when you search it, you only get about a page of websites referring to it.

I've never quite understood why such an important conceptual device as his triangle seems to draw so little interest. I presented it in my first book, then—after no one mentioned it in reviews and discussions of my book—I brought it back in my *Houston* book in a section called "Back by Unpopular Demand." I'm determined to show how important it is.

What the triangle conveys is the interaction between narrative structure and audience size. There is one form of narrative structure that is termed "Classical Design," which underlies the oldest, greatest, most enduring and broadly popular stories of all time. It is found from the ancient myths all the way up to today's blockbuster franchises like *Star Wars*.

McKee talks at great length about classical design, which he also calls "Archplot."

For the other two corners of his triangle, he has the opposite of Archplot, which he terms "Miniplot." This is a form of story that plays more to the "arthouse" audience and the more cerebral film critics. It is more characteristic of pieces of art, but, as a result, generally reaches a smaller audience.

Then he has a third corner of his triangle for the extreme statements against structure, which he calls, "Antiplot." These are films that refuse to yield to ABT dynamics. They range from the stream-of-consciousness art films, like *Meshes of the Afternoon*, which we had to watch in film school, to rebellious comedies, like *Blazing Saddles*, which throw storytelling out the window in the end. (Though keep in mind that any silly comedy that is popular still has a huge amount of ABT at work on the smaller scale.)

So let's ignore antiplot, as it is the refusal to engage in narrative, and let's just look at archplot and miniplot as two ends of a spectrum. Archplot is mass entertainment, while miniplot is arthouse entertainment. Archplot is ABT, while miniplot is AAA or DHY.

Furthermore, there is a whole set of characteristics that go with the two forms. Archplot structure is characterized by:

1) One main character
2) The character is active
3) Linear timeline
4) Complete causation
5) Closed ending

These are age-old principles of narrative that McKee explores in depth. They refer to the need for 1) one main character, not an ensemble group of equally important characters. (This is what Nicholas Kristof discussed, as I mentioned in Chapter 2.) Second, the character must be actively fighting for something in the world, not be just a victim of events.

Third, the events must be told one after another, in chronological order, not jumping around. Fourth, the events must have complete causality, meaning that everything happens for an understandable reason — someone dies because of a disease, but not just randomly for no reason. And fifth, the story must have a closed ending in which all the main questions are answered: Who committed the murder, where did a character who vanished in the middle of the story go, where did they live happily ever after?

The opposite of all these attributes is what characterizes miniplot, the form of arthouse movies that challenge the mind and make the critics swoon but draw only small audiences. Those films have ensemble casts where everyone is equally important. They feature characters who are just the victims of bad luck, they love to feature "non-linear timelines" where we jump around in time — something that is stimulating to intellectuals but often tedious and confusing to the masses.

The films feature events that have no clear causation (*Chinatown* ends with the line, "Forget it, Jake, it's Chinatown," meaning, essentially, don't go looking for the standard logical explanations.) And arthouse films love to end with mysteries unresolved, just like in the real world; sometimes we don't get our happy ending, and not everything in the world makes sense.

This fundamental divide between archplot and miniplot is important in everything. You see politicians who try to deliver the truth, as boring and confusing as it might be (miniplot), and lose, then you see politicians who deliver a happy, engaging, logical, albeit fabricated, story that the masses love (archplot). The Toad would be the prime example of the latter—endlessly, speech after speech — always the happy ending with that guy.

Is one more virtuous than the other? Who knows? I only know that most brains are programmed to seek archplot more than miniplot. And that's a pretty important thing to know if you're in business, politics, entertainment, science or religion. It's how the brain is programmed. It's humanity, as we'll discuss in the final chapter.

A IS FOR CONTEXT: DRAMA VERSUS MELODRAMA

Since first presenting the ABT Framework in 2013 at TEDMED, I've gotten a large group of friends and colleagues who are now on this journey with me, trying to figure out how the ABT dynamic works, and what the basic rules are. One shift many of us have undergone over the past five years is a growing appreciation for the "AND" part of the template.

In the beginning we were drawn to the obvious importance of the "BUT" element—the contradiction. People like to talk about how the media are so "conflict-driven"—the basic, "if it bleeds, it leads." But what ought to be said is that the media, and pretty much everything in life, is "contradiction-driven." Conflict is one of many forms of contradictions. Others include mystery, suspense, curiosity, intrigue. For all of these dynamics there is a norm, and then something arises that differs from the norm. That difference fires up the brain, starting the narrative process.

So if you then start thinking more deeply about it, you begin to realize you can't have contradiction without first having something to be contradicted. That something is the opening element of agreement—the "setup" for the contradiction. It's also the context (or "frame," as we discussed in the politics chapter).

This is what we have increasingly found to be the most neglected and under-appreciated of the three forces. And quite possibly the most important. If you don't set up this initial context, then you're not going to have much depth of impact. This is what melodrama is about: the absence of much context.

At the start of this book I mentioned that in our first semester of film school at USC we had to take a class in "The History of Silent Cinema." That class was such an eye-opener to human culture in general.

One of the things we learned about was what the first great film directors had to say about storytelling. From Rex Ingram to Cecile B. DeMille, they all felt that movies had to tell great stories that had a mighty setup with backstory and character development. Basically they were big believers in the A of the ABT.

But then along came a whole bunch of other filmmakers who realized that all you really need to grab the eyeballs of most viewers (even the most intellectual) is a big dose of B. They realized all you gotta do is tie a woman to the railroad track and have a train coming towards her, and the audience will sit up straight with its eyes wide open. They won't care who she is or where she grew up. This genre of films came to be known the "Serial Queen Melodramas" — basically the first popcorn/action movies — with films like *The Perils of Pauline*.

The key point is that the mass audience doesn't need all that A material before they get to their B and T. But ... if you largely skip the A, you end up with melodrama, which is shallow, ephemeral and potentially even meaningless.

In fact, this is the real, functional definition of the word "melodrama." It is broadly defined as "exaggeration," but what it's really about is "unjustified drama." The stereotypical melodramatic scene is the villain twirling his mustache as the femme fatale puts the back of her hand to her forehead and swoons.

But here's the thing: Think of some of the most powerful dramatic scenes in great movies. Brando, Bogart, Hepburn, Streep, Nicholson, Pacino — most of their greatest moments, taken out of context (meaning looking only at the B, without the A or C), actually seem pretty melodramatic.

Brando shouting at "Stelllll-aahhhhhh" in *A Streetcar Named Desire* plays as over-the-top melodrama by itself. But when you spend two hours in a play or movie slowly building the context, laying out all the exposition through a rising series of ABTs, until you finally reach this well-constructed climax, then the same scene doesn't feel the least bit melodramatic. You have built the dramatic context that enables the intense drama to work.

Which means "the A and the T matter," and that is exactly what comedian/news critic John Oliver underscored recently.

JOHN OLIVER KNOWS THE ABT

For the past few years, comedian John Oliver has had a very smart team of writers helping him craft clever and powerful monologues about societal issues for his HBO show, *Last Week Tonight*. In March 2019, he took on the topic of internet shaming by specifically delving into one of the iconic instances of it from 2015, in which an aunt supposedly sued her nephew for accidentally injuring her.

She came to be known as the "worst aunt ever" and "the Auntie Christ," as the Twittersphere unleashed its pent-up bile. Her eight-year-old nephew had given her an "exuberant hug," in the process of which they both fell over, and she broke her wrist. When she filed a claim against her relatives' home owners' insurance, the boy, not the insurance company, was named as the defendant, resulting in the media claiming she was suing her nephew.

The truth was that it was just a formality required by the state of Connecticut— that an individual must be named—not anything personal for her. She and the nephew appeared on talk shows trying to make this clear. But the initial media coverage didn't mention this, so the Twittersphere took the story and ran with it, portraying her as a hideous villain.

In editorializing about the whole mess, John Oliver said, "At some point it is incumbent on everyone to consider context and consequence." That was, of course, music to my ears, as what he was basically saying was, "To make sense of the B, it is incumbent on everyone to consider the A and the T."

The truth is, in the long run, humans do seek to understand the world around them. And this is why Twitter eventually doubled the length of tweets from 140 to 280 characters. This was a prediction I made in 2015 in the second appendix of my *Houston* book. I had already begun to realize that a typical ABT needs about 300 characters. Which meant that Twitter would either have to increase the length of tweets, or the public would eventually lose interest. I will present this in greater detail in the last chapter — providing a bit more A and T to the story, if you know what I mean by now.

THE ABT IS EFFECTIVE SHORTHAND

So this is about as much as I want to say on the ABT and movies. The ABT Framework ought to eventually be taught in all writing classes because it's such a powerful and simple tool for "finding the story" that you're working on. In particular, it provides the sort of short, simple analytical labels that are needed for the three main states of narrative you deal with in telling a story: boring (AAA), confusing (DHY) or interesting (ABT).

Actually, looked at another way, it's like the ABT is the next level of shorthand, following on the heels of Christopher Vogler. In the last chapter I will discuss his 1992 book, *The Writer's Journey: Mythic Structure for Storytellers and Screenwriters*, in detail. For now, suffice it to say that Vogler's book is the more contemporary presentation of Joseph Campbell's *Hero's Journey* model that underpins storytelling. The preface to the second edition, *The Writer's Journey: Mythic Structure for Writers* (2007), is packed with story wisdom. One thing Vogler says is, "… new terms and concepts are always being created to reflect changing conditions."

What he's talking about is the idea of narrative selection. As the environment changes so does the culture. What I'm introducing with the ABT Framework is simply the next set of terms for the Information Society.

With these simple analytical tools, you can start to ask deeper questions about art itself. The AAA and DHY forms almost certainly have unique powers of their own. A lot of the greatest, most epic novels ever written have very, very long stretches of AAA. Some stretches of a story might, taken in isolation, seem like DHY, but if you keep reading, what was initially totally confusing might start to become clear. This form of problem-solution dynamic can be the most deeply satisfying experience imaginable — "I once was lost, but now I'm found."

Novelists have been at this stuff for a lot longer than the makers of film and television. They have had centuries of exploration and experimentation. So now let's take a look at their world through the ABT prism.

3.2) BOOKS

THE NARRATIVE INDEX APPLIED TO AUTHORS

Novels present large amounts of text — far beyond the 1,000 words I require of a speech before I think the Narrative Index (BUT/AND ratio) has much meaning. On the following page are scores for a variety of some of my favorite novels (plus a few other books) with both the Narrative Index and the "And Frequency" (AF, the percentage of total words that are "and") of each.

When it comes to number of words, on the upper end is *War and Peace*, checking in at over a half-million. Such large sample sizes mean that a difference of three or four points in the Narrative Index probably is significant where it wasn't for individual speeches.

So let's look at a few of the interesting patterns. We'll start with the leader of the pack: Barbara Cartland, the legendary British author who holds the record for most romance novels. She published 723 novels, many of which were bestsellers. She was enormously popular. And not coincidentally, she's the only novelist I've found who was able to reach the upper deck with a Narrative Index score above 30.

N.I.	A.F.	TOTAL WORDS	TITLE	AUTHOR
37	2.4	40,570	*Love in the East*	Barbara Cartland
33	2.2	53,282	*Fear and Loathing in Las Vegas*	Hunter S. Thompson
29	2.3	101,737	*To Kill A Mockingbird*	Harper Lee
28	2.7	74,474	*The Catcher in the Rye*	J.D. Salinger
27	2.2	107,626	*1984*	George Orwell
26	3.6	178,289	*Lord of the Rings, Book 1*	J.R. Tolkien
26	2.4	77,868	*Harry Potter and the Sorcerer's Stone*	J.K. Rowling
25	2.1	136,292	*The God Delusion*	Richard Dawkins
24	2.5	58,664	*The Dragons of Eden*	Carl Sagan
23	1.6	41,228	*The Double Helix*	James Watson
23	2.4	131,130	*Even Cowgirls Get the Blues*	Tom Robbins
23	2.1	25,501	*The Panda's Thumb*	Stephen Jay Gould
23	1.8	164,540	*The Hunt for Red October*	Tom Clancy
22	2.2	32,427	*Astrophysics for People in a Hurry*	Neil Degrasse Tyson
21	2.6	65,652	*Go Set a Watchman*	Harper Lee
21	2.6	149,681	*The Mismeasure of Man*	Stephen Jay Gould
21	3.2	86,282	*Darkness*	Ursula Leguin
20	2.6	217,798	*The Origin of Species*	Charles Darwin
20	2.3	129,680	*Jurassic Park*	Michael Crichton
20	3.5	176,848	*For Whom the Bell Tolls*	Ernest Hemingway
20	2.9	162,442	*The Shining*	Stephen King
20	2.8	50,917	*The Mist*	Stephen King
19	2.7	152,080	*The Dead Zone*	Stephen King
19	4.6	27,089	*The Old Man and the Sea*	Ernest Hemingway
19	3.0	54,372	*The Bluest Eye*	Toni Morrison
18	3.9	584,715	*War and Peace*	Leo Tolstoy
18	2.8	125,745	*Surely You're Joking, Mr. Feynman*	Richard Feynman
16	3.4	127,879	*Death in the Afternoon*	Ernest Hemingway
16	2.6	75,486	*The Tipping Point*	Malcolm Gladwell
16	2.8	131,644	*Black Hawk Down*	Mark Bowden
15	2.9	270,621	Tytler's 1839 *Universal History*	Alexander Tytler
15	3.4	48,396	*The Great Gatsby*	F. Scott Fitzgerald
14	2.5	50,386	*Bridges of Madison County*	Robert James Waller
14	3.1	174,705	*The World is Flat*	Thomas Friedman
14	3.7	136,220	*The Firm*	John Grisham
13	2.8	79,242	*The Perfect Storm*	Sebastian Junger
13	3.2	180,835	*The Grapes of Wrath*	John Steinbeck
12	3.1	128,724	*Consilience*	E.O. Wilson
11	2.5	58,386	*Breakfast of Champions*	Kurt Vonnegut
11	2.4	76,267	*Sirens of Titan*	Kurt Vonnegut
10	2.8	49,991	*Slaughterhouse Five*	Kurt Vonnegut
10	2.6	270,531	*Ulysses*	James Joyce
8	3.3	68,350	*The Sun Also Rises*	Ernest Hemingway
8	5.2	15,677	*Evangeline*	Henry Wadsworth Longfellow
8	2.2	645,990	*Biology* (College Textbook)	Raven & Johnson, 11th Edition

N.I. - Narrative Index (ratio of BUTs/ANDs x 100)

A.F. - And Frequency (percentage of total words that are the word "and")

But … if you look at her novel *Love in the East* (which may or may not be representative of the other 722 novels she wrote, I don't know, I've never read any of them), you'll see the score is not surprising — every page is packed with twists and turns.

Here's a random sample:

"But I am not the only one pretending," she answered, looking at him and remembering Lionel's mysterious words. He did not answer, but stayed as he was, regarding her with a puzzled expression in his eyes. Suddenly the boat lurched again, throwing her off-balance. She grasped wildly for something to hold onto, but could find nothing. He reached out to save her and the next moment she had fallen against his chest. For what seemed like an eternity, but was only a split second, he held her tightly against him in an echo of the previous night.

Think of what that is doing to the brain of the reader. It's moment after moment of contradiction. Not just with the action, but with the description as well. If we can accept that contradiction is the central element of brain stimulation (and by the way, a neurophysiologist said to me recently that in his opinion almost all behavior just comes down to dopamine addiction — we are drawn to whatever will stimulate the release of dopamine in the brain, leading him to suggest all this stuff may be as simple as the word "but" causing more dopamine squirts than anything else), we can see that she is doing an awful lot of brain stimulation — at least for non-intellectual brains. (Most intellectuals would find her books brain deadening.)

Of course close behind her melodrama is the drug-fueled melodrama *Fear and Loathing in Las Vegas*. It's a darkly comic tale of paranoia, in which nothing turns out to be what it seems or should be — all of which is punctuated by the word "but." Here's a choice sample of three "but's" in four sentences:

It was closed, but the salesman said he would wait, if we hurried. But we were delayed en route when a Stingray in front of us killed a pedestrian on Sunset Boulevard. The store was closed by the time we got there. There were people inside, but they refused to come to the double-glass door until we gave it a few belts and made ourselves clear.

Next down the list is the book that psychotic killer Mark David Chapman held in his hands as he shot John Lennon. There was always a cultish aura around that book. I remember reading it obsessively in eighth grade; one of my older sister's boyfriends gave it to me. The whole book was about contradiction, the alienated young man feeling out of synch with all that is ordinary in the world. It's highly stimulatory to young minds. It's not surprising it would have so much contradiction.

Now look at the consistency of many authors. Stephen King hovers around 20 for the Narrative Index. Kurt Vonnegut, with his eternally droll, deadpan, piercing view of humanity is down around 10. His books are characterized by tediously dull long stretches (probably all AAA), punctuated by sudden twists, which unleash laughter that would make me stop reading to laugh uncontrollably. Those moments stay with you for a lifetime. Such is the art of this AAA/ABT dynamic.

THE CURIOUS CASE OF ERNEST HEMINGWAY'S "AND"s

The AF (And Frequency) tells us something, too. Look at the curious case of Ernest Hemingway. Just about all of these authors have an AF right around the well-edited optimum of 2.5 (remember in Chapter 2, I told the story of the Stanford Literary Lab study that identified this optimum, plus my own short study of ten articles each in *The New Yorker* and *The New York Times* that all converged on this value).

But then look at Hemingway. He's over 3.0 with all of his scores and as high as 4.6 for *The Old Man and the Sea*. That score is amazing. It's getting up there in the range of government reports—like the legendary World Bank annual reports that suffer from "Bankspeak."

Now see what it actually looks like in action. Here's a random sample from the text:

They sat on the Terrace and many of the fishermen made fun of the old man and he was not angry. Others, of the older fishermen, looked at him and were sad. But they did not show it and they spoke politely about the current and the depths they had drifted their lines at and the steady good weather and of what they had seen.

He's Mister And, And, Andy, but there's also something very soothing about the prose. "And" is the most common word of agreement. He was clearly drawing on that power in using it so much.

This tells us that the AF for non-fiction (meaning more literal texts) is reflective of how boring something is—like the long-winded World Bank reports. But when you enter into art, it's probably a different dynamic. Exactly what that dynamic is remains to be studied and clarified.

BLIND TEXT ANALYSIS

What's also interesting is to look at the typical blindness of so many people doing "text analysis." It's so common now to just measure the hell out of everything in search of possible patterns, then call yourself an "expert." (I'm looking at you, 538.com.) This was what happened with The Toad-Clinton election—so many pollsters citing all their numbers with the lethal combination of blind belief in numbers and an absence of intuition.

In scientific research there's a term for this approach: inductivism. It basically means conducting research without using your brain in hopes of not biasing what you're doing because of what you already know. You go out into nature, measure 37 different variables, not knowing which is likely to be important, then see what you get for patterns.

The opposite approach is called hypothetico-deductive. This is where you go ahead and use your brain and even intuition to avoid wasting time. You look at the 37 variables, decide that 34 of them are probably not important, then do a really good job of measuring only the three you think are worth it.

A classic example of the inductivist approach can be seen on a website called LitCharts. In January 2018, Justin Rice posted an article called "What Makes Hemingway Hemingway?" It's a classic "cast the net wide" approach; he presents a ton of graphs and numbers analyzing the bejesus out of Hemingway's writings, but he only mentions the word "narrative" once—in the opening sentence of the article. He presents the frequencies of a number of words, but the words he chooses don't include the two most important narrative words—"and" and "but."

This matches what I mentioned in Chapter 2 about the field of "sentiment analysis." They begin by throwing out these two key narrative words (but, and), viewing them as "without sentiment" and thus meaningless.

And they are meaningless. Except in the world of narrative structure, which is kind of everything in communication.

And yes, I know that what I am presenting here is so "reductionist" and analytical that it makes the stomachs of literary folks churn. My heart is with you. It's terrible to watch art be dissected. And yet ... it's happening everywhere now, as computers analyze everything within reach.

In fact, here's another study.

THE GREAT AMERICAN WORD MAPPER

After giving a talk about the Narrative Index at the 2018 South By Southwest Interactive Festival, I was contacted by Jack Grieve, a "forensic linguist" at Ashton University in Scotland. He and a couple of colleagues in the U.S. used Twitter to look analytically at regional variation in word usage in the U.S.

It turns out that when you send out a tweet, it has attached to it the GPS location of where it originated. They gathered the data for over 10 million tweets and came up with what they call "The Great American Word Mapper." It allows you to enter any word, and then it shows you the frequency of usage of the word (in tweets at least) throughout the United States.

After seeing me tweet about the But/And ratio, this is what he sent: the plots for the two words. Look where "but" appears the most in tweets: the South. Why might that be?

He said they felt it was from the greater use of "but" by the

African-American community, which has a large population in the South. But ... I would suggest otherwise.

The Center for the Study of Southern Culture is located at the University of Mississippi. It's the only such institute in the country. There is no Center for the Study of Northern Culture. Or Eastern or Western. Only the South.

Years ago, I saw a talk by the director of the institute. He began by explaining how the only original art form the United States has given world culture is jazz music, which originated in the South. He added that the South has given rise to more great novelists than any other part of the country, from William Faulkner to Thomas Wolfe to Alice Walker. It is the heart of storytelling in America. You would expect it to be the heart of "but" usage.

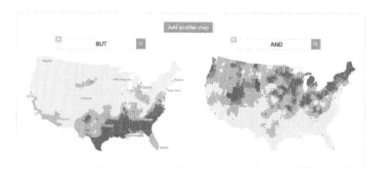

THE GREAT AMERICAN WORD MAPPER LOOKS AT "BUT" AND "AND." Using the geographic locations of over 10 million tweets, the Word Mapper shows the south loves its "buts'" while the north is more fond of "and's."

Conversely, look who likes to use the word "and" in their tweets. You wouldn't want to imply the people from North Dakota or Wisconsin or Maine are boring, but ...

And going back to those southern novelists, here's something about one of the greatest — Harper Lee.

THE NARRATIVE INDEX AS FINGERPRINT: TO KILL A MOCKINGBIRD

As I've said, when you get to the size of entire novels, you're dealing with a large sample size that probably allows for a level of precision not possible with speeches. A five-point difference in the Narrative Index of two books is probably significant.

In 2015, 65 years after Lee Harper published her Pulitzer-Prize-winning literary masterpiece, *To Kill a Mockingbird*, her second novel, *Go Set a Watchman*, was published to a collective groan of, "boh-ring." *Entertainment Weekly* said this about it: "it reads, for the most part, like a sluggishly-paced first draft, replete with incongruities, bad dialogue, and underdeveloped characters." It came out just months before her death at age 89, when she was in pretty much of a fog of decline.

The literary world set to work as detectives, trying to figure out the exact origins of the book. The overall conclusion seems to be that it was a first draft of *Mockingbird*, and not a very good one.

Well, what did screenwriting guru Frank Daniel have to say about first drafts? He said we always begin with the dreaded "and then, and then, and then," narrative structure — meaning AAA. Which means, all else equal, you would predict that the Narrative Index of a first draft would be considerably lower than the finished draft.

So look at the Narrative Index for *Mockingbird*. It was a very powerful 29. Now look at the same index for *Watchman* — a 21.

There you go.

The masterpiece was ABT. The weird leftover manuscript that was probably a first draft was much more AAA. All of which figures.

On that note, let's move on to more lyrical communication.

3.3) MUSIC/POETRY

DYLAN, ELVIS, TAYLOR SWIFT

You see the ABT everywhere with things that are big in space (large audience) or time (persist over the ages).

In the last chapter I will go into my theory of narrative selection, but in simple terms, it's this: AAA and DHY material may stimulate people in the short term, but those forms reach limited audiences and don't last. Because they are hard to absorb, hard to remember, and don't reach deep inside of you, they get selected against.

Take a look at nursery rhymes. (There's a few in Appendix 3.) They're just about all ABT-structured. There may well have been some that have arisen over the ages that were AAA-structured, but due to narrative selection, they either changed or died. Either they became ABT-structured, or kids quit telling them because they couldn't remember them.

In the beginning, it might have been, "Jack and Jill went up the hill to fetch a pail of water. AND Jack tied a rope around the handle, AND Jill pulled out a tiny candle. AND Jack lowered the bucket into the well, AND Jill held up the candle saying, 'isn't this swell.' AND as Jack hoisted the bucket with all his strength, Jill talked politics at great length. AND ..."

By the time a kid got to that point, one of his friends would have said, "Um, excuse me, but where's this going?" as someone else said, "THEREFORE ... ?" That would have been narrative selection at work, as the kid stopped the rhyme and said, "Okay, gotcha, lemme work on this one," and eventually found his way to the contradiction of Jack falling down and breaking his crown.

The same is true for most music. Start with the most popular song ever: "Happy Birthday to You." Think more of the feel of it than the words. The first two lines are set up, the third line identifies the recipient ("Happy birthday, dear Jayde") and has a different melody that has just the tiniest bit of contradiction/climax feel to it. Then the last line relieves the tension with a "therefore" feel of resolution. It's the same old three-part structure.

Now apply the same analysis of tone to Bob Dylan's classic, "Stuck Inside of Mobile with the Memphis Blues Again." It has nine verses, each one repeating the same basic ABT structure like this:

Oh, the ragman draws circles
Up and down the block
I'd ask him what the matter was
But I know that he don't talk
And the ladies treat me kindly
And they furnish me with tape
But deep inside my heart
I know I can't escape
(BUT) Oh, Mama, can this really be the end
(THEREFORE) To be stuck inside of Mobile with the

There it is, ABT, plain as day. Over and over again for each verse. There's no overarching ABT to the song — it's flat as a narrative pancake, and probably as a result, it's not on anybody's list of Top 100 Songs of All Time. But it's definitely an ABT workout.

Actually, an interesting fact to notice about that verse is there are two "but"'s in the agreement material, then none in the contradiction. This is important to note, as it shows how it's not as simple as just looking for the key words. You have to develop a feel for which narrative force is at work.

And then you look at Elvis, ABT-ing about his blue suede shoes (thanks to Mike Strauss for this one):

Well, it's one for the money
Two for the show
Three to get ready
Now go, cat, go
But don't you
Step on my blue suede shoes
Well (THEREFORE) you can do anything
But stay off of my blue suede shoes

Or John Lennon singing, "Imagine":

You may say that I'm a dreamer
But I'm not the only one
(THEREFORE) I hope someday you'll join us
And the world will be as one

And then there's Taylor Swift's ultra-megahit of 2014, "Shake it Off." The music video of it has nearly 3 billion views. Here's the opening verse—pure ABT:

I stay out too late, got nothin' in my brain
That's what people say, mmm hmm, that's what people say, mmm hmm
I go on too many dates, but I can't make 'em stay
At least that's what people say mmm mmm, that's what people say mmm mmm
But I keep cruising, can't stop, won't stop moving
It's like I got this music in my mind, sayin' gonna be alright
'Cause the players gonna play, play, play, play, play
And the haters gonna hate, hate, hate, hate, hate
(THEREFORE) Baby, I'm just gonna shake, shake, shake, shake, shake
I shake it off, I shake it off

The fact is just about every song has a basic beginning, middle and end. That means you can find elements of the ABT somewhere within a song. But all of these examples (and countless others; I'm constantly getting emails from friends saying, "Did you see how this song has the ABT?") are just a small sample. Narrative structure is how we communicate— even in songs.

SONATAS

I'm not going to even try to pretend like I know anything about classical music or rap. I don't. But take a look at the Wikipedia page for classical music forms. A sonata is defined as having five parts: introduction, exposition, development, recapitulation, coda.

It's basic three-act structure. Act one is introduction and exposition: the set-up. Act two is development that builds to a climax: the problem. Act three is recapitulation: the solution. Coda, as we know, is just a bit tacked on after the story.

THE NARRATIVE INDEX FOR MUSIC

If the word count (meaning sample size) of speeches is at the lower end of reliable, songs are way below it. Bob Dylan's nine verses of "Stuck Inside of Mobile with the Memphis Blues Again" is a lengthy 616 words, but that's not even near the 1,000 words I like to see for a speech. When you look at the Narrative Index for it—a gigantic 267—you need to consider that it's the result of only 8 BUTs, 3 ANDs.

So let's not try to use the Narrative Index for songs. Except … a friend asked, "What about really angry rap songs?" Well, I looked at NWA's foundational album, *Straight Outta Compton*. The song with the title scores 111 (10 BUTs, 9 ANDs). Five of the other songs have scores over 50.

What's maybe a little more significant is that all 13 songs on the album combine for a Narrative Index of 53 (95 BUTs, 193 ANDs), with a total number of words at 10,348. That's starts to be a little more reliable.

But … when we compare it to Barry Manilow's Greatest Hits album, there's no difference. His average is 47, with a range from 0 to 300 around it. Which means lots o' noise.

Bottom line, let's not try and use the Narrative Index for songs—the sample size is just too small. But it does look like maybe they average around 50, which is way more than speeches. But who knows, maybe someone else can pursue this in more detail, along with everything else to do with the

Narrative Index. I'm only hoping to sow some seeds of inquiry.

POETRY?

Poetry and I go together like the opera and Cheetos. I have zilch to say on the subject, but ... fortunately, I have a good friend who writes poetry. His name is Paul Cummins. He's an amazing guy—a PhD from Stanford in literature from two decades ahead of my time. He was the founder of a series of hugely successful and innovative schools in Los Angeles, with The Crossroads School of Santa Monica being his flagship achievement.

That's his original poem at the start of this book. He is someone who instantly "got it" on the ABT, the first time he heard it. And to prove it, the next time I saw him he gave me a copy of a famous poem that's as much ABT ideal form as the Gettysburg Address.

Here's the poem. It might offend the #Metoo movement, and it's clearly a little behind the times—kind of like 330 years behind the times. It was published in 1681 and written by English author and politician Andrew Marvell. The title is, "To His Coy Mistress," and, to be crude about it, it's about a guy trying to get laid.

Here's the poem:

Had we but world enough, and time,
This coyness, Lady, were no crime
We would sit down and think which way
To walk and pass our long love's day.
Thou by the Indian Ganges' side

Shouldst rubies find: I by the tide
Of Humber would complain. I would
Love you ten years before the Flood,
And you should, if you please, refuse
Till the conversion of the Jews.
My vegetable love should grow
Vaster than empires, and more slow;
A hundred years should go to praise
Thine eyes and on thy forehead gaze;
Two hundred to adore each breast,
But thirty thousand to the rest;
An age at least to every part,
And the last age should show your heart.
For, Lady, you deserve this state,
Nor would I love at lower rate.

But at my back I always hear
Time's wingèd chariot hurrying near;
And yonder all before us lie
Deserts of vast eternity.
Thy beauty shall no more be found,
Nor, in thy marble vault, shall sound
My echoing song; then worms shall try
That long preserved virginity,
And your quaint honour turn to dust,
And into ashes all my lust:
The grave's a fine and private place,
But none, I think, do there embrace.

Now therefore, while the youthful hue
Sits on thy skin like morning dew,
And while thy willing soul transpires
At every pore with instant fires,
Now let us sport us while we may,
And now, like amorous birds of prey,
Rather at once our time devour

Than languish in his slow-chapped power.
Let us roll all our strength and all
Our sweetness up into one ball,
And tear our pleasures with rough strife
Through the iron gates of life:
Thus, though we cannot make our sun
Stand still, yet we will make him run.

Okay, let's not talk about the content, at all. It was three centuries ago; things were different. As with everything in this book, we're not here to talk about CONTENT; we're only interested in FORM. And that's why I present it.

Look at the form. Pure ABT. He even uses the words BUT and THEREFORE to start the second and third paragraphs.

This is before the philosophers of the 1800's, like Hegel, who identified the triad of thesis, antithesis, synthesis. This might have been one of the works he was studying as he came to the realization of the three-part nature of communication.

And now, let us not languish in his "slow-chapped power." Instead, we shall roll all our strength and all our sweetness up into one ball, and move on to the last section of this chapter. It's time to talk about a group that has shown not just a lack of interest in the ABT but, in some cases, an overt spurning of the ABT for its "overly reductionist" nature.

It's time for the journalists.

3.4) JOURNALISM: WHY THE LONG FACE?

This is going to be one of the more contentious sections. Journalists haven't taken to the ABT. It may be a cultural thing. The ABT template arises from Hollywood. Journalists as a group don't care for what Hollywood has done to our culture.

I want to be delicate about this because our bombastic president, Mr. Toad, has attacked journalists relentlessly, and I don't support any of that. They are clearly embattled.

But that said, I expressed my frustrations in Chapter 2 when I told the story of my teaming up with James Carville to try and get the Hillary Clinton campaign to realize how lethally non-narrative their whole program was. I also tried to get a wide range of journalists to listen. Even the publicist at University of Chicago Press joined in, using his media contacts, trying to get journalists to consider my editorial on Trump and the Narrative Index in the fall of 2015 as my *Houston* book came out, but they all dismissed the ABT as a piece of elementary school trivia.

You would think they would listen, given that their job is supposed to involve listening and reporting. But the truth is a lot of journalists don't listen very well.

And actually there was one journalist who not only didn't care to listen—he attacked. He is a Pulitzer Prize winner. He tweeted at me in August of 2017 that he was "losing patience with your hyper-reductionist" approach to my analyses of The Toad's speeches. I did nothing to provoke such an outburst other than do my standard "hyper- reductionist" ABT analysis of The Toad on my blog—so I guess I was basically guilty as charged, but can't you at least go a little further than plugging your ears and singing "la-la-la-la-la"?

I'm not the only one to hear such caustic comments about the ABT. My friend Park Howell uses it in his workshops with business folks. He had one woman who seemed more of the literary persuasion lash out at him, calling the ABT "reductive and insulting."

Maybe. But what do you do when you see thousands of people benefit in their daily lives from the ABT Framework, especially through our Story Circles Narrative Training program, as I've now seen over the past decade?

There's an element of cultural elitism to the dismissiveness of some journalists and even humanities folks—like a connoisseur driving by a McDonald's and cringing. Sorry, the masses have a right to understand narrative as much as anyone. We'll have more on this later.

So here's two examples of the ABT at work all day, every day in the world of journalism, whether journalists care to recognize it or not.

GOOD ABT IN JOURNALISM: NEW YORK TIMES FRONT PAGE "BUT PARAGRAPHS"

Think about the front page of *The New York Times*—could there be an any more intensive incubator for narrative structure? It has the highest daily circulation in the United States. You know there's lots of eyeballs at work each day, selecting and shaping the content on the front page. As a result, the ABT is there, hard at work, every single day.

You see the clearest mark of the ABT on the front page through what I call "But Paragraphs." This term refers to paragraphs that start with the word BUT.

Back in elementary school (when I was taught a really lousy and fractured version of grammar and writing), we were told that you can never start a paragraph with BUT or AND.

But ... somewhere over the ages that rule got dumped. A few years ago, on *The New York Times* blog "After Deadline," the host addressed this issue for the newspaper. He cited The New York Times *Manual of Style and Usage* as the ultimate source. It says this on the subject:

Q: "Should a Sentence Ever Start With 'And'?

A: Another pet peeve of some commenters is the use of "but" or "and" to begin a sentence. I don't see any basis for their objections. It shouldn't be overdone, but using coordinating conjunctions this way can provide a handy and very efficient transition. "But" is certainly preferable in many cases to the stilted "however," and "and" is simpler than "in addition" or similar phrases.

So what I began to notice is that on any given day, there are almost always two or three articles on the front page of The New York Times that have a paragraph beginning with BUT. These are tightly ABT-structured stories. They begin with two or three paragraphs of statements: all the AND material. Then there's the But Paragraph that establishes the narrative core of the story.

So what I began to notice is that on any given day, there are almost always two or three articles on the front page of The New York Times that have a paragraph beginning with BUT. These are tightly ABT-structured stories. They begin with two or three paragraphs of statements: all the AND material. Then there's the But Paragraph that establishes the narrative core of the story.

"BUT PARAGRAPHS" ON THE FRONT PAGE OF THE NEW YORK TIMES. Here's the front page for April 13, 2016. There are two "But Paragraphs" as well as a sub-headline that has a "but."

You see it over and over again. So much so that I had an assistant do a little project in August 2016. I had her purchase five newspapers every day for three weeks and record the number of But Paragraphs on the front page of each for each day. The newspapers were "Big News" (New York Times, Washington Post), "Business-Oriented" (Wall Street Journal), and "Local News" (Huntington News, Long Islander News).

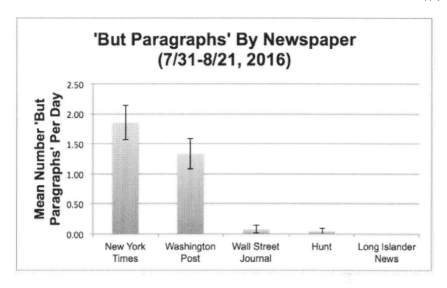

DAILY OCCURRENCE OF "BUT PARAGRAPHS" (PARAGRAPHS STARTING WITH THE WORD "BUT") ON THE FRONT PAGE OF 5 NEWSPAPERS. "Hunt" is Huntington News, a local New York newspaper.

Look at the pattern—it's so clear. The Big Papers have lots of "But Paragraphs"; the small papers have almost none. There's two hypotheses to explain what you see.

The first is just style: the Big Newspapers allow "But Paragraphs," and the Business- Oriented and Local Newspapers don't allow them, but let a few slip by.

The other hypothesis, which is more logical given that there are a few "But Paragraphs" that occur, is that the Big Newspapers are working to reach the Outer Circle (as defined in Chapter 1 of this book) on their front page. But both *The Wall Street Journal* and the small local papers are playing to their Inner Circle audience.

People buy *The Wall Street Journal* primarily because they're interested in business news. People buy a local paper because they're interested in what's happening locally. There's no need to put the story of a local bake sale on Long Island into a broader context using the ABT.

But if it's the front page of *The New York Times*, you'd better have some ABT to help your audience understand why in the world you're telling the story of a bake sale.

A sub-hypothesis to this is that on the front page of *The New York Times*, stories that are about urgent, intense breaking news don't need to bother with the ABT structure. It's similar to what I said about the CDC communicating about a disease outbreak — the interest of the public is already activated. But that "slower" story about a growing problem of water shortages in Gabon might need to have a good setup that makes clear why the reader should care, before getting into the details of the problem.

Urgent stories don't need much setup.

BAD ABT IN JOURNALISM: USA TODAY AND "NARRATIVE FABRICATION"

USA Today is such a piece of trash newspaper. It really is. I've followed it since its inception in the 1980's, when it was immediately nicknamed "McPaper." I was friends with a writer there for years who told me inside stories of all the high school interns who run much of the operations at their headquarters in McClean, Virginia.

For more than a decade I've had it as the home page on my browser so that I get to see the levels they routinely stoop to in manufacturing stories. It's not quite *The National Inquirer*, but if you look close you'll see it's not far behind.

USA Today is constantly trying to grab eyeballs, so it's constantly finding and pumping up, or manufacturing, controversy. This means they need an endless supply of voices of contradiction.

They have realized that to meet this need, they can find the endless amounts of contradiction on Twitter. So they end up using it for crafting headlines.

Here's a typical example. On January 23, 2019, their front page screamed out, "Twitter Rips Samantha Guthrie for 'Appalling' Interview." As if Twitter were some institution with a singular voice.

For this particular article, Samantha Guthrie on NBC's *The Today Show* had interviewed the Kentucky high school kid who had been at the center of a protest incident in Washington, D.C. According to *USA Today*, Twitter was "ripping" Guthrie, but when you look at the voices they cite from Twitter, they all have minuscule followings. The numbers of followers for the first five Twitter comments being cited were 1423, 184, 640, 37, and 48.

How long does it take to get 37 followers? One high school intern can produce that in fifteen minutes.

If the paper had integrity it would establish some set procedure for what qualifies quantitatively as "the voice of Twitter," but they don't. This is the sort of "false equivalence" that the science world has long complained of. At *USA Today* it's just the daily crafting of the ABT structure to reach the non-AAA-reading masses.

3.5) SUMMARY: HOW CAN THE ENTERTAINMENT WORLD USE THE ABT FRAMEWORK?

This chapter got to the core of the ABT because the template itself arose from the world of entertainment. I don't think I would recommend the ABT to poets; it's maybe a little too literal for their art-driven world. Song writers start to get closer to needing it. But when it comes to television and movie screenwriters, it's all about the ABT. Every screenwriter should be using **1) THE NARRATIVE SPECTRUM** in spotting parts of a script that are too much AAA or DHY. For the theme of a work, the **2) DOBZHANSKY TEMPLATE** is just a simple one-sentence tool to help articulate it. When it comes to great stories or TV series, the structure is **3) NESTED ABT's** in creating overlain story arcs. Writers hoping to reach the broadest audiences should be aware of the **4) NARRATIVE IMPERATIVE**. Any text or script should be quickly and repeatedly assessed with the two key text indices: **5) THE NARRATIVE INDEX (NI)** and **6) THE AND FREQUENCY (AF);** the former reveals a lack of narrative strength, while the latter shows long-windedness unless "and" is being used for art. **7) THE "AND"** part of the ABT is essential for context, depth and impact. And lastly, **8) THE ABT DYNAMIC** overall provides the path to reaching the broader, Outer Circle of an audience.

4) SCIENCE

4) SCIENCE - The Scientific Method is ABT

Now it's time for my home turf. I was once a scientist, AND I achieved tenure as a professor of biology, BUT I developed a bigger interest in mass communication, THEREFORE I resigned and went to film school. There's the ABT of my life's journey.

The fact is that I've been involved with the communication of science for over four decades. I was in graduate school in 1980, which was a landmark year for the subject, as two highly commercial magazines for science launched: *Discover* and *Science 80* (the latter eventually folded and was absorbed by the former, which still exists).

I have a lot to say on the communication of science, though my 2015 book *Houston, We Have a Narrative* covered a great deal of it for me, so this chapter won't be quite as long as the previous three.

I'm going to follow "the old triad thing" of the nineteenth-century philosophers and structure this chapter around the elements of thesis, antithesis, synthesis. I'll do this by delivering: first, the bad news (how things have traditionally been for science and communication); second, the good news (some changes for the better over the ages, though unfortunately these are offset somewhat by technology); and third, the most important news that needs to be realized and worked on if scientists are ever going to be understood.

If you're a scientist, please keep in mind I am 100% pro-science. I loved my science career and the vast majority of scientists have taken to the ABT Framework eagerly, producing countless great collaborations. But ... there is still that literal minded element with some scientists. It happens. I know of what I speak — I have 40 years of experience with science to draw upon. Okay, here we go.

4.1) THE BAD NEWS

LIKE A NAIL IN THE FOREHEAD

Have you ever seen the humorous video of the woman with the nail in her forehead complaining to her boyfriend about not knowing what's causing her piercing headache? He keeps trying to point out that there's a nail in her forehead. She dismisses him, saying, "No, it's not that simple." He reluctantly says, "Actually, I kinda think it is."

Well, it's kinda been the same story for some scientists and the ABT.

It's an age-old stereotype that scientists are terrible with communication. There are countless TV shows and movies, from *The Big Bang Theory* to *Revenge of the Nerds*, that have exploited this. So you'd think that when a powerful, simple communications tool like the ABT comes along, the science community would embrace it enthusiastically. But nope.

In 2013, I presented the ABT in detail in a keynote address to 1,000 scientists at the annual meeting of the biological society of which I used to be a member. During the reception afterwards a friend told me she was listening to the conversations. She said, "The scientists think the ABT is a 'neat trick,' but that it's *too simple* for their communications needs."

Too simple …

Like the boyfriend pointing out the nail in the forehead as she basically replies, "No, it's not that simple," and he says, "I kinda think it is."

SCIENTISTS LOVE THEIR AAA, ALL THE WAY UP TO THE NOBEL PRIZE

Scientists, bless their hearts, love, love, love their information. I did a workshop with postdoctoral fellows at the National Institutes of Health. I had them try to craft the "conversational" version of the ABT (presented in Chapter 1), which involves stripping the narrative to its structural bare bones, leaving it devoid of information. So many of the postdocs just didn't want to let go of their beloved details, like this …

The goal of that exercise is to take an ABT and strip it to its narrative core. It might start with, for example, "The key neurotransmitter receptors of microglia are well known …" For this, I would explain how the idea is to strip it down to just, "A thing is well known."

The postdocs would say okay, got it, then read their revision, "The neurotransmitter things of microglia are well known …" I would say, no, you need to remove ALL content. They would say, okay, right, right, then the new draft would be, "The things of microglia are well known …" And I would have to say, no, I mean ALL content — we want it to be totally generic.

You could feel them not wanting to let go of information. It was kind of comical, but at the core, it's a serious problem.

It's the assumption that the entire world is part of your inner circle: abreast of the science, eager to hear about your research. But the world isn't.

You can see this bad habit all the way up to the highest pinnacle of the science world: the Nobel Prize recipients. NobelPrize.org is a website with all of the Nobel Laureates' speeches. The prizes in physics and literature both began in 1901. Working with a couple of assistants, we calculated the Narrative Index for each speech up to 2016.

What would you expect to see? Based on all their training in narrative, the literary folks ought to be a little more narrative-driven. That would mean a higher Narrative Index, right?

Sure enough, it's what you see, plain as day (Thanks to Bill Dennison and his graduate students for these calculations). Nearly a third of the physics laureates gave speeches that were in "The Land of And," but almost none of the literary types were so non-narrative.

Now that's not to say that all scientists are weak with narrative. Carl Sagan's media-career-making first book, The Dragons of Eden, scores a 24 for the Narrative Index.

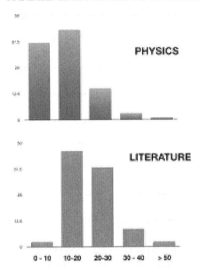

NARRATIVE INDEX FOR
NOBEL LAUREATE SPEECHES

PHYSICS

LITERATURE

0 - 10   10-20   20-30   30 - 40   > 50

NARRATIVE INDEX VALUES FOR THE SPEECHES OF NOBEL LAUREATES IN PHYSICS VERSUS LITERATURE. Narrative Index scores are grouped in increments of 10.

In fact, look at the classic science-themed books I included in the list in the last chapter:

25	2.1	136,292	*The God Delusion*	Richard Dawkins
24	2.5	58,664	*The Dragons of Eden*	Carl Sagan
23	1.6	41,228	*The Double Helix*	James Watson
23	2.1	25,501	*The Panda's Thumb*	Stephen Jay Gould
22	2.2	32,427	*Astrophysics for People in a Hurry*	Neil Degrasse Tyson
21	2.6	149,681	*The Mismeasure of Man*	Stephen Jay Gould
20	2.3	129,680	*Jurassic Park*	Michael Crichton
18	2.8	125,745	*Surely You're Joking, Mr. Feynman*	Richard Feynman
12	3.1	128,724	*Consilience*	E.O. Wilson

Clearly scientists (with editors) can tap into narrative structure when they need to. So why don't they, more often?

STORYPHOBIA

Science is meant to be a clinical, cold, objective, repeatable, tightly controlled, rigorously executed profession. It's at its best when conducted this way — meaning basically robotically.

Storytelling, on the other hand, is at its best when filled with human attributes such as emotion and humor. These are properties that lead to irrationality, which is the enemy of the rational mind of the scientist.

So you can start to see the basic problem. As we all know, "To err is human," but for science, "To err is not science." Scientists dream of being devoid of errors. So why would a scientist want to bring in the human element and foul everything up?

The result is widespread suspicion about "the telling of stories" in science, and even outright efforts to banish the practice. For example, in 2014, *Nature Methods* published a series of editorials debating this. One of them, from an M.I.T. scientist, was titled "Against Storytelling of Scientific Results." (By the way, I love pointing out that the author used the ABT structure for the opening of his essay — gotcha!)

I actually think the problems go very deep. I know most people like to be told that they can do anything, but I kinda think sometimes it's good to know the limits. Telling a kid who grows up to be five-foot two that he can one day play professional basketball if he just puts his mind to it isn't really helping the kid.

Towards that end, nobody ever told me at age 38, when I moved to Hollywood, that my brain had probably already been programmed irreversibly in a non-narrative direction. I don't even know that it's true, but I think it's worth considering now in light of the following.

THE BRAIN AND NARRATIVE: THE "OBVIOUS VERSUS INTERESTING" QUESTIONS

The meeting of brain science and narrative is just in its infancy. Lots of people — especially journalists — are eager to tell big stories about how "we are wired for storytelling."

Well … that statement is actually pretty obvious. We're also wired for compliments and anything else that we enjoy, but exactly how that wiring works at the cellular and molecular level is not at well-known so far.

For the past decade I've repeatedly cited the work of Princeton neurophysiologist Uri Hasson on this subject. He and his colleagues established the subfield of "neurocinematics," which they define as the study of how the brain responds to movies. Using functional MRI scans, they have subjects watch video clips that have narrative structure (e.g., a suspense movie) versus clips that lack narrative structure (e.g., a video of people walking randomly in a park) in order to examine how the brain responds to videos.

The major observation they found that I cite frequently because it is so simple, so robust, and so important is that narrative material stimulates the brain a lot, non-narrative material, not so much. That's all that I take away from the studies so far.

In my discussions with him he warned me repeatedly about reading too much into the work done. It is still very limited, and there is lots of skepticism about the precision of Functional MRI.

In Chapter 2 I mentioned that Adam Gopnik had a great article in The New Yorker in 2013 called, "Mindless: The New Neuro-skeptics," in which he related how much excessive extrapolation takes place these days in the whole field of neuroscience. The caption to the artwork accompanying the article summarizes the problem nicely by saying, "Neuroscience can often answer the obvious questions but rarely the interesting ones."

Of course, the fact that neuroscience can't answer the interesting questions doesn't stop plenty of journalists from pretending it can. So many journalists want to tell big, bold stories with complete certainty about how the brain works, regardless of whether the scientists actually know these things. Why?

Think back to screenwriting guru Robert McKee's defining characteristics of archplot. One of the key elements is complete certainty. It's what mass audiences want, and many journalists can't resist. To satisfy the audience, they tell bogus tales of neuroscience. That's what Gopnik's article was about.

So when it comes to neurobiology and storytelling, I'm inclined to go with that artwork caption. We're on solid ground with answering the obvious question—Is the brain stimulated by narrative (meaning basically contradiction?) Yes. But the interesting, more specific questions, like, "Is the brain more stimulated by mystery or fantasy, romance or action, etc."? He assures me they're not even close to starting to answer questions at that level.

So keeping that in mind, here's what I think may be the most interesting question of all when it comes to scientists and communication …

IS SCIENCE EDUCATION A ONE-WAY NEUROLOGICAL TRIP?

Back to my "brain transplant experiment." At age 38, I essentially transplanted my own brain from a largely non-narrative environment (at a university where I was a professor of marine biology) into an intensely narrative environment (USC Cinema School, where they talked about story structure endlessly). So we have two environments.

Scientists live their lives on a mental diet that is rich in non-narrative material. They consume facts and information all day without demanding that the material be told as a story. Sometimes it is, but that's more of an extra benefit than a requirement.

Humanities folks live their lives on a mental diet that's rich in narrative material. They read hundreds and hundreds of novels and short stories. A novel or short story generally needs to tell a story—it's kind of obligatory. So those folks end up developing narrative intuition from the world they live in just through osmosis.

Now here is the key element. We know pretty clearly these days that the brain is not finished developing until around age 25. Up until then neurons are being added and different parts continue to grow.

So what if ... what if it makes a huge difference whether, during that time, the brain is being stimulated by a large amount of engaging narrative material, or deadened by being force-fed the drudgery of non-narrative content?

What I'm suggesting is that a science education might have developmental consequences that limit flexibility later in life. I'm hypothesizing that there could end up being such a thing as a "non-narrative brain," versus a "narrative brain."

Most science students start getting serious about the subject around age 15. I know I locked onto marine biology around that age. As you get serious about science, you start reading books that have little narrative structure—they're just mountains of facts, the ultimate And, And, And material.

By college you're reading tons of these books. They rarely tell stories. You can see one of them in the list of books in Chapter 3. It's at the bottom of the list. It's the popular college biology textbook by Raven and Johnson. It scores a dull 8. This means it's just above a State of the Union address by George W. Bush. (Though also note that the And Frequency is 2.2, which means it's not nearly as And, And, Andy as World Bank annual reports that reach over 5.0.)

Back when I applied to undergraduate programs I was so fixated on marine biology that I thought I was ready to study nothing but that one subject. I would have jumped at the chance to do just that. But everywhere I turned I got the same advice: "you need to first get a solid, broad education as an undergraduate, and then in your last two years start to take the more specialized courses that start to prepare you for graduate school, where you will specialize."

That old advice was based on solid intuition. Today, I think that, looking at it from the perspective of narrative versus non-narrative training in relation to brain development, it makes good sense.

But the trend in our education system has been to cave in to students as consumers. It was happening when I left academia in the mid-'90's. I remember our biology department didn't offer a course in whale biology, but so many students demanded it that we found somebody to do it.

These days, the students run the show. So now undergraduates obsessed with science can bypass most of the humanities requirements at most universities. I wrote about this at length in the *Houston* book in a section titled, "Sprinting past the humanities."

Even more, where I live, there is a "marine science elementary school" that prides itself on teaching kids lots of science, starting from the earliest ages. But what if this is doing something to their narrative ability down the line?

Who knows? It's one of those interesting questions (as opposed to obvious questions) that neuroscience has not yet begun to address.

I know from my experience that I've managed to get a whole lot better at narrative since moving to the world of filmmaking at age 38. But despite the improvement, I knew from the start of film school that I wouldn't be able to compete with the 21-year-olds in my class who had just completed degrees in the humanities, in the process of which they had read hundreds of novels. It was clear from the start that they were grasping story structure and narrative dynamics far more easily and at a deeper level than I.

Make no mistake, I got better. But 25 years later, when I talk story with those folks, I'm just not on the same plane. They can conceptualize intricate screenplays that work on multiple levels in ways that I couldn't start to do.

I'd be willing to bet that the degree of exposure to narrative during that window from ages 15 to 25 is hugely important, and the lack of it is to some extent irreversible.

4.2) THE GOOD NEWS

Despite the professional impairments, the science world has been working on these problems for a long while. So here's some of the good news.

IMRAD: SCIENCE YIELDED TO OUR NARRATIVE-DRIVEN WORLD LONG AGO

In the beginning, scientists tried to be AAA with their communication. As we know, the real world is more And, And, And in its narrative structure. As Frank Daniel said, diaries and journals (which tend to be a direct recounting of the real world) are written with that structure, but scripts are not. Neither are scientific papers. This is what the science world came to realize over time.

The first scientific journals began appearing in the 1600's. They were largely AAA. The articles were long rambling discourses filled with observations, experiments and theorizing on nature with no clear narrative shape or form. But by the 1800's, they began to change. They knew that for knowledge to be shared it had to be at least somewhat standardized in how it was assembled.

Scientific papers began to take on the ABT form. Most of them were three sections: basically beginning, middle, and end, in the form of theory, experiment, and discussion.

In the early 1900's, science further institutionalized this by creating a standardized, more detailed structural convention. The narrative template they agreed upon is today know by the acronym IMRAD.

The letters stand for the four main sections you see in most scientific papers (with "and" added to make the acronym work better):

I - Introduction
M - Methods
R - Results
(A - And)
D - Discussion

This figure shows the adoption of the IMRAD template in the last century in the four major medical journals.

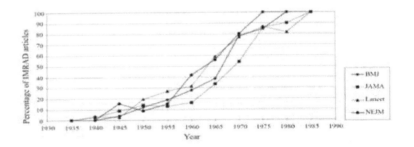

ADOPTION OF THE IMRAD (Introduction, Methods, Results, And Discussion) NARRATIVE TEMPLATE. You might think a good idea would be incorporated overnight, but it took 50 years for the top four medical journals to fully adopt the IMRAD form.

So here's the key point—the IMRAD template is just an extended version of the ABT. The Introduction is ABT in form. It has the basic shape of Graff's *They Say, I Say* structure. It begins with a review of the basic history of the scientific topic being investigated, relating the "they say" of what previous research tells us.

Then comes the presentation of the "I say" element from the author(s), which points to the research that needed to be done. This launches the reader into the "journey" of the Methods that were used and the Results that were found. Eventually the paper concludes with the overall THEREFORE of the study in the form of the Discussion section.

It's pure ABT dynamics, start to finish. Which means that although scientists aspire, dream and even pretend to be AAA in their communication, over a century ago they established this convention to force them all to be mostly ABT.

The crazy part for scientists is that while they hate "storytelling" and warn of all the pitfalls of rearranging their information to concoct better stories, they never seem to even question the sacred IMRAD narrative template. Nor do they call it "confining," "homogenizing," or all the other tenuous criticisms that have been offered up for the ABT. I'm guessing this is because they were imprinted and weaned on the IMRAD from their very first exposures to science. Why would you question something so foundational to your training?

SCIENTISTS WORK ON BEING MORE HUMAN

So by the 1950's, the science world had stamped out a lot of the irregularity in how science was written up professionally. With this reduction in individuality also came a sort of robotic view of "the scientist." Within the profession this was expressed not just by the structure of papers, but also with the actual style of writing. To make the whole process of science feel more objective, the style was shifted to using the third person. This meant that papers reported things like, "The investigators drew samples, and reagents were applied."

This style persisted into the 1970's, when I first started reading scientific papers. I used to wonder why in the world the writing was so strangely inhuman.

By the 1980's, things began to change, as some journals started allowing the use of the first person. This meant the scientist could write, "I took samples and applied reagents." This is more human, but it was of course off-putting to the old-school scientists.

Today, the style of communication in science continues to change. Our entire society is saturated with social media, resulting in scientists being nowhere near as objectified and portrayed as inanimate as in the old days. With this has come a greater acceptance and realization that scientists are in fact human.

And yet, just as society seems to be invading the world of scientists, there are also opposite trends. On college campuses, the sciences have trampled over the humanities. Visit almost any university, and you'll see huge and exciting new buildings for molecular biology, biomedical engineering, particle physics — and on and on.

What you won't see are any huge and exciting new buildings for literature, history or philosophy. Okay, I'm sure there's a few exceptions, but not many. I do lots of university visits for my films and training. I hear about it everywhere. The best you can hope for is an exciting and new building for something like computational linguistics — using science to analyze the humanities.

The sciences have beaten down the humanities. Which means

that the very thing the scientists needed help with—being more human—they have kicked to the curb. I will explore this theme in more detail in the final chapter.

HOPE FOR HUMANITY: THE ABT FRAMEWORK IN SCIENCE

I'm sure this is going to sound self-serving, but I do see one ray of possible hope for the long term: the introduction of the ABT Framework into science. It's been seven years now since I had my first exposure to the ABT elements. It was in November 2011, when I saw the *South Park* documentary on Comedy Central.

Two months later, I presented the ABT to 1,000 scientists in Anchorage, Alaska, at the Alaska Ocean Science Conference. My talk was on the opening day. I left Alaska early the next morning. By the end of the week I had a stack of emails from attendees telling me about how many people ended up adopting it immediately. Multiple speakers began their talks with, "I'm going to be speaking about …" then read their one-sentence ABT—often to applause at the end.

That was all it took for me. Those emails were all the proof I needed: the ABT works. And needs to be propagated.

Since then I've pounded away, slowly but surely, preaching the gospel of the ABT. Here are some of the initial landmarks of the past few years.

You may recall that in the Introduction I mentioned the two studies that showed how the IPCC (Intergovernmental Panel on Climate Change) was getting worse with their broad communication over time. Well, in 2017, they added a full-page presentation of the ABT to their Communications

Handbook.

There's now daily activity on Twitter, with people attending sessions in which the speaker presents the ABT, or professors introduce it in their classes. For at least some courses in the communication of science, they are seeing the power of the ABT.

The National Park Service — in addition to becoming major fans of our Story Circles Narrative Training program — is using it as a narrative template for case studies in their reports. And several scientific journals have added the structure to their Guidelines for Writers sections.

And yet, I don't think the trend lines are good. As the science world developed more awareness of structure over the past century, it fell victim to obfuscation, as Michael Crichton pointed out in his 1975 short paper. Here's a rather bleak and pivotal paragraph from his discussion that hammers home the obfuscation problem:

Contrary to popular belief, there is little historical precedent for bad writing. Scientific prose is usually said to begin with Galileo, and the Starry Messenger is a classic of vigorous exposition. Even as late as the 19th century physicians stated their views with strength and conviction. Only in the 20th century has obfuscation become widely acceptable.

I wish the science world could come together and grasp how large of an enemy the problem continues to be, but the deck appears stacked against that. Complexity creep appears unstoppable.

4.3) THE MOST IMPORTANT NEWS

All is not rosy in the land of science. Much of the problems arise from scientists failing to have even an accurate perception of themselves and their profession. This starts with their whole work practice, called "the scientific method."

IS THERE EVEN SUCH A THING AS THE SCIENTIFIC METHOD?

Is there really such a thing as "the scientific method"? As a scientist I never felt there was.

From the beginning it seemed to me like, what's the big deal? How is this any different from the thought process of a car mechanic, or baker, or gardener trying to figure out what's killing the petunias?

They all identify problems, they all generate "multiple working hypotheses" (the title of an important paper published in *Science*, the most important American scientific journal, in 1965, that was all about the best method for doing science). The car mechanic does the same thing, thinking, "It could be the spark plugs, or it could be the transmission, or it could be the alternator." Those are all multiple working hypotheses.

Yes, there might more rigor to what scientists do, and yes, they might be thinking a little more in the big picture of the entire body of "the scientific literature." But if a car mechanic, in trying to fix the car alarm on a Subaru Outback, realizes that faulty programming is the reason it keeps going off when you unlock the car (as happened to a good friend), he or she will probably contact national headquarters to let them know, and they will issue a notification nationally. Isn't that functionally about the same as publishing a peer-reviewed paper?

So if you are a non-scientist and in the business of making the work of scientists seem mystical (as, for example, a journalist or screenwriter), then yes, you want to focus on and even exaggerate the differences. But if you're more concerned with the truth and even humanizing scientists, then you should probably look at the similarities, which is the focus of this book, which shows how everyone employs the ABT dynamic.

Joseph Campbell faced this issue in the 1940's when conducting his foundational research on storytelling around the world. Near the start of his landmark 1949 book, *The Hero of a Thousand Faces*, he said:

There are of course differences between the numerous mythologies and religions of mankind, but this is a book about the similarities.

Campbell knew that the power of understanding comes in searching for the similarities. This is one of the major challenges of science in looking for patterns in the natural world. Campbell knew explanatory patterns are usually best revealed by focusing on similarities. It's how evolutionary relationships between organisms are determined — by focusing on the "derived characters" that species share, rather than on how they differ.

So this, as I say, leaves me skeptical of how unique science is.

IS THERE EVEN SUCH A THING AS SCIENCE COMMUNICATION?

And furthermore …

I've been bothered by this term, "science communication," ever since I started seeing the similarities between the communication of science and the communication of everything else. Joseph Campbell could have focused on "Asian storytelling" versus "African storytelling" versus "European storytelling." I'm sure there were differences. But as he said, he saw more power in emphasizing the similarities.

I feel the same way about communication (thus the five core chapters of this book). There's no reason for scientists to feel that special when it comes to communication. The core principles of communication lie in narrative structure, and that, as I showed in the Introduction with the three forces of narrative, is universal.

So the principles are the same, but … there is a conceptual divide. At the simplest of all levels, it's a difference in the perception of the number one. And I think it might be the biggest stumbling block to communication that all scientists face. So here we go with the big challenge.

YES, SCIENTISTS ARE HUMAN, BUT THEY DEFINITELY ARE DIFFERENT WHEN IT COMES TO PERCEIVING NARRATIVE

Scientists actually are different from non-scientists in how they think. That's what we need to begin with. Remember Jerry Graff's book title and general template for argumentation? His book is titled *They Say, I Say*. Let's use that as our template for where we are so far in our journey through these five broad topics.

"They say" is our first three chapters (business, politics, entertainment). Just about everyone involved in those worlds accepts the importance of the singular narrative. Business people know you want to focus on the one main thing that distinguishes your product from the pack. Politicians know they need a clear singular message. And for the entertainment world, the question of "Whose story is it?" is the basic concession that you need to have one central narrative thread and stick to it if you want to tap into the power of Archplot (classical design) to reach a large audience (meaning the Outer Circle).

In 2012, the bestselling book *The One Thing* was voted one of the top ten business books of all time on the website Goodreads. It was custom-made for the business world, but it didn't begin to suggest applying singular thinking to the world of science. Here's why.

THE FUNDAMENTAL CONUNDRUM: THE SINGULAR NARRATIVE VERSUS GIANT SAMPLE SIZE

Scientists love big numbers—especially when it comes to sample size. As a scientist, you spend your life gathering and analyzing data. There is always this relentless force driving you to obtain larger sample sizes. It gets programmed into your psyche: big number good, small number bad. The worst number of all is one, the "anecdote."

When you listen to a talk and the speaker says "exactly 40 percent of the moths were white," you get a squeamish feeling. You think, "please don't tell me you observed only five moths, and two were white …"

But then the speaker puts up the data and the value mentioned is actually 40.246%. You begin to relax. And then you see the sample size was 1,283,472 moths, and you say to yourself, "Wow. Over one millllllllion moths!"

You feel very, very good just looking at that large number on the screen. At the same time, you retain your dread fear of a sample size of just one. And of course that's what an anecdote is: a single instance. It's "n equals one," in the parlance of scientists.

ANECDOTES: THE BANE OF SCIENCE

Storytellers love the singular narrative, which means they love the anecdote. Take a look at any issue of *The New Yorker*, and you'll find at least one article that opens with an anecdote about one person.

In fact, let's put this to the test right now. I'm opening up the March 18, 2019, issue of *The New Yorker*, which I just received yesterday. I'm seeing an article called, "The Perfect Paint: Farrow and Ball's Selective Palette Is Creating a New Kind of Decorating Anxiety." I'm turning to the article, and I'm reading the first paragraph, which begins with, "When Haley Allman and her husband bought an Edwardian town house … " And there you have it — it opens with the story of one person, Haley (her husband is just an added detail) — the classic anecdote.

You can find at least one major article in just about every issue of *The New Yorker* that starts like this. The singular anecdote provides immediate focus and locks in your interest while conveying the basic theme of what's about to be explored. But to scientists, it's fundamentally wrong.

I developed an intimate familiarity with this in my science career. For example, one of my marine biological projects involved diving under the ice in Antarctica. The climate there was brutally cold, and for one starfish species we studied, I was only able to find one individual of the species and make one measurement. When it came time to publish a paper about the project, there was discussion over whether I should be allowed to mention that one observation, since it was "just an anecdote."

The discussion came down to the question of whether the world of science would be better off knowing this one tidbit of unreplicated information, or whether science would be better if no one ever even heard it. It's a bit like a judge ruling on whether hearsay evidence is admissible in court. We chose to not mention it. (P.S. The only recording of that one measurement was in a notebook that was in my house that burned down, so the world will never know that tiny piece of starfish data, boo hoo.)

This is how scientists are absolutely different from non-scientists. You are trained to be suspect and spurn anecdotes and be suspicious of them. And yet, the brain of the average human loves them — as exemplified in the extreme with the examples from Nicholas Kristof I mentioned in the first chapter about the advertisements of children dying in Africa. That communication was at its most powerful when the sample size of individuals being talked about was one.

So scientists dream of communicating in this somewhat non-human, anecdote-free manner that involves the luxury of running through all 43 points you want to make. When I work with them I can usually convince them that 43 is too much. But when you start to get down to their wanting to tell three stories versus my recommending they yield to Dave Gold's single Christmas-tree model — that's where it can get ugly.

They will push back, saying there is no one single story. I will push forward, saying, "Maybe there is, and you just haven't realized it yet." They will say three is good enough, I will try to point out there is greater power in the singular narrative and they will start to glare at me as though I am the enemy. I've been through it many times.

Scientists are different this way. I know because I used to be one. They yearn for an AAA-accepting world, but the truth is, they are the ones who have produced the technology that has glutted our world with information, resulting in even less tolerance for the AAA form. The world used to be more AAA, but narrative selection has changed the landscape — which will be our major topic for Chapter 6.

4.4) SUMMARY: HOW SCIENTISTS CAN USE THE ABT FRAMEWORK

This chapter was different from the previous three. The others introduced a variety of narrative tools, then talked about the variety of ways the ABT Framework can be put to work.

The tools are laid out in those first three chapters. My advice to scientists still rests in the title of the second chapter of my first book: "Don't Be So Literal Minded."

If you are a scientist, I recommend you put that thinking to work by reading in detail the first three chapters and realizing that all of those applications of the ABT Framework in the worlds of business, politics and entertainment apply just as much to science.

You're no different at the core.

You write proposals, you give presentations, you write papers, and you make videos. For all those central elements of your entire profession, you need to have a command of narrative. The principles you need for mastering narrative structure have nothing to do with science.

They are universal and they pervade all aspects of humanity, because … narrative is everything.

5) RELIGION

5) RELIGION - THE DOUBLE-EDGED SWORD

5.1) I HAVE NOTHING TO SAY ABOUT RELIGION

Of course, there are lots of books on preaching, and you can bet there's heaps of ABT dynamics throughout them, but I won't be examining any of them. It's not that I have anything against religion—I don't. It's just that I was raised in Kansas, where we were taught to not talk about politics or religion at the dinner table.

Given how deeply I have waded into politics, I'm going to avoid religion entirely. But I am going to use the topic to offer a cautionary warning about the ABT that I will call "the double-edged sword of simplicity."

5.2) MICHAEL CRICHTON TRIED TO WARN OF THE TOAD

You saw in Chapter 2 that I've spent a lot of time reading and thinking about great American speeches. I'm a big fan of the core principles of this country, but there are two aspects of communication that I believe in most strongly.

The first is that the communication landscape of our society has changed drastically in the past four decades. It began with the information explosion in the 1980's, followed by the internet and social media. We first increased the amount of information, then we increased the speed of communication. We are now in the Information Society.

The second thing I believe is that perhaps the most important and under-appreciated speech in the history of our society is not one of the great historical speeches from politicians that I presented in Chapter 2, but, rather, a speech to scientists that fell largely on deaf ears. I shall now tell about the message of this speech, then come back to the topic of religion.

MICHAEL CRICHTON'S PRESCIENT 1999 SPEECH

I'm pretty sure Michael Crichton viewed himself as similar to Humphrey Bogart in *Casablanca* — the jaded, cynical loner who does his best to maintain the facade of not caring about anything, when in fact he cared deeply.

I've spent a lot of time studying his life. My best friend and Hollywood mentor Mike Backes worked closely with Crichton throughout the 1990's. He wrote the screenplays for two of Crichton's novels (*Rising Sun*, which used his draft, and *Congo*, which didn't). He was business partners with Crichton and read the first drafts of most of his later novels. The two men and their wives were good friends. Mike and I have had a lot of discussions about Crichton.

Michael Crichton was a complex character. For 25 years, he

did his best to offer guidance to the world of science in two ways. First, he wrote a series of hugely popular techno-thrillers, classic "cautionary tales" about the potential power for science to do both good and bad.

The other help he offered society was 25 years of speeches and essays, again warning of the risks of "science gone wrong." His efforts began with the 1975 article about obfuscation that I mentioned in the Introduction. His attempts to contribute constructively to guiding society had a last gasp in 1999. It seems that after hitting a brick wall with his final speeches to the science world, he sadly drifted to the dark side.

By 2007, when I traded three months of emails with him as I was making my climate mockumentary film, *Sizzle: A Global Warming Comedy*, he had demolished his credibility with the science community. He had bought into the climate-skeptic movement, I think largely through anger, disgust and frustration with mainstream scientists. He wrote a thinly veiled anti-environmental-rant novel, *State of Fear*, then ended up being a partner to a ragtag crew of opponents of climate science.

But before he jumped ship, he offered a very powerful warning that should have been heeded.

MICHAEL CRICHTON'S 1999 WARNING OF THE TOAD TO COME

There has never been an American with more combined practical knowledge of science and media than Michael Crichton. He was a Harvard-educated doctor who left a promising medical career for Hollywood. In 1994, he became the first person to ever score the entertainment media triple play of simultaneously having the #1 book, movie and TV show. My career pathway from science to the entertainment industry followed in his footsteps, sort of. (Though where he earned hundreds of *millions* of dollars, I earned little more than hundreds ... of dollars.)

He had so much to offer the science world in terms of guidance, and he tried. But once you leave the ivory tower, you're pretty much considered a pariah—especially if you engage with Hollywood. One of the greatest scientists to ever step into the mass entertainment world, Carl Sagan, eventually paid the price by being rejected by the National Academy of Sciences despite his more-than- sufficient qualifications for the Academy.

So in 1999, Crichton was invited to give the keynote address at the annual meeting of the American Association for the Advancement of Science (AAAS). I know a lot about his speech because the fellow who invited and hosted him, Mike Strauss, is today one of my Story Circle Narrative Training co-developers. He has told me about the experience in detail.

Crichton gave a powerful speech, which you can find online. It was an ABT tour de force, as he laid out a series of problems the science world faces in dealing with the media dynamics of our society. The Narrative Index score was a 35. He was trying to warn of the changes to our society that he could see coming. If anyone should have been listened to about the future, he was the one. The man was, after all, a futurist in his writings.

In his speech he warned about the loss of control of scientific information with the advent of the internet, and of basically the inevitability of today's "fake news" problem. But his most important and prescient quote was this:

The information society will be dominated by the groups of people who are most skilled at manipulating the media for their own ends.

That was it. Right there—the warning that The Toad was coming. He was trying to say, "Watch out, when we finally create the Information Society, it's going to create openings for people who understand mass media and how to use the newly created lightning-fast social media that will saturate our brains."

Well, it was the wrong audience. As Mike Strauss has told me, in the Q&A nobody asked about his warnings. No, the main topic of the questions from the scientists was, "How can we make more movies like *Jurassic Park*, which will encourage kids to go into science?" They just wanted to know how to make their profession more popular.

And so now we've created the Information Society Crichton warned of, and The Toad is in charge and tweeting up a storm. And even worse, for the first couple of years of his reign, his opponents could think of nothing to do other than berate him. It was taboo to suggest he was actually one of those people "skilled at manipulating the media" that Crichton warned of.

Over the past year there have finally been concessions that The Toad does understand the media. He knows how it works and how to use it, though not analytically. He could never teach a course on how to do what he does with media.

He is definitely a toad, but there has to be a concession of his skills. Which then leads to my concerns about society in general and religion specifically.

STEREOTYPES: THE OTHER EDGE OF THE SIMPLICITY SWORD

In a world of too much information, the selection for simplicity is more intense than ever. This is the premise of this entire book and everything I have to say.

I've spent the whole book advocating the understanding and use of simplicity, but now it's time to consider the dark side of simplification. We all know stereotypes are harmful, but why do they arise, and why do they persist?

There are plenty of explanations from the world of psychology. These include socialization, upbringing, illusory correlation, correspondence bias and plenty of other complicated terms.

I don't know about all those terms, but what I do know is what I have cited repeatedly, which is the programming of our brains for the singular narrative. Kristof explained it in simple terms in his *Outside Magazine* article that I mentioned in Chapter 2, and then Keller and Papasan took the concept to the bank with their bestselling book *The One Thing*.

Kristof expressed disgust with what research on the singular narrative shows (not with the research itself, just with what it shows about how the brain works). In talking about the experiments on donors and singular versus multiple subjects, he said, "Donors didn't want to help ease a crisis personified by a child; they just wanted to help one person and to hell with the crisis." Talking about the findings of social psychologist Paul Slovic, he said, "Slovic found that our empathy begins to fade when the number of victims reaches just two. As he puts it: 'The more who die, the less we care.'"

So this is the more complicated dimension of all this narrative stuff. Our brains are programmed to seek the singular narrative; that needs to be accepted and understood. But along with all of the ways to play to that programming for good, it must be understood that it can be exploited just as easily for bad. Which leads us back to The Toad.

As I said earlier, I don't understand why The Toad has been allowed to get away with his large-scale, long-term use of one-word insult names. From Crooked Hillary to Little Marco to The Failing *New York Times*. Why haven't his opponents pointed out that this is the same as the use of stereotypes?

Minorities figured out long ago that there needs to be resistance to the use of stereotypes in communication. It's clear that he's playing a delicate game — choosing insult names that are amusing and not quite blatantly racist or sexist — but just the establishment of the practice opens the door for the damaging effects that are well-documented for stereotypes.

GREAT POWER

So this becomes my final overall message about the ABT dynamic: It is like a superpower — it can be used for good or evil. With great power comes great responsibility. Beware the simple narrative.

6) NARRATIVE SELECTION: THE FUTURE

6) Narrative Selection - The Future

SPOILER ALERT: If you are of the archplot persuasion and need your stories to have happy, closed endings, then let me give you the quick exit line now—here we go—"We're all gonna live happily ever after!" Okay, close the book, you're done.

For the rest of you: You're clearly able to handle the miniplot nature of the real world. Keep this problem in mind when you read the bit about artificial intelligence and the endings of science fiction stories.

So here we go: my grand synthesis.

INTRODUCING "NARRATIVE SELECTION"

What is the significance of the ABT in the end? Is it a "neat trick," or is it a shorter version of "The Handbook for Life"? In this final chapter I will argue for the latter.

Let me begin by talking about two forms of evolution: biological versus cultural. The former is what Charles Darwin studied; the latter is what anthropologists have spent decades trying to precisely theorize, as the larger and older field of evolutionary biology often pushes back.

What I am now going to take a shot at is a new, broader and simpler look at cultural evolution from the perspective of narrative. I see that the term "narrative selection" has been mentioned on the internet previously, but I don't see any details on how exactly the mechanism might work. I am introducing the term here with a much more specific, analytical definition. It's built around the idea that ABT structure is the defining element of "fitness" that determines what does and does not get selected for over time.

Overall, I am suggesting that there are parallel mechanisms of natural selection (for nature) and narrative selection (for culture).

THIS (ABT) VIEW OF LIFE

Back when I was an evolutionary biologist, I learned about evolution by means of natural selection from arguably the greatest evolutionist since Charles Darwin. His name was Stephen Jay Gould. He was a professor at Harvard University for most of his legendary career. He published 28 books, wrote a monthly column in *Natural History Magazine* for over 25 years and was a powerful speaker.

Gould was in his prime when I was a graduate student. I spent as much time as I could around him, by sitting in on his Tuesday lunch paleontology discussion group, serving as a teaching fellow in the introductory biology course in which he taught and by hosting him for lunch with the undergraduates twice at Winthrop House in my role as resident biology tutor. He was mesmerizing (though he was a lousy and annoying poker player). The only other human I've ever met whom I have found as brilliant and intimidating is Quentin Tarantino.

So what I picked up from him, more than anything else, was

my basic understanding of natural selection—the driving force of evolution that Charles Darwin had first detailed. Gould emphasized constantly that natural selection is a *simple* two-step process consisting first of VARIATION—the random production of offspring by a species—and then SELECTION—the non-random differential survival of those offspring. The selective agent (the environment) kills many, but not all. This ratcheting, iterative process, generation after generation, produces the diversity of patterns we see in nature among the countless species.

Learning about natural selection can be life-altering. It's such a powerful mechanism that once you absorb it, it changes how you view the world. That was what Charles Darwin himself said. He felt it was one of those things that, once you see it, you can never un-see it. Kind of like the arrow in the FedEx logo, right?

6.1) CHARLES DARWIN AND EVOLUTION: "THIS VIEW OF LIFE"

Darwin's most important and enduring work was formally titled *On the Origin of Species by Means of Natural Selection*. For ease of reading I'm going to go with the title of the 6th edition, which was just *The Origin of Species*.

It was a popular book in its time. Not surprisingly, the Narrative Index for it is 20. Qualitatively you can see the ABT structure throughout.

Darwin ended his book with a final "therefore" statement.

His very last sentence refers to what he called "this view of life." You can feel how well the word "therefore" could have worked to start the last sentence. Here is the version that appeared at the end of the first edition:

[THEREFORE] *There is grandeur in this view of life, with its several powers, having been originally breathed into a few forms or into one; and that, whilst this planet has gone cycling on according to the fixed law of gravity, from so simple a beginning endless forms most beautiful and most wonderful have been, and are being, evolved.*

A century later the line resonated so deeply with Stephen Jay Gould that he used it for the title of his column in *Natural History Magazine*, "This View of Life."

I am arguing for the parallels and even convergence of natural selection with narrative selection. Natural selection sculpts nature; narrative selection sculpts our culture. They are equally important forces of creativity, and, I think, follow the same basic two-step mechanism.

Species produce variation in offspring. Humans produce variation in culture. The environment determines which offspring survive. The brain (which is programmed to seek narrative structure) determines which pieces of culture survive.

6.2) CHRISTOPHER VOGLER AND NARRATIVE: A COMPLETE "HANDBOOK FOR LIFE"

Darwin spoke of "this view of life" as being one that was enlightened by the knowledge of natural selection. I think there is a similar quotation for narrative.

It comes from what I would say is the closest equivalent to *The Origin of Species* for narrative. It's a book titled *The Writer's Journey*, by Christopher Vogler (who was at USC Cinema School a few years before me), first published in 1992. It is currently in its third edition and has become the central resource of Hollywood screenwriters for learning the basics of story structure.

The book is a more formal and in-depth presentation of what mythologist Joseph Campbell first labeled as "the Hero's Journey" in the 1940's. Vogler's title is a play on that term. (If you're not clear on the Hero's Journey, see Appendix 1 for a brief explanation.)

For the second edition Vogler wrote a powerful and concise 14-page preface, which, near the start, says this:

I came looking for the design principles of storytelling, but on the road I found something more: a set of principles for living. I came to believe that the Hero's Journey is nothing less than a handbook for life, a complete instruction manual in the art of being human.

Using the Dobzhanksy template (Chapter 2), Vogler said basically that nothing in human culture makes sense except in the light of the Hero's Journey. This is what Joseph Campbell had come to realize a generation earlier.

So the ideas are huge and parallel. Natural selection is the handbook of biological life. The Hero's Journey is the handbook of human life.

6.3) CULTURAL EVOLUTION BY MEANS OF NARRATIVE SELECTION: THE SHIFT FROM AAA TO ABT

Had we but world enough, and time …

Uh oh, that's a flashback to the forbidden poem.

Sorry. But what I want to say here is that I wish I had a couple years' time to research and write this section. Darwin famously burned up most of the decade of the 1850's mustering the evidence for his theory of natural selection, and even then he wasn't planning to present it until Alfred Russel Wallace looked ready to beat him to the punch.

I'm no Darwin, and I don't have a decade to dwell on this. Therefore … it's fairly skimpy what I'm going to present here, but I think a simple "you get the idea" should suffice for most readers. What I'm presenting here is how the "narrative landscape" has changed over the past century from AAA to ABT, to put it simply. This is how I view the world today, and I invite you to think it through and see if it makes sense to you.

So let's take a look at a few cases in more recent times of the changes in form of various media. These are examples of narrative selection in action.

MOVIES: THE CRAP IS LOST

Edward Dmytryk was a legendary director from the golden era of Hollywood who spent his last years teaching at USC's film school in the 1990's. In addition to the treat of taking Frank Daniel's class, I also was lucky enough to take Intermediate Directing from 86-year-old Eddie.

He directed 74 Hollywood movies, including such timeless classics as *The Caine Mutiny*, and *Young Lions* with Marlon Brando and Montgomery Clift. He was also a co-founder of the entire genre of film noir.

But the important point that Eddie always made to us as he talked about the old classic movies was, "People don't realize how much crap was made that didn't survive." There were thousands and thousands of films produced that were terrible. None of those survived.

Think of that quote in terms of Darwin's "survival of the fittest." Same thing. Large numbers of offspring are produced, only a few survive. He was talking about narrative selection.

What survived from back then and are still popular are the movies with solid ABT structure. From *Gone with the Wind*, to *Casablanca*, to his classic, *The Caine Mutiny*, they are all "good stories." None of them bore, none of them confuse. The narratively weak were long ago culled from the herd and lost to time.

TELEVISION: THE NETWORK EVENING NEWS

In May of 1990, the feature article on the cover of *The New Republic* was titled "The Incredible Shrinking Sound Bite," by Kiku Adatto of Harvard University. In the wake of George H. W. Bush's 1988 presidential campaign, which included some ruthless tactics (like the infamous Willie Horton commercial), Adatto quantified some of the shifts in how the network evening news covered presidential campaigns. The shifts reflect narrative selection at work.

Here are three key metrics she presented:

	1968	1988
AVERAGE SOUND BITE (seconds)	42.3	9.8
"THEATER CRITICISM"	6%	52%
CAMPAIGN COMMERCIAL EXCERPTS ON THE NEWS	2	125

The 1980's was the decade of the information explosion. It saw the advent of such lifestyle upgrades as home computing and cable television. Adatto's news-coverage numbers reflect that change.

The first thing to note is the reduction in the length of sound bites. In 1968, candidates were allowed to speak for over a minute at times, indulging in AAA material in prime time. By 1988, their sound bites had shrunk to less than ten seconds. Part of what took place was that the news commentator became the voice of the candidate.

By 1988, instead of letting the candidate explain themselves slowly, the anchor did most of the talking. The anchor would set up the clip by saying something like, "Today the candidate presented his tax plan, which will cut taxes on the wealthy, which he feels will stimulate economic growth," then run the 10-second clip of the candidate saying, "Support my plan, and you'll see a new, more vibrant economy."

This is narrative shaping—condensing down AAA material into tighter, more-ABT-shaped form.

The second metric shows the shift from content to form. In 1968, the focus was on what the candidate was saying, meaning that the media would not often critique the "theatrics" of the candidate. By 1988, there was a shift away from *what* was being said to *how* it was being said; about half of the news reports on the candidates in 1988 focused on what Adatto called "theater criticism." In other words, it was the shift from content to form, or from substance to style.

And third, in 1968, there was almost no news interest in campaign commercials, but by 1988, they were a major focus of campaign coverage. Commercials tend to be highly ABT (needing to exceed the Narrative Imperative to qualify for television airtime), whereas the campaign as a whole is more AAA.

TELEVISION: THE LOCAL NEWS

Here's an anecdote (the bane of scientists!) to add at the local level: I had a friend who was a field correspondent for New England Cable News in Boston. She had previously worked "out in the sticks" of Bangor, Maine.

She told me that her job of interviewing people in the field was much easier in Maine. Those people were less "media-savvy." When you asked them a question, they would jump into AAA mode—going on and on and on, telling you everything they knew on the subject. The result would be huge amounts of material you could pick and choose from to edit your story, finding exactly what you want them to eventually say, as you reshape their AAA material down to

ABT.

In contrast, people around Boston, because they watch so much television news, tended to speak in short, concise sound bites that were much more ABT. You ask them about the car crash, and they give you a short, punchy ABT, like, "Oh, it was terrible, but thankfully nobody was killed, so I think everyone will be okay in the end." As a result, she had to keep cueing them on and on: "Okay, tell me more."

Narrative selection ends up being tighter in urban environments. People live faster lives, so they have less time for the long-winded AAA structure. This is true the world over.

NEWSPAPER: THE NEW YORK TIMES FRONT PAGE

In Chapter 3, I showed how the front page of *The New York Times* is the ultimate ABT incubator. At least that's how it is today, but it wasn't always so "ABT-structured."

The New York Times published a wonderful book in 2008 (and they keep updating it), which is a collection of their front pages over the years. It's huge in size—a giant coffee table book—with the front pages going all the way back to 1851.

Using the same index of narrative strength—the prevalence of "But Paragraphs" (paragraphs that begin with the word "But")—you can see the changes over time.

DECADE	AVERAGE NUMBER OF "BUT PARAGRAPHS"	PERCENT with 0
1920's	0.43	62%
1930's	0.38	67%
1940's	0.17	90%
1990's	1.50	17%
2000's	1.60	10%
2010's	1.19	14%

CHANGE IN NARRATIVE STRUCTURE OF THE NEW YORK TIMES FRONT PAGE. For each decade at least 20 front pages were examined for the presence of "But Paragraphs" (paragraphs that begin with the word "but"). The second value is the percentage of all the front pages examined that had zero "But Paragraphs."

In the introductory text accompanying the book, the lead author, Bill Keller, says, "The byline, you will notice, was a relatively late embellishment in *The Times* — nonexistent until the early 20th century; and relatively scarce until after mid-century ... Now we are promiscuous with bylines."

In the 1800's, there were almost no instances of "But Paragraphs." Back then the newspaper mostly just reported the previous day's events with no setup, no background, no interpretation. But by the second half of the 20th century, most front-page articles had a byline, the famous reporters emerged, and the voice of the newspaper shifted from just AAA to the broader, more narrative ABT form.

NOVELS: WHERE DO WE FIND THE DEAD BODY?

This is just a tidbit, but it's the same ABT selective pattern. In 2009, I attended Book Expo in New York City. They had a panel discussion with three veteran editors of best-selling novels, moderated by a literary critic. For the last question of the panel he asked each one to offer up a prediction for the future of novel-writing.

The third panelist said, "In the future, instead of having your dead body appear on page 50, it will have to appear on page 5." The other two immediately agreed.

What he was saying was that the shortening attention span of readers is forcing authors to minimize the A material at the start of their story and quickly get to the B. And of course they didn't even bother to mention artsy miniplot AAA books. It was implicit that there would be minuscule audiences for that material in the future.

SOCIAL MEDIA: TWITTER WAS NARRATIVELY SELECTED (AS PREDICTED IN 2015)

There are countless examples of narrative selection in action on the internet, but let me show you a simple, recent one that I predicted in print in 2015. My prediction can be found at the end of my 2015 book *Houston, We Have a Narrative*.

I looked at the lengths of tweets on Twitter back then (140 characters), saw they were too short for ABT structure and thus predicted Twitter would change or go extinct. The detailed account of my prediction before it came true — complete with Stephen Colbert quote — is on page 237 of the book.

We began counting the number of characters that participants in our workshops needed to "naturally" write their narrative using the ABT template. The sentences averaged around 300 characters — double the length of tweets back then.

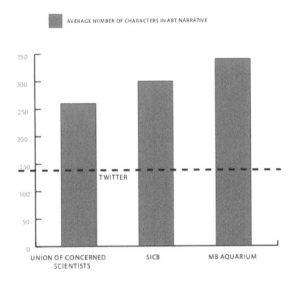

AVERAGE NUMBER OF CHARACTERS IN ABT NARRATIVE

TWITTER WAS NARRATIVELY SELECTED. This is from Houston, We Have A Narrative. Twitter initially limited tweets to 140 characters, but that was half the average length of ABT sentences. In 2017, the length of tweets was doubled.

This meant that in order to tweet something, you either had to shrink all three elements way down to half their natural lengths, or … just use the most powerful element — the piece of contradiction — the "but."

Guess which solution prevailed. Twitter soon became a place for little more than contradiction and all the rancor that accompanies it.

In 2017, Twitter finally yielded to the problem by doubling the length of tweets to 280 characters. It was narrative selection in action: adapt or die.

A similar data point comes from my Story Circles co-creator Jayde Lovell, who worked for Weber Shandwick, one of the world's largest PR firms, for several years. She was part of a study they did looking for the optimal length for their Facebook posts.

They found there was an optimum amount of text. Too little, and nobody understood what you were saying (confusion); too much, you lose the reader (boredom); just the right length, and it works (interesting). Guess what the optimum length was? Same, same — 280 characters.

In the world of evolutionary biology, this would be called "stabilizing selection."

6.4) "A FIXED NARRATIVE": THE ONE-WAY STREET TO ABT

There are so many parallels between narrative selection and natural selection. One common attribute of genetics is what are called "fixed traits." This refers to a gene that used to have variation, but the variation has gone away, either through selection or happenstance. It is no longer variable and is thus "fixed."

I've seen a similar thing with ABT structure. A filmmaker friend edited a feature documentary about mobsters in Florida that aired on Showtime. The movie opens with a screen of text setting up the story. He had been discussing the ABT Framework with me for a few years. The text he wrote for the opening screen had simple ABT form.

Referring to the mobsters, the opening text basically said, "They were this, they were this, they were this, but they were never this …"

In ABT terms, it was saying, "They were this (AND) they were this (AND) they were this, (BUT) they were never this ... (THEREFORE) ..."

Once you knew those three opening statements about what they were, and then you saw the key thing they were lacking ("they were never this"), it gave you the whole predicament of what would follow, which was the entire movie.

In the year he spent editing the movie, there were at least 5 producers and other editors who reworked that opening graphic, changing words to suit their ideas. By the end of the editing the entire thing had been rewritten multiple times, BUT ... despite changing every word in the text, nobody changed the form — it still had the same ABT shape at the end. They only changed the content.

The idea (or hypothesis) I would offer to explain this is that once you land on the ABT structure, it's difficult to argue that it should be changed to AAA or DHY. Just like the genetic trait I mentioned, it becomes fixed.

Another friend was tasked at a conference with writing the mission statement for a Hawaiian national park. She wrote a first draft, which several people set to work rewriting. She witnessed the same thing. Her draft was ABT-structured. The others rewrote all the content in their revisions, but nobody changed the ABT form. Again, it was fixed.

Once you solve a problem of structure, it's rare that someone wants to unsolve it.

And speaking of movie openings, if you want to see instant ABT in action, just watch the start of the blockbuster movie of 2017, *Dunkirk*. In little more than a minute it sprints through the basic ABT of the movie.

It opens with a screen of text telling the audience that Hitler had surrounded the British forces at the start of World War II and driven them to the coastal town of Dunkirk. AND then it cuts to a single soldier (the power of the individual narrative!) running frantically down streets. AND then he runs out onto a beach.

BUT at the beach he sees massive lines of soldiers waiting to be transported back to England; there were no sources of transport.

THEREFORE ... the rest of the movie — trying to get the troops off the beach and back home. There was virtually no further background or character development provided in the movie (the one big criticism from the critics), but who cares? Remember my mention of the Serial Queen Melodrama movies in Chapter 3? The genre lives on today with action movies like *Dunkirk*.

6.5)   THE PAST IS VISCERAL, THE FUTURE IS INTELLECTUAL

So where is all this headed?

Here's one very practical thing narrative teaches you: The past is visceral, the future is intellectual.

Our knowledge, understanding and connection to the past comes from experience. It's based on things we or someone else has experienced. As a result, we have a deep and human connection with the past.

Just about all great speeches begin in the past. I had mentioned this in Chapter 2 with the Barbara Jordan speech. Whether it's our childhood, nostalgia or historical events, we feel a deep emotional connection. This is the essence of the famous quote from author William Faulkner: "The past is never dead. It's not even past."

The past can make the masses cry. But the future? How many people really cry about the future?

The future is different in terms of narrative. As far as we know, no one has experienced the future yet. Which means there can be no clear gut feelings about it. It's purely intellectual. This is a lot of why it's so difficult to motivate people about climate change.

So I want to end this book on what (at least in theory) should be a non-emotional note. I'm going to consider the future of two aspects of our society: first, the Democratic party, then humanity itself.

THE NARRATIVE LANDSCAPE HAS CHANGED: THE INFORMATION SOCIETY CALLS FOR NEW THINKING

This is my general concern — that the environment has changed, but the thinking has not. All of the examples of narrative selection above reflect communication dynamics in the earlier, more AAA, environment of the last century, rather than today's. The old narrative environment was reflected by *The New York Times* front page that didn't need to resort to ABT structure to grab interest and by the network evening news that enjoyed the luxury of lengthy AAA soundbites from candidates.

We're now in the Information Society, which is characterized by both large amounts of information and rapid communication. As I've said, the core of my concern is the 1999 Michael Crichton prediction that the Information Society will be dominated by those most skilled at manipulating the media. With that speech he basically predicted The Odious Toad who now inhabits the White House.

The Toad came out of the television world of the Narrative Imperative. He was pre-adapted for the ABT landscape. He trained with *The Apprentice*, an extremely short attention span show punctuated by its catchphrase, "You're fired." Today he is up against the earnest warriors from "The Land of And." It's not a fair fight.

The predictable casualty of this fight is the party that shuns the whole idea of media manipulation. It's an admirable attitude, but it's also a handicap in today's political environment. So let's take a look at that party in light of today's narrative landscape.

THE DEMOCRATIC PARTY: MALADAPTED?

I'm going to use the term "maladaptation," which refers to something that is not suited for the current environment and will be selected against unless it is dealt with, somehow.

I have voted Democratic throughout my adult life, so please don't take this as an attack on the values of the party. I share their goals but am constantly disappointed at their lack of political savvy. Just dreaming of a perfect world isn't enough to make it happen. You have to understand the landscape in which you live, then work within the constraints.

What has driven me crazy about the Democratic Party in recent years is the absence of a core message, which as we know from Chapter 2 means the absence of an understanding of narrative. Take a look at this quotation from a staff editorial in *The New York Times* just a few weeks after the failed campaign of Hillary Clinton.

> "Democrats have been sidetracked by trying to accommodate the various needs of a diverse America and thus have failed to promote a **unifying narrative**."

-NY Times, Jan 19, 2017

That was from the left-leaning *New York Times*. They're not saying the goals are wrong; they are saying that the Democrats are not managing to figure out how to create the essential element of the unifying narrative.

It's two years later. The party still suffers from the lack of a unifying narrative.

So I totally support the goals of the Democratic Party, but I ask whether some of its core principles are fundamentally maladaptive. If they are, it doesn't mean the goals need to be changed; it only means that a different approach is needed. It's not impossible to succeed with a maladaptive trait, but it definitely takes extra effort.

MALADAPTATION #1 - INCLUSIVENESS?

I ask this only as a question. I am deeply in favor of inclusiveness. In my career I've experienced both sides of the inclusiveness issue — both the privilege of exclusivity and the pain of discrimination. I was treated to the spoiled indulgence of exclusivity by attending Harvard University, then subjected to a lifetime of discrimination and snubs by leaving the almighty ivory tower of academia.

Let me begin with the subject of "mush." A few years ago a friend working with a government agency called me, filled with frustration. He complained about a meeting he had just gotten out of. He said, "We always start these meetings with the best of intentions, and it seems so clear what our problem is and how we need to solve it, but by the time we finish, we end up with a document that includes a little bit of everyone's voices — no matter how good or bad their ideas are — just so we can achieve 'inclusiveness.' The end result is vague, unfocused mush."

Two months later I gave a talk at a conservation biology conference. My title was "Fighting Mush"; I opened with my friend's story and a photo of a bowl of porridge. The talk resonated so deeply with one conservationist that he ended up bringing me to his home state, where they had just lost a huge conservation campaign. They had sponsored a ballot initiative in which their side presented a giant laundry list of disconnected ideas (= mush) against their opponents, who waged a very simple campaign, with a singular core message of, "We don't need any of this." The conservation groups were crushed, 80-20.

Again, I wholeheartedly support the notion of inclusiveness and diversity, and I even agree with the idea of quotas to achieve diversity. But it worries me when I see laundry lists of demands presented in AAA form with no awareness of the narrative landscape. You can't bore the public and expect support.

Which do you want, leadership or inclusiveness? The environmental movement, for one, doesn't seem to know there's any divergence between these two. But a leader provides a single direction; inclusiveness points in countless directions. The two *can* be resolved, but it doesn't happen through the AAA approach of laundry lists. It happens through accepting how narrative works.

There is a way to turn inclusiveness into a singular narrative that can comply with the narrative landscape. And yet I've attended countless workshops where nobody wants to pick a single direction, so they do the easy thing—they defer to all directions.

The singular narrative is not a luxury item; the narrative landscape now demands it.

MALADAPTATION #2: NON-JUDGMENTALISM?

These maladaption traits overlap with each other. Non-judgmentalism is inherent in inclusiveness, but it has further dimensions, such as the soccer trophy syndrome of wanting there to be no winners and losers in life.

The problem is, it doesn't work within the dynamics of narrative. Look at the three forces of narrative.

First there is agreement, which is positivity—everyone's a winner! Then there is contradiction—sad face, everything is not in agreement, and there's probably even someone losing. Lastly there's consequence, when we square it all away and the world moves on.

These are the three forces. They are eternal. They are what all brains seek, all day, every day.

The entire idea of non-judgmentalism means deleting contradiction—the central, most powerful element of narrative. It's more than just maladaptive; it's not human.

Even if you are the greatest peace-loving, anti-violence, anti-conflict hippie in the universe, you still enjoy a good story about peace and love. If it's a good story, I guarantee you it has contradiction at the core of it.

Look at the stories of Gandhi, Mother Teresa, Martin Luther King, Jr. They were all engaged in fighting for something. That involves contradiction, which involves making judgements. It's only human, which means it involves narrative.

And most important of all is that judgmentalism, being central to narrative, ends up being central to leadership. It's not that you can't be non-judgmental; just realize the consequences of it within the narrative landscape. It's the opposite of leadership, so just don't be surprised when it leads to poor leadership.

MALADAPTATON #3: POLITICAL CORRECTNESS?

The Odious Toad has made fighting political correctness one of the fundamental planks of his administration. His tactics helped earn him the label of "odious."

I don't support any of the repulsive things he's said and done, but I do understand the core elements of narrative he's using to his advantage.

A major part of the politically correct agenda (which could be called the dignity and respect agenda) is combatting stereotypes. But what I fear is not appreciated is the extent to which the narrative landscape favors stereotypes. This was what Chapter 5 was all about: the double-edged sword.

You might say that you don't want to live in a world that favors stereotypes. Well, you'd better start working on some sort of genetic manipulation that can change the structure of the brain because unless something changes, we're going to be ABT-seeking creatures for a long time to come. ABT points to the singular narrative, and the singular narrative points to the stereotype.

As minority groups know, stereotypes can be combatted, but it takes major effort, in large part because you're battling the basic programming of the brain. But that's okay. Most of what civilization is about is creating structure to prevent what the brain will do if there isn't any structure.

We know it is possible to stop stereotypes, and it's worth doing … unless of course Artificial Intelligence takes over. Then all bets are off, as none of this matters.

Which leads to my final statement about narrative and the potentially grim future ahead.

THE FUTURE OF HUMANITY: WILL NARRATIVE BE OUR FINAL UNDOING?

Human culture is fading away. It kind of feels like we're the character Brophy in Mel Brooks' comedy classic, *High Anxiety*. He was constantly picking up heavy items, saying, "I got it. It got it. I got it. I ain't got it."

For a few thousand years humans thought they got it when it came to documenting and understanding human culture. By the end of the last century it was looking like we really did have it. But now things appear to be taking a U-turn. We ain't got it.

We're losing our grip on culture. As I talked about in Chapter 4, the humanities are getting eaten up by the sciences. History is becoming a lost cause—a product of lost interest and endless possibilities for revisionism.

Kids are no longer reading novels. Even adults are no longer reading novels. The 2010 book *The Shallows* documented the effects of the internet on the brain. There's a tidal wave of weird transitions taking place.

The downward spiral of culture began long ago. It's been the major story of my adult life. Just after I got to graduate school in 1978, ambitious and ready to do great things, the information explosion of the 1980's erupted, and suddenly everyone seemed confused by society. Everything has been downhill since.

The U.S. elected a dummy for a president—the biggest clown since Warren Harding (though at least Harding wasn't a toad). By 1987, E.D. Hirsh published *Cultural Literacy*, which was the first book that opened my eyes to the idea that our knowledge of culture might be limited and reversible.

So where is it all headed? There's now a wealth of speculation on the future of A.I. (artificial intelligence). In the debate between determinists (who think we are destined to be replaced by machines) and instrumentalists (who think we can keep the machines in check as nothing more than our instruments), I tend to lean in the determinist direction.

Sure feels to me like we're losing our privacy and thus our control over our lives and eventually our culture. The singularity (when robot intelligence replaces human intelligence) doesn't feel that far off.

So let me close with how narrative comes into play.

THE STORYTELLERS HAVE LET US DOWN

It's anybody's guess whether A.I. will be benevolent or malevolent in the long run. As I said, the future is intellectual; I can't get that worked up about it. But I have found one person's perspective on A.I. to be more interesting than all the rest so far.

It's James Barrat's. He wrote *Our Final Invention* in 2013. That's the book that caught the interest of Elon Musk, Bill Gates and lots of other very smart people who began to look at A.I. differently. They began to question whether we should be doing so much cheerleading for all the new inventions and suggested that maybe we should instead spend a little more time thinking about where it might be leading.

The element that intersects with narrative is the problem that Barrat points out with regard to the age-old tradition of "cautionary tales" presented by the greatest of science fiction writers. From *Frankenstein* to 2001 to *Terminator*, there's a recurring problem, which is the need for archplot narrative structure.

If you want the masses to listen, you'd better conform to the age-old principles of archplot as outlined by Robert McKee. One of the most fundamental of those properties is the need for the "Closed Ending." Mass audiences want their story to come full circle (straight out of the monomyth template, which you can read more about in Appendix 1) and conclude by answering all questions, tying up all lose ends and having the protagonist win.

By definition, the protagonists are us — the humans. We are fighting the fight, and we have to win. If we don't, you end up violating one of the key principles of archplot, landing you in the artsy world of miniplot.

James Barrat was a guest on the podcast *After On* in late 2017. After a reservedly grim assessment of the future of A.I. and humanity, the co-hosts discussed what he said. They talked about this problem of all the sci-fi tales ending with humanity winning.

One of the co-hosts mentioned the one prominent recent movie that is an exception to the happy ending stories, saying this about it:

To me the best recent big screen treatment was definitely Ex Machina, *which came out in 2015, and I'm sure that a lot of our listeners have seen it, but it's amazing how many people have not seen it — it actually was not a very big grossing movie.*

There you have it. Not a very big grossing movie, because humans didn't win. (Sorry if that just spoiled it for you — boo hoo, we're talking about the fate of humanity here, deal with it). The opposite story of the mega-blockbuster *Terminator*.

Our poorly programmed brains may turn out to be unable to respond to the eventual source of our demise. As Barrat says, it's like the CDC issuing a warning about vampires; generations of fiction teach us they're not a real threat. Same with A.I. — it's going to be our friend, right?

You might as well be under the impression that lions are happy, fun, friendly creatures as one finally approaches you on the Serengeti, licking its chops.

CAN WE OVERCOME OUR POOR NARRATIVE PROGRAMMING?

This then ends up being my final question for humanity. Yuval Noah Harari points out at the start of *Homo Deus* that humans have managed to overcome the traditional big three threats of plague, famine and war.

Of the three, only one of them — war — involves narrative. Famine and plague have been conquered through our actions that have cured diseases and improved food production. But war has been (hopefully) solved by overcoming our poor programming of narrative.

Once again, at the core of narrative is contradiction. In its most extreme form, contradiction is all-out conflict. We continue to be driven by this central force. The endless rage of Twitter, among other recent innovations, has shown that we still have an attraction to it.

But since the war horrors of the first half of the last century, there has been a great deal of conflict avoided. This suggests that we do have the ability to overcome the flaws in our narrative programming.

SO WHAT'S IT GONNA BE, PUNK, CLIMATE CHANGE OR A.I.?

Now we face the two existential threats of climate change and A.I. Both of them run the risk of being underestimated due to narrative dynamics.

Climate change is not only firmly planted in "The Land of And," given the glacier-sized amount of information around it, but it is also a deeply intellectual threat. The future threat of war can be emotionalized with all the countless dramatic stories of pain and suffering from past wars. But climate change?

What can we point to in our past to illustrate the pain of climate change? There are apparently some civilizations that have fallen victim to changing climates, but theirs are distant tales, and even then, their demise occurred gradually, not dramatically.

As for artificial intelligence, it's something we haven't experienced any bad consequences from yet, so we need to be told stories about how it works. But as James Barrat warns: If it's a popular, well-known story, by definition it has to have a happy ending for the humans, causing the public to not worry. "A.I.? It's our friend!"

So this is where humanity now is—facing two threats that circumvent our narrative brains. One is too boring; the other, too happy. Which leaves us with a simple final question—are we better than our narrative programming?

And there's your non-archplot ending. Sorry.

APPENDIX 1 - Defining "Story" Versus Narrative

In 2011, my improv-instructor buddy Brian Palermo began making a bit of a noodge of himself in our workshops. I would use the words "story" and "narrative" liberally. He finally asked, "What's the difference?"

I scoffed, obfuscated (the very thing I complained about in this book's Introduction) and said, "You can't separate them." I told him the terms are too broad and all-encompassing to parse. He said bullshit.

We had that exchange enough times that I began to think about what he was saying. He was right. I was being lazy. So I put the same question to a senior communications professor at USC who had been a huge help over the years. He scoffed, obfuscated and dismissed me, saying, "You can't separate them." I wanted to say bullshit, but was a little more polite.

By 2014, I had figured out what I feel is an effective set of working definitions for the two terms which I presented in *Houston, We Have a Narrative*. It's now five years later. I not only stick with the definitions, I also think they are important, and that most people using these terms are just being lazy in not thinking this through.

We live in an information-overburdened world now. We know that narrative structure is at the core of what we have to say. But you can sense the two words are not identical just by how people respond to them. Story has a sense of human warmth to it, while narrative is more cold and analytical.

So here are my analytical definitions of the two.

THE MONOMYTH-BASED DEFINITIONS

Famed mythologist Joseph Campbell did a comparative study of storytelling among the various religions and cultures of the world and found that their stories follow a basic form, which he called "the monomyth."

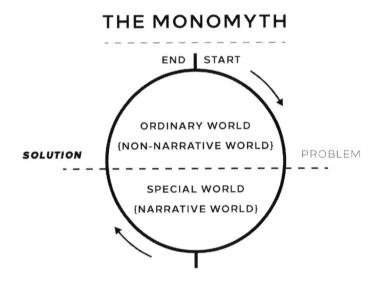

THE MONOMYTH

JOSEPH CAMPBELL'S MONOMYTH MODEL FOR A STORY. A "story" is this entire diagram. "Narrative" refers to just the bottom half—the problem-solution part of the journey—which is the driving force of a story.

He defined the structure of a story as a circular journey that begins and ends at the same place. Along the way, it passes through three phases:

1) THE ORDINARY WORLD (NON-NARRATIVE) - The first phase is what he called the "Ordinary World." I would re-label this the "Non-Narrative World." This is the initial part of the story, which is usually called "exposition." It is largely intellectual. Information is presented, but there has yet to be a problem encountered, which means that the problem-solution part of the brain has not yet been activated. This is the A material in the ABT template. If it goes on for too long it will become the AAA template and bore everyone. We've all seen movies that left you wondering, "When is this going to start to get interesting?"

2) THE SPECIAL WORLD (NARRATIVE) - The second phase begins when the problem is encountered. This is usually referred to as, "When the story begins." The common expression in Hollywood is, "A story begins when something happens." This is where that something happens. Before this we weren't really telling a story.

The "something" that initiates the problem can be finding a dead body, having the ship hit an iceberg, or having a tornado take a little girl to a new world. The corresponding problems are: whodunnit, how are we going to save everyone on the ship, and how is the little girl going to get back home?

All of these problems activate the narrative process, which activates the narrative part of the brain. Joseph Campbell called this part of the journey the "Special World." I would rename it the "Narrative World."

3) RETURN TO THE ORDINARY WORLD (NON-NARRATIVE) - The third part of the story starts when the problem is solved. The murderer is found, the people are saved, and the little girl returns home. This allows the narrative part of the brain to relax (mission accomplished) and return to a resting state. The final part is similar to the first part—i.e., more intellectual—now synthesizing and philosophizing about what was learned in the course of the journey.

So this becomes the distinction. "Story" is the entire package. It's the whole journey, from start to finish. It consists of both narrative and non-narrative material. It's warm, human and multi-dimensional.

As I mentioned in Chapter 2, Ronald Reagan was a storyteller. He would take the time to set up a story, providing human details to make it relatable. Then he would end it with some element of how the story relates to our world.

Donald Trump is not a storyteller. He hates small talk, which is what he would call the details of the Ordinary World (the intellectual part—not his strength). He prefers to just "cut to the chase," by starting with the problem.

THE DEFINITIONS

So here is how I roughly define the two terms:

NARRATIVE - The series of events that occur in the search for the solution to a problem.

STORY - The complete circular journey from non-narrative to narrative, then back to non-narrative.

What this means is that "a series of events" that never gets out of the And, And, And mode of the non-narrative world is not, technically speaking, a story. This means that a resume or chronology is not a story. A series of events doesn't become a story until a problem is established, which sets up the narrative part of the journey, which is the heart of the story.

APPENDIX 2 - Narrative Training

Nothing in Story Circles Narrative Training makes sense except in the light of the Cueing Video.

"NARRATIVE INTUITION": THE "THEREFORE"

By the time I was done writing the *Houston* book, it was clear to me that the central challenge for communication is the need to master narrative structure. In fact, I got my final inspiration on this point from Matt Stone and Trey Parker, the co-creators of the animated series *South Park*.

You may remember that they were the guys from whom I first heard about the importance of the three words (*And, But, Therefore*) — in their 2011 Comedy Central documentary, *Six Days to Air*. Just as my *Houston* book was coming out, a Hollywood friend mentioned he was buddies with Matt Stone. I had him send an email to Matt with the chapter from my book in which I told of learning the ABT elements from their documentary. Matt wrote back a very nice email, in which he said, "If there's anything Trey and I work hard on, it's structure. It's so important and so, so hard to get right."

And there it was, from the horse's mouth, from the mind of the hugely successful duo, with their seven Tony Awards and the massive success of *South Park*. Look at what he said: that structure is "SO" important, yet "SO, SO" hard to get right. Yes, it's important, but it's incredibly hard to get right.

Without a grasp of narrative structure, you are doomed to bore or confuse. You can dazzle and excite people in the short term with fun facts and eye-grabbing visuals, but whether you actually convey a deeper message over the long term—that's dependent upon your grasp of narrative.

Which then takes us back to the two fundamental parts to communication: content (the information you want to convey) and form (how you put it together). Content is the easy part—it's what you already know—all the facts, and bits of humor and emotion. Form is narrative structure. As Matt Stone says, it's the hard part—basically solving the puzzle of how the information goes together to be best understood.

Furthermore, just memorizing narrative templates isn't enough. You need to move that information from your head to your gut. This is what Malcolm Gladwell talked about in *Blink: Thinking Without Thinking*. It's the development of intuition—the gut feel for something.

In Hollywood, in the best books on screenwriting, they refer to what they call "story sense." This is the same thing as the intuition Gladwell talks about—developing "a feel" for story dynamics at the intuitive level. When it comes to story dynamics, you need to be able to hear it, see it, speak it, sense it, and ultimately feel it at the gut level.

It was from these sources that I devised the term "narrative intuition" in *Houston*. It is the ultimate goal. Which then begs the question of how to strengthen narrative intuition.

I ended that book by recommending a form of training I called Story Circles. At the start of 2015, we began the development of our Story Circles Narrative Training program. The training is essentially groups of five individuals meeting for 10 one-hour sessions. In the four years since, we've completed more than 60 circles involving a range of government agencies and universities.

In this chapter I will talk about the inspirations I drew from for the specific elements of Story Circles, how the training works, the "proof" that it works and what we've learned so far.

DESIGN: IMPROV- AND MEISNER- INSPIRED

The starting point for narrative training was my years of working with improv actors in Hollywood and hearing them talk about their own training. Improv actors like to say, "Improv is like a muscle; it has to be conditioned over time."

That began to resonate with my thoughts on narrative, especially as I looked at the fMRI work of neurophysiologists. They talk about major parts of the brain being involved in narrative – as we would expect, given what a primal element narrative is for humanity itself.

Improv actors end up being like athletes: They know they need to "stay in shape," and that requires ongoing conditioning. It's also true for comedians. They, too, have to stay in shape if they are going to succeed at holding the interest of audiences.

One thing I noticed in the 1990's about comedian Jay Leno matched this. Every Sunday when I was in film school at USC, I would see advertisements that he would be performing at a small comedy club in Hermosa Beach. He was host of *The Tonight Show*, making millions of dollars a year, yet he couldn't have been earning more than a few hundred a night with that Sunday show (if he even bothered to have them pay him). I used to wonder, why would he waste time on such a financially trivial activity?

I came to realize he did it for "conditioning." Comedians, actors, athletes — they all know they need this ongoing training. But for some reason most people who communicate to audiences as part of their job don't seem to grasp this.

And so this became one of the core principles for narrative training — the need for repetitive activity to stay "in shape," just like physical fitness. As Jayde Lovell and I set to work creating the training program we began to develop the analogy of physical fitness. We like to say, "You can no more go to the gym for one day and expect to go home buff than you can do a single-day workshop on narrative and think you will master it." It takes a long-term commitment, and that's the core philosophy Story Circles is based upon.

IT'S ALL ABOUT REPETITION

The second inspiration for narrative training came from the intensive Meisner acting program I went through in the mid-1990's, which changed my life. My first book was filled with stories of "the crazy acting teacher" who taught the course. She was the most abusive instructor I've ever experienced, yet also the best.

The core principle and goal of the Meisner technique is the need for the development of "intuition" when it comes to acting. You need to get beyond just thinking about the principles of acting; you need to absorb them so deeply you can feel them in your gut. Moving this knowledge from the brain to the gut is achieved through repetition.

Again, this is what Gladwell talks about in *Blink*. He cites professional athletes and performers needing 10,000 hours to achieve the shift. This is the same thing Meisner training is about: repetition to achieve this shift.

THE BASIC HOUR SESSION

Each hourlong "workout" consists of two parts. The first half hour is the ANALYSIS of the narrative structure of other people's material using the ABT Template. Everyone is given five narratives, which are either the Abstract sections of published research papers (the first three) or synopses of movies (the fourth and fifth).

You read the samples and score them from 1 to 10. A score of 10 means you felt the sample had perfect ABT structure, versus a score of 1, which means it had almost no narrative structure. You read and score all 5 samples, and then the group discusses each one for three minutes each.

The discussion begins with each person telling what score they gave that abstract. There are frequent outbursts of laughter when someone announces that their score for an abstract is a 2, and then the next person, having read the same abstract, gives it a 9. Those moments are the start of realizing how variable a process narrative can be.

The second half of the hour is spent working on the DEVELOPMENT of the material of one member of the circle. It's sort of like Jerry Graff's They Say, I Say. The first half hour is "they say" (other people's material). The second half hour is "I say" (your material).

To keep everything on track we created a CUEING VIDEO,

which can play on the laptop of a member of the circle. It's exactly 60 minutes in length, and it cues the various smaller segments to start every 2 to 10 minutes during the hour.

The cueing video turned out to be the heart and soul of the training. Narrative needs structure. So does training. If you just pull people together for an hour of blabbing about story structure, it's not going to work. You'll get the dominant people taking over as the quieter people sit quiet. You need the cueing video to prevent this. I'll say more about it in a bit.

ADDITION OF THE DEMO DAY

In 2015, we started the narrative training program by creating four prototype circles. Each one consisted of participants at different levels: undergraduates, graduates, postdoctoral scientists, professional scientists. Over the next few months the circles met for 10 one-hour sessions, intended to be once a week, but less frequently if there were scheduling problems.

One of many things we learned with the prototype circles was that basically "you have to want it" for the training to work. It's not designed for short-attention-span, overly busy people who already think they're great with communication. Nor is it meant for someone who is such a quick study that all they need to know is the three words — and, but, therefore.

Those types of people hear the three words and say, "Okay, I got it, all done."

But no, you don't got it. Nobody gets it in one day. Trust me on this, we've been doing it for a lot of years now. Narrative takes time. There is no way around that. None. Sorry, mister busy guy. It's all about time.

Because of this I decided there needed to be a "weeding out" step in the form of what we call the "Demo Day." It's a single-day event, usually from 10 a.m. to 4 p.m., where roughly 40 participants are given a clear understanding of what the training will involve. There's two hours of lecture in the morning, and then in the afternoon we conduct the standard one-hour session but expand it out to three hours, so there's time to ask questions and discuss. By doing this no one signs up without knowing what they are committing to.

At the end of the Demo Day participants sign up for the circles. Over the next few weeks the host institution sorts them into the circles of 5 individuals who will meet for the 10 one-hour sessions.

The sessions take place either in person in a conference room or via teleconferencing. Early on we ran both and determined that the remote sessions are equally effective because there's so little to the training that's visual. (It's not like improv.)

The first session runs for two hours and has one of our people present so everyone can ask questions and clarify details. Then we let the circles run on their own for the rest of the sessions, with no involvement from us. This initially felt neglectful and like a recipe for a disaster until we realized it works great, as I'll explain.

RESULTS: IT WORKS

ASSESSMENT

It's been five years now, we've completed about 60 circles, every one of them has gone the distance, none have disbanded and we now have countless examples of people applying the ABT Framework. Suffice it to say, it works.

The first question we faced was how to assess how well it works. For the initial four prototypes we did what was essentially "B.S. metrics." We videotaped all the sessions (4 circles, 10 sessions, one hour each, equaling 40 hours of video), then had them transcribed.

We set about analyzing the transcripts and eventually found that, yes, the participants did say the words "and, but, therefore" more by the end than at the start, but so what? The increase was slight, and it wasn't even clear what that would mean. That was clearly bullshit. Here's what was much more significant …

THE PROTOTYPE CIRCLE OF USDA RESEARCH SCIENTISTS

Of the four prototypes, the one that came to life immediately and worked best was the one with research scientists at the USDA. That circle was organized by Mike Strauss, the long-time head of their Office of Science Quality Review (who subsequently became the most important member of my Story Circles team). At the end of that circle I videotaped interviews with all the participants, asking them to share the details of the experience, eagerly anticipating their raves about how it had changed their lives.

What I got was disappointing. They said the training was "interesting," but … they couldn't tell yet whether it was definitely worth the time. I went away a little jilted. We had invested a lot of energy in developing the circles, and all my intuition told me it should work, but they weren't sure it was worth it?

But ... (time for the ABT twist) ... a year later we ran a Demo Day at USDA. At lunchtime we had two members of the prototype circle take part in a lunchtime panel to discuss their experiences. I braced for the same equivocal message, but what I heard that day was the opposite.

One of them said, verbatim, "Over the past year — as we've put the training to work — it has changed how we talk, write and even think about our science."

That was the golden moment. That was the day I knew we were on the right track.

OUR FIRST SURVEY OF STORY CIRCLE GRADUATES

In the spring of 2019, after nearly five years of developing the program and completing over 50 circles with around 300 graduates, we finally decided to run our first survey of graduates.

We assembled a short, very focused set of six questions, plus three blanks for them to tell us any examples of how they have put the ABT Framework to use for their own work or with others. We sent it to 120 recent graduates, hoping for a 10% response rate.

The first shocker was the response: We got 101 replies in just 10 days. Many of them thanked us for making it so short and to the point. It wasn't the shotgun questionnaire we did for the prototypes, which was so useless. This one was very focused.

The two specific points we found were that the majority of

graduates did not feel that the length of training needed to be fewer than 10 sessions, and when asked if they thought it should be compressed into just three weeks, an even larger majority said no.

But the most powerful part of the surveys was what the graduates entered into the blanks for their stories of applying the ABT Framework. We posted 130 of their accounts of applying the knowledge to a huge range of activities, including proposal writing, presentations, press-release writing, staff training, video scriptwriting and lots of other situations, including even using the ABT to help their kids with college applications.

There is an old adage for effective communication: "Don't tell me, show me." Having a number that says 80% of recipients found the training valuable tells you it's important, but having 130 specific stories of the graduates using the training in the real world shows you how important it is.

WHAT WE'VE LEARNED SO FAR ABOUT NARRATIVE TRAINING

NARRATIVE TAKES TIME

I can't say this enough. Therapists have a favorite expression for patients: "You can't rush the river." They use it when patients come to them with major psychological problems that they want to fix overnight. I first heard it from a therapist when I was getting divorced, and then I heard it again years later from a therapist trying to help my sister deal with the death of her daughter.

You can't rush the river — in life or with narrative. It takes time. There's no getting around that. None.

Of course you can try rushing it and end up with poor quality. There's that. But if you want to communicate effectively, you have to grasp narrative structure, and if you want that, it's going to take time.

And this is why I have gravitated to the basic policy of "One-day workshops don't work." There is no "one and done" pathway. Sorry.

THREE MYTHS BUSTED: YOUNG PEOPLE, OLD PEOPLE, AND ACADEMICS

Let me now share a few more realizations we've come to after five years of running Story Circles.

1) YOUNG PEOPLE

In the beginning, we heard one thing over and over, and we believed it ourselves: "It's today's kids who are so good with communication with all their social media. They're the ones who are gonna take to this training so well."

Nope. Wrong.

Let me give a simple explanation of why this didn't happen, which is that you don't want to provide solutions to people who don't think they have a problem.

This is an age-old problem of the environmental movement. I've watched so many environmentalists come up with big solutions to environmental problems only to find that the public (for whom the solutions were intended) doesn't think there is a problem and thus isn't likely to listen.

Same thing for young students. They don't know yet that they have any problems with communication. The first thing we saw with the prototype circle of undergraduates was that they were the most enthusiastic participants ever, but ... they didn't get it. When we got to the last three sessions, where we shift from analyzing abstracts to rewriting them, it became clear they were totally lost on what the ABT really meant and how you use it.

A year after the prototypes we ran a Demo Day with Master's students in a program for forestry and environmental studies. They were new students, not yet involved in writing papers and proposals or giving major talks. Of the 50 students, 26 signed up to join circles.

But a week later the head professor emailed to say he couldn't even find enough students for one circle. Most had signed up just to make us feel good. They didn't really intend to do the full training; they couldn't see the value of it because they didn't feel they had any serious communications problems.

And then the biggest realization hit us when a university with a conservation biology master's program added Story Circles to the first-semester orientation course for new students. They formed two circles, but by the seventh session they were ready to mutiny.

I conducted an hourlong conference call with them. They said they "got it" on the three words the first day. They couldn't understand why week after week they had to work with the same three words. Instead, they wanted classes on how to write proposals and papers — skills they had not even begun to acquire.

And that's when it hit me—you have to have a problem for Story Circles to work. You need at least some experience with failed communication in order to see why the training is valuable.

We got the confirmation of this in 2019 with the three circles of upper-level graduate students from U.C. Davis. They were 5th- and 6th-year PhD students who had already written proposals, published papers, given talks and produced videos. They had a context in which to apply the training. They did the full 10 one-hour sessions and emerged deeply appreciative of the experience and with a clear understanding of how to apply the knowledge.

So this is firming up into one of our basic realizations. Story Circles is not meant for young students. The participants need to have enough practical experience for the training to be meaningful. Otherwise it just becomes boring working with the ABT template week after week but not understanding what it's for.

2) OLD PEOPLE

You ever heard that expression that you can't teach an old dog new tricks? The flip side of what we heard about young people (above) was what people warned us about older participants: they wouldn't get the ABT Framework.

Wrong again. And this is important at a deeper level because it addresses the misconception that, "Some people are meant to be communicators, but others are hopeless." I firmly believe everyone can get better with narrative structure.

The fact is, giving a presentation that has AAA structure is fine, so long as it is accurate. But there exists a higher level of achievement with the ABT structure. If this has never been pointed out to you, there's probably a lot of improvement that can be accomplished right off the bat.

A prime example of this is Liz Foote, an environmental activist who wrote to me in 2014 about using the ABT. She had spent years giving talks that were just AAA in structure. But after hearing about the ABT she tried using it for the first time for a talk.

She experienced three things for the first time: the talk was easier to rehearse, during the talk she could feel that the audience was more engaged than usual and after the talk she saw people on social media regurgitating her core message exactly as she had presented it.

The whole experience made her such a believer that she's been one of our main Story Circles trainers ever since. And she wasn't exactly a kid when she had this experience. Everyone, regardless of age, can make immediate, rapid improvements in their communication simply by shifting from AAA to ABT structure.

3) ACADEMICS

This one taps deep into my programming long ago as an academic snob. In my younger years I spent time around a lot of academic superstars, both as an undergraduate in the Zoology Department at the University of Washington, then as a graduate student at Harvard.

When you're not yet 25 years old, your brain is still being heavily programmed by your environment. When you hear very bright professors and graduate students constantly saying that government-agency scientists are second-rate, you begin to absorb that as a core belief. And it can stay with you for a lifetime.

As a result, when I began creating Story Circles at age 60, I warned my group that the "second-rate" government scientists probably wouldn't be bright enough to grasp what we were saying, but that the brilliant scientists of academia would take the ball and run with it. Boy, was I stupid.

Wrong for a third time.

Numerous academics chewed up and spat out Story Circles at universities, starting with the University of Chicago. We ran two of our prototypes there (grad students and postdocs). Some of their faculty felt they already knew how it worked, so they didn't hesitate to change several basic aspects of it to suit their ideas.

This started with them doing their own questionnaire of their participants, not at the end of the 10 one-hour sessions, but instead on the first day, after we ran the orientation sessions and left. They asked the participants five questions that basically implied that we didn't know what we were doing with the training. They sent us the results.

By the time they were done running the circles they had misconstrued so many things and bent so many of the basic rules, even letting one participant quit (the only person to quit to date out of more than 60 circles, and part of why we eventually added the whole element of the Demo Day), that I wanted to pull the whole plug on them. They sent us a pile of criticism on how to actually do Story Circles, but in the meanwhile the prototype at USDA ran perfectly, so we knew the basic model was fine.

Since then I've had a number of other run-ins with academics who: A) feel they are great communicators (their students tell them that every day) and B) think they know how to teach narrative just fine their own way. Whatever.

What we know right now, after five years, is that my brain was programmed completely wrong back in the 1970's. The government-agency folks have proven to be the ones most capable of listening, implementing and learning. And as a result, they have been a joy to work with.

My experiences with academics have frequently circled back to the first two chapters of my first book, which were titled, "Don't Be So Cerebral" and "Don't Be So Literal Minded." Such is the bane of academics when it comes to communication.

And actually, the last laugh on the University of Chicago came at a final lunch there, where it was clear they had made a mess of the training and as a result no one was enjoying it. As I shook my head in confusion, the graduate student sitting next to me quietly said, "Don't you know the nickname of this university? It's called the place where fun comes to die."

Yikes. It's true. Search it. Worst place ever for Story Circles.

THREE SURPRISES: THE COHESION, THE DOBZHANSKY, AND THE CUEING VIDEO

NOBODY QUITS

As I mentioned, we were braced for all sorts of setbacks with Story Circles, starting with some circles falling apart. People get so busy, we figured a certain number of circles would be disbanded halfway through.

To our delight it has never happened. Even at Genentech, where their schedules are so incredibly intense it took one circle nearly a year to go the distance. Even they managed to do all 10 one-hour sessions.

Part of it was the implementation of the Demo Day. That makes sure no one joins a circle without knowing exactly what they are signing up for. This is very important. We learned long ago you can't force the training on participants. It requires a lot of effort during the hour. The members of the circle need to be motivated.

NAILING IT WITH THE DOBZHANSKY NARRATIVE TEMPLATE

Story Circles is built primarily around the ABT as the central tool, but there are also several other elements. One of them is the Dobzhansky Narrative Template — the tool for finding the one word at the core of a narrative.

In the beginning it was just one of several narrative tools, but over the course of five years we've heard repeatedly that it emerges as everyone's favorite tool. We've had several circles tell us, when I've interviewed them after their circle completed, that it was the Dobzhansky that provided the most powerful and even surprising breakthroughs on people's narratives.

Week after week they find themselves working on someone's narrative of a project they are doing. They craft the ABT for the project and have a hard time getting to a consensus, but then they get to the Dobzhansky, someone blurts out a word they hadn't considered, and in an instant the entire group says, "Wow, that's it."

When that moment happens, it can be so powerful, it's inspiring. It's the Dobzhansky that seems to provide more of those moments than any other tool.

THE WONDERS OF THE CUEING VIDEO

The last big surprise has been the cueing video. I came up with the whole idea the night before the very first circle we ever ran. I knew there was a list of segments with specific times that I wanted to have happen during the Story Circles hour. It seemed like having the video would make it easier than having someone looking at a watch.

What I didn't know was all the wonderful side benefits the cueing video would bring, starting with removing the element of personalities.

If you pull together any average group of five people, you're going to have a range of personalities. Inevitably you'll have domineering types in conversation (i.e., loudmouthed jerks, like me, sometimes), as well as quiet types who have trouble interrupting the flow of a group (not ever like me). You'll eventually have complaints from the quiet types, who get tired of the domineering types.

We've never had a single complaint about personalities. This is because the cueing video forces the group to move along. Every two to ten minutes the cue goes off. The rules are, whoever is speaking must stop mid-sentence, no matter how brilliant the point was that they were making. It becomes comical when someone thinks they were saying something brilliant, the alarm goes off, and the group (following the rules) cuts them off.

All of which leads to this final point that is the most profound thing of all.

COMMUNICATION IS NOT ABOUT PERFECTION

More than anything else, this is what Story Circles has taught us. Research is absolutely about perfection. When you're conducting research, whether it is in the field of history, geography, political science, economics or science itself, you absolutely want to be driven by the desire to measure and record things as perfectly as possible.

But when it comes time to communicate what you've found, you have to be careful about perfection. Yes, you want to make sure your content is perfectly accurate, but the overall form has to be the best approximation.

The problem is that you're dealing with so much natural variation. In Story Circles you can see how variable everyone's minds are when it comes to narrative. When you do the exercise analyzing the abstracts and hear people read the same abstract and give it scores as different as a one and a ten, that is when you're seeing the real variation in the perception of narrative.

This means that there is no perfect narrative form that will match all the brains in an audience. You have to just give it your best shot and move on. To try and stop things until you've got it exactly right would be foolish.

It's about iteration and moving on. Just like in the real world. And this then becomes one of the most gratifying things of all to witness: Participants beginning to see how variable communication is in the real world, and how you deal with that variation. That's what Story Circles is all about.

SO DOES STORY CIRCLES NARRATIVE TRAINING WORK FOR THE WORLDS OF BUSINESS, POLITICS AND ENTERTAINMENT?

Of course. Three things.

First, Story Circles is non-discriminatory. It's about form, not content. Every group has different content, and maybe at the very detailed level might also have some differences in form. But at the core level of shaping the narrative — the toughest part of all communication — the principles and attributes are universal.

I am constantly being invited to institutions, organizations, businesses, and activist groups for which I know zilch about their content. And in fact, I don't even want to know about their content. They start to describe their awesome marketing plan or political strategy or the details of their screenplay and I just say, "Stop ... please ... I don't want to know the details — I just want to help you with the FORM of what you're wanting to communicate."

Second, there is no effective "one and done" strategy for communication. One day workshops not only accomplish very little, they can be deceptive. People go home thinking they've "nailed it," but very little sticks. You have to have the repetition for things to take. It's about the long term commitment to strengthen the "narrative muscle." If you look at the Survey of Graduates on our Story Circles website you'll see people tell about sharing the ABT Framework with their team or assistants. What they say is that it's definitely useful, but … they can tell the people don't "get it" quite the same as investing the time for the 10 one hour sessions.

It's like the old "give a man a fish," adage. I get brought in to coach people on their individual presentations using the ABT Framework. That can be somewhat gratifying, but if they lack narrative intuition, they will revert to AAA after I leave. What I much, much prefer is to run them through Story Circles. It is more the "teach a man to fish" approach to the problems.

Third, there's not any effective shorter version of it. You get back what you put in. I met with a big boss at a big agency who said he liked the sound of the program, but time is just too short for his people. He said they were ready to dive in if we could shorten the training to just 5 sessions.

I had my colleague Mike Strauss write a detail email basically saying no. It's in the second 5 sessions that the groups begin to show the first evidence of narrative intuition, which is the ultimate goal. They get to the point where they no longer need to look at their notes for how the hour schedule goes, they no longer need to look at their cards we give them with vocabulary and the narrative templates. And most impressive of all, many get to the point where they know by heart, not just the shorter templates, but all 12 stages of the Story Cycle and the 9 parts of the Logline Maker. They start to "feel" the narrative structure of material — able to glance at a block of text and say, "This feels very DHY." That's when it's working.

That sort of intuition is essential to shaping the narrative of any text, from business to politics to entertainment.

APPENDIX 3 - Narrative Analysis Examples

The ABT template provides an objective structure for narrative but is still very subjective with how you implement it. Here are some examples where I give: 1) The original text, 2) The format-coded text, and 3) my ABT rewrite. None of the weak texts are "wrong" per se, they are just easier to read and absorb with better narrative form.

Achieving the best structure is still subjective so in the rewrites you may see ways to do it better. That's why we create groups of five individuals for a Story Circle — you can't do a very good job of shaping narrative alone — you need other voices.

Here are the examples:

I.   EXAMPLES OF WEAK NARRATIVE STRUCTURE
        - Domestic Violence Mission Statement
        - Gun Control Mission Statement
        - Media Matters Mission Statement
        - *Science* Summary: Oceanography
        - Hilary Clinton Speech Excerpt
        - *Clerks* Movie Synopsis
        - Extinction Editorial

II.   EXAMPLES OF STRONG NARRATIVE STRUCTURE
        - Nursery Rhymes
        - Gettysburg Address from Abraham Lincoln
        - *I Have A Dream* from Martin Luther King, Jr.
        - Oprah Winfrey 2018 Golden Globes
        - Nixon First Inaugural opening

- Obama National Academy of Sciences opening
- NY Times Editorial: Miss America
- *Science* Summary: Neuroscience
- *Wonder Woman* opening narration
- *Call Me Maybe* from Carlie Rae Jepsen

I. EXAMPLES OF WEAK NARRATIVE STRUCTURE

Here are six examples of narrative gone weak. Sadly, the world is filled with countless examples of poor narrative structure. This is not to say that everything should have the ABT form. Of course we want a world filled with variation, and much of art demands deliberate deviation from the simple triadic structure. But this book is not about art, it's about effective broad communication. Therefore, let's have a look at a few examples that could use some narrative improvement (and notice this paragraph is an ABT).

1) NO "B": Mission Statement for Domestic Violence Group

ORIGINAL:

Our mission is to transform society's response to sexual assault, domestic violence, and child abuse, support survivors' healing, and end this violence forever.
While we understand that our vision may not be achievable in our lifetimes, we firmly believe that violence and abuse are preventable. In support of our vision and mission, we have

developed and adopted a set of values and guiding principles that inform and inspire our approach to all that we do:

•   Our Values are the foundation of our organization and guide our thinking, actions, decisions, responses, and priorities.

•   Our Guiding Principles serve as a compass both individually and organizationally. They are the application of our core beliefs that help to shape and direct our work. We approach all we do and every decision we make with the Guiding Principles in mind.

FORMAT-CODED:

Our mission is to transform society's response to sexual assault, domestic violence, and child abuse, support survivors' healing, and end this violence forever.
While we understand that our vision may not be achievable in our lifetimes, we firmly believe that violence and abuse are preventable. *In support of our vision and mission, we have developed and adopted a set of values and guiding principles that inform and inspire our approach to all that we do:*

•   *Our Values are the foundation of our organization and guide our thinking, actions, decisions, responses, and priorities.*

•   *Our Guiding Principles serve as a compass both individually and organizationally. They are the application of our core beliefs that help to shape and direct our work. We approach all we do and every decision we make with the Guiding Principles in mind.*

ABT REWRITE:

Domestic violence touches everyone's lives in America. More than 1.75 million workdays are lost each year because of it AND programs do exist to combat it, **BUT current efforts are not enough,** *(THEREFORE) society's overall response needs to be transformed.*

We have developed and adopted a set of values and guiding principles that inform and inspire our approach to all that we do:
• *Our Values are the foundation of our organization and guide our thinking, actions, decisions, responses, and priorities.*
• *Our Guiding Principles serve as a compass both individually and organizationally. They are the application of our core beliefs that help to shape and direct our work. We approach all we do and every decision we make with the Guiding Principles in mind.*

COMMENTARY:

The original text cuts right to what the group is doing, making the assumption that everyone knows the problem, why it is important, and what needs to happen (to transform society's response). The rewrite attends to these details first, before saying what the group is doing.

2) SCRAMBLED ABT: Mission statement of gun violence group

ORIGINAL:

Guns Down is fighting back against the National Rifle Association and the gun lobby with the simple premise that our communities are safer with fewer guns. If we're serious about saving lives, we need to build a bolder, broader movement that finally tackles the problem at its core.

America has far more gun deaths than our peer nations. We use our guns to kill each other at a rate that's 25 times higher than people in any other high-income country in the world and we use our guns to kill ourselves at a rate that's eight times higher. Guns exist for the sole purpose of killing, and they'll continue to devastate our families and communities until we dramatically limit their availability. Unfortunately, the National Rifle Association has spent millions of dollars advancing its guns everywhere agenda, buying off members of Congress, and spreading lies about gun reform. In 2016, the lobby invested over $30 million to elect Donald Trump and spent another $20 million electing gun extremists to Congress. Guns Down is taking on the NRA on all sides, by exposing the true cost of its guns-everywhere agenda and challenging those who do business with the NRA. #GunFreePolls: In the lead-up to the 2016 elections, law enforcement agencies were increasingly concerned about the threat of armed intimidators at polling locations. Guns Down established a helpline for those who witnessed such incidents. FedEx: Guns Down is pushing FedEx to pull out of the NRA's Business Alliance, which offers FedEx discounts to NRA members. Tell FedEx not to fund gun violence. Gun violence is a major threat facing our country today. Every day, 48 children and teens are shot. Seven of them die. Mass shootings, in which four or more people are shot, have occurred in more than 100 metropolitan areas since 2015.

FORMAT-CODED:

Guns Down is fighting back against the National Rifle Association and the gun lobby with the simple premise that our communities are safer with fewer guns. **If we're serious about saving lives, we need to build a bolder, broader movement that finally tackles the problem at its core.** America has far more gun deaths than our peer nations. We use our guns to kill each other at a rate that's 25 times higher than people in any other high-income country in the world and we use our guns to kill ourselves at a rate that's eight times higher. Guns exist for the sole purpose of killing, **and they'll continue to devastate our families and communities until we dramatically limit their availability. Unfortunately, the National Rifle Association has spent millions of dollars advancing its guns everywhere agenda, buying off members of Congress, and spreading lies about gun reform. In 2016, the lobby invested over $30 million to elect Donald Trump and spent another $20 million electing gun extremists to Congress.** *Guns Down is taking on the NRA on all sides, by exposing the true cost of its guns-everywhere agenda and challenging those who do business with the NRA.* **#GunFreePolls: In the lead-up to the 2016 elections, law enforcement agencies were increasingly concerned about the threat of armed intimidators at polling locations.** *Guns Down established a helpline for those who witnessed such incidents. FedEx: Guns Down is pushing FedEx to pull out of the NRA's Business Alliance, which offers FedEx discounts to NRA members. Tell FedEx not to fund gun violence.* Gun violence is a major threat facing our country today. Every day, 48 children and teens are shot. Seven of them die. Mass shootings, in which four or more people are shot, have occurred in more than 100 metropolitan areas since 2015.

ABT REWRITE:

America has far more gun deaths than our peer nations. We use our guns to kill each other at a rate that's 25 times higher than people in any other high-income country in the world and we use our guns to kill ourselves at a rate that's eight times higher. Guns exist for the sole purpose of killing. Gun violence is a major threat facing our country today. Every day, 48 children and teens are shot. Seven of them die. Mass shootings, in which four or more people are shot, have occurred in more than 100 metropolitan areas since 2015. (BUT) If we're serious about saving lives, we need to build a bolder, broader movement that finally tackles the problem at its core. (GUNS WILL) continue to devastate our families and communities until we dramatically limit their availability. Unfortunately, the National Rifle Association has spent millions of dollars advancing its guns everywhere agenda, buying off members of Congress, and spreading lies about gun reform. In 2016, the lobby invested over $30 million to elect Donald Trump and spent another $20 million electing gun extremists to Congress. In the lead-up to the 2016 elections, law enforcement agencies were increasingly concerned about the threat of armed intimidators at polling locations. *(THEREFORE) Guns Down is fighting back against the National Rifle Association and the gun lobby with the simple premise that our communities are safer with fewer guns. Guns Down is taking on the NRA on all sides, by exposing the true cost of its guns-everywhere agenda and challenging those who do business with the NRA. Guns Down established a helpline for those who witnessed such incidents. Guns Down is pushing FedEx to pull out of the NRA's Business Alliance, which offers FedEx discounts to NRA members. Tell FedEx not to fund gun violence.*

COMMENTARY:

There's nothing wrong with how the original text is written. It's perfectly understandable, but it's a mess when it comes to narrative structure. Instead of following a smooth, logical flow, it jumps all over the place. Yes, it may be a little more attention grabbing to start by having a statement of action (saying they are fighting back against the NRA), but the average reader is left wondering what exactly is the problem you're addressing and how are you doing something different about it from all the other people working on it. The rewrite presents the set up, problem (need a broader movement) and solution (the actions being taken by Guns Down). In simple terms, it tells a story. And also could probably be much shorter without losing any impact.

3) NO "B": Media Watchdog Group Mission Statement

ORIGINAL:

Launched in May 2004, *Media Matters for America* put in place, for the first time, the means to systematically monitor a cross section of print, broadcast, cable, radio, and Internet media outlets for conservative misinformation - news or commentary that is not accurate, reliable, or credible and that forwards the conservative agenda - every day, in real time.

Using the website mediamatters.org as the principal vehicle for disseminating research and information, *Media Matters* posts rapid-response items as well as longer research and analytic reports documenting conservative misinformation throughout the media. Additionally, *Media Matters* works daily to notify activists, journalists, pundits, and the general public about instances of misinformation, providing them with the resources to rebut false claims and to take direct action against offending media institutions.

FORMAT-CODED:

Launched in May 2004, Media Matters for America put in place, for the first time, the means to systematically monitor a cross section of print, broadcast, cable, radio, and Internet media outlets for conservative misinformation - news or commentary that is not accurate, reliable, or credible and that forwards the conservative agenda - every day, in real time.

Using the website mediamatters.org as the principal vehicle for disseminating research and information, Media Matters posts rapid-response items as well as longer research and analytic reports documenting conservative misinformation throughout the media. Additionally, Media Matters works daily to notify activists, journalists, pundits, and the general public about instances of misinformation, providing them with the resources to rebut false claims and to take direct action against offending media institutions.

ABT REWRITE:

By 2004 conservative media had established an overwhelming presence across print, broadcast, cable, radio and internet, **but there was no organization able to systematically monitor them for news or commentary that is not accurate, reliable or credible.** *Media Matters for America was created to meet this need, every day, in real time. Using the website mediamatters.org as the principal vehicle for disseminating research and information, Media Matters posts rapid-response items as well as longer research and analytic reports documenting conservative misinformation throughout the media. Additionally, Media Matters works daily to notify activists, journalists, pundits, and the general public about instances of misinformation, providing them with the resources to rebut false claims and to take direct action against offending media institutions.*

COMMENTARY:

It's not that their version is wrong, it's just that it fails to draw on the power of narrative structure to tell a story about a problem that existed, and the solution provided by *Media Matters.*

4) SCRAMBLED ABT: Summary of ocean science research

from Science magazine

ORIGINAL:

Scientists are retrieving data from the largest effort yet to monitor the Atlantic conveyor belt, a set of powerful ocean currents with far- reaching effects on the global climate that has mysteriously slowed over the past decade. Five research cruises this spring and summer will fetch data from the 53 moorings in an array called Overturning in the Subpolar North Atlantic Program (OSNAP), which stretches from Labrador to Greenland to Scotland. The array's measurements of temperature, salinity, and current velocity will be key to understanding the Atlantic Meridional Overturning Circulation (AMOC), and how it is affected by climate change. The AMOC currents include the Gulf Stream, which brings shallow warm waters north, nourishing fisheries and warming northwest Europe. The warm waters give up their heat in the bitterly cold regions monitored by OSNAP, become denser, and sink, forming ocean-bottom currents that return southward, hugging the perimeter of the ocean basins. Models suggest that climate change should weaken the AMOC as warmer Arctic temperatures, combined with buoyant freshwater from Greenland's melting ice cap, impede the formation of deep currents. BUT so far, limited ocean measurements show the AMOC to be far more capricious than the models have been able to capture.

FORMAT-CODED:

Scientists are retrieving data from the largest effort yet to monitor the Atlantic conveyor belt, a set of powerful ocean currents with far- reaching effects on the global climate that has mysteriously slowed over the past decade. *Five research cruises this spring and summer will fetch data from the 53 moorings in an array called Overturning in the Subpolar North Atlantic*

Program (OSNAP), which stretches from Labrador to Greenland to Scotland. The array's measurements of temperature, salinity, and current velocity will be key to understanding the Atlantic Meridional Overturning Circulation (AMOC), and how it is affected by climate change. The AMOC currents include the Gulf Stream, which brings shallow warm waters north, nourishing fisheries and warming northwest Europe. The warm waters give up their heat in the bitterly cold regions monitored by OSNAP, become denser, and sink, forming ocean-bottom currents that return southward, hugging the perimeter of the ocean basins. Models suggest that climate change should weaken the AMOC as warmer Arctic temperatures, combined with buoyant freshwater from Greenland's melting ice cap, impede the formation of deep currents. **But so far, limited ocean measurements show the AMOC to be far more capricious than the models have been able to capture.**

THE ABT REWRITE:

Atlantic conveyor belt is a set of powerful ocean currents with far- reaching effects on the global climate that has mysteriously slowed over the past decade. The Atlantic Meridional Overturning Circulation (AMOC) currents include the Gulf Stream, which brings shallow warm waters north, nourishing fisheries and warming northwest Europe. The warm waters give up their heat in the bitterly cold regions monitored by OSNAP, become denser, and sink, forming ocean-bottom currents that return southward, hugging the perimeter of the ocean basins. Models suggest that climate change should weaken the AMOC as warmer Arctic temperatures, combined with buoyant freshwater from Greenland's melting ice cap, impede the formation of deep currents. **BUT so far, limited ocean measurements show the AMOC to be far more capricious than the models have been able to capture.** *(THEREFORE) Five research cruises this spring and summer will fetch data from the 53 moorings in an array called*

Overturning in the Subpolar North Atlantic Program (OSNAP), which stretches from Labrador to Greenland to Scotland. The array's measurements of temperature, salinity, and current velocity will be key to understanding the AMOC, and how it is affected by climate change.

COMMENTARY:

Once you start to get a feel for the ABT basic pattern of narrative structure, you kind of look at a piece of text like this and wonder what the author was thinking. The ABT elements were all there, but for some reason he decided to end it with the statement of the problem? I guess he thought that was a suspenseful ending, but Science isn't an environmental suspense magazine — it's a scientific journal. Of course, keep in mind that it takes extra effort to get narrative structure straight.

5) WEAK ABT: Hillary Clinton speech excerpt

Excerpted from a speech given by Hillary Clinton during her presidential campaign in 2016.

ORIGINAL:

Tonight I am looking forward to the opportunity to discuss how we knock down the barriers that stand in the way of people getting ahead and staying ahead, starting with the economic ones. My focus is on more good paying jobs with rising incomes for families and how we prevent corporations from taking jobs out of our country by imposing an exit tax, making them pay back any tax breaks they've gotten.

But we also need to be having a positive agenda for manufacturing, for small businesses and entrepreneurs.

FORMAT-CODED:

Tonight I am looking forward to the opportunity to discuss how we knock down the barriers that stand in the way of people getting ahead and staying ahead, starting with the economic ones. *My focus is on more good paying jobs with rising incomes for families and how we prevent corporations from taking jobs out of our country by imposing an exit tax, making them pay back any tax breaks they've gotten.*

But we also need to be having a positive agenda for manufacturing, for small businesses and entrepreneurs.

ABT REWRITE:

People work hard in this country and have a right to expect a good life, but they encounter barriers. My goal is to knock down those barriers. **But how do we do this?** *With more good paying jobs. We also prevent corporations from taking jobs out of our country by imposing an exit tax, making them pay back any tax breaks they've gotten. That's how we start to fix things, but there's much more needed. We need a positive agenda for manufacturing, for small businesses and entrepreneurs.*

COMMENTARY:

In the rewrite I've revised the opening set up a bit to put it in a broader, simpler context before getting to the simple statement of the problem leading to the actions she is proposing.

6) INTENTIONAL AAA: Synopsis of the movie, "Clerks"

ORIGINAL:

Dante Hicks is not having a good day. He works as a clerk in a small convenience store and is told to come into work on his day off. Dante thinks life is a series of down endings and this day is proving to no different. He reads in the newspaper that his ex-girlfriend Caitlin is getting married. His present girlfriend reveals to have somewhat more experience with sex that he ever imagined. His principal concerns are the hockey game he has that afternoon and the wake for a friend who died. His buddy Randal Graves works as a clerk in the video store next and he hates his job just about as much as Dante hates his.

FORMAT-CODED:

Dante Hicks is not having a good day. He works as a clerk in a small convenience store and is told to come into work on his day off. Dante thinks life is a series of down endings and this day is proving to no different. He reads in the newspaper that his ex-girlfriend Caitlin is getting married. His present girlfriend reveals to have somewhat more experience with sex that he ever imagined. His principal concerns are the hockey game he has that afternoon and the wake for a friend who died. His buddy Randal Graves works as a clerk in the video store next and he hates his job just about as much as Dante hates his.

ABT REWRITE:

None. You don't mess with masterpieces.

COMMENTARY:

This is our favorite movie synopsis for the Narrative Analysis part of our Story Circles Narrative Training program. Initially spotted by Jayde Lovell for our very first session, it has become "Exhibit A" for the entire concept of "And, And, And" structure. "Clerks" was the iconic film for the generation known as "slackers" of the 1990's. They felt their lives were filled with trivial events. The movie was a perfect reflection of that, which meant it had to be AAA, not ABT. It knew what it wanted to be, which was intentional AAA. It also mostly bores people who are not part of the Inner Group (i.e. slackers).

7) DHY HOME RUN: Washington Post extinction editorial

This is an editorial published in December, 2017 which so inflamed the evolution and conservation biology world it received over 4,000 comments in just a few days.

ORIGINAL:

Near midnight, during an expedition to southwestern Ecuador in December 2013, I spotted a small green frog asleep on a leaf, near a stream by the side of the road. It was *Atelopus balios* , the Rio Pescado stubfoot toad. Although a lone male had been spotted in 2011, no populations had been found since 1995, and it was thought to be extinct. But here it was, raised from the dead like Lazarus. My colleagues and I found several more that night, males and females, and shipped them to an amphibian ark in Quito, where they are now breeding safely in captivity. But they will go extinct one day, and the world will be none the poorer for it. Eventually, they will be replaced by a dozen or a hundred new species that evolve later.

Mass extinctions periodically wipe out up to 95 percent of all species in one fell swoop; these come every 50 million to 100 million years, and scientists agree that we are now in the middle of the sixth such extinction, this one caused primarily by humans and our effects on animal habitats. It is an "immense and hidden" tragedy to see creatures pushed out of existence by humans, lamented the Harvard entomologist E.O. Wilson, who coined the term "biodiversity" in 1985. A joint paper by several prominent researchers published by the National Academy of Sciences called it a "biological annihilation." Pope Francis imbues the biodiversity crisis with a moral imperative ("Each creature has its own purpose," he said in 2015), and biologists often cite an ecological one (we must avert "a dramatic decay of biodiversity and the subsequent loss of ecosystem services," several wrote in a paper for Science Advances). "What is Conservation Biology?," a foundational text for the field, written by Michael Soulé of the University of California at Santa Cruz, says, "Diversity of organisms is good ... the untimely extinction of populations and species is bad ... [and] biotic diversity has intrinsic value." In her book "The Sixth Extinction ," journalist Elizabeth Kolbert captures the panic all this has induced: "Such is the pain the loss of a single species causes that we're willing to perform ultrasounds on rhinos and handjobs on crows."

But the impulse to conserve for conservation's sake has taken on an unthinking, unsupported, unnecessary urgency. Extinction is the engine of evolution, the mechanism by which natural selection prunes the poorly adapted and allows the hardiest to flourish. Species constantly go extinct, and every species that is alive today will one day follow suit. There is no such thing as an "endangered species," except for all species. The only reason we should conserve biodiversity is for ourselves, to create a stable future for human beings. Yes, we have altered the environment and, in doing so, hurt other species. This seems artificial because we, unlike other life forms, use sentience and agriculture and industry. But we are a part of the biosphere just like every other creature, and our actions are just as volitional, their consequences just as natural. Conserving a species we have helped to kill off, but on which we are not directly dependent, serves to discharge our own guilt, but little else.

Climate scientists worry about how we've altered our planet, and they have good reasons for apprehension: Will we be able to feed ourselves? Will our water supplies dry up? Will our homes wash away? But unlike those concerns, extinction does not carry moral significance, even when we have caused it. And unless we somehow destroy every living cell on Earth, the sixth extinction will be followed by a recovery, and later a seventh extinction, and so on.

Yet we are obsessed with reviving the status quo ante. The Paris Accords aim to hold the temperature to under two degrees Celsius above preindustrial levels, even though the temperature has been at least eight degrees Celsius warmer within the past 65 million years. Twenty-one thousand years ago, Boston was under an ice sheet a kilometer thick. We are near all-time lows for temperature and sea level ; whatever effort we make to maintain the current climate will eventually be overrun by the inexorable forces of space and geology. Our concern, in other words, should not be protecting the animal kingdom, which will be just fine. Within a few million years of the asteroid that killed the dinosaurs, the post-apocalyptic void had been filled by an explosion of diversity — modern mammals, birds and amphibians of all shapes and sizes.

This is how evolution proceeds: through extinction. The inevitability of death is the only constant in life, and 99.9 percent of all species that have ever lived, as many as 50 billion, have already gone extinct. In 50 million years, Europe will collide with Africa and form a new supercontinent, destroying species (think of birds, fish and anything vulnerable to invasive life forms from another landmass) by irrevocably altering their habitats. Extinctions of individual species, entire lineages and even complete ecosystems are common occurrences in the history of life. The world is no better or worse for the absence of saber-toothed tigers and dodo birds and our Neanderthal cousins, who died off as Homo sapiens evolved. (According to some studies, it's not even clear that biodiversity is suffering. The authors of another recent National Academy of Sciences paper point out that species richness has shown no net decline among plants over 100 years across 16,000 sites examined around the world.)

Conserving biodiversity should not be an end in itself; diversity can even be hazardous to human health. Infectious diseases are most prevalent and virulent in the most diverse tropical areas. Nobody donates to campaigns to save HIV, Ebola, malaria, dengue and yellow fever, but these are key components of microbial biodiversity, as unique as pandas, elephants and orangutans, all of which are ostensibly endangered thanks to human interference.

Humans should feel less shame about molding their environment to suit their survival needs. When beavers make a dam, they cause the local extinction of numerous riverine species that cannot survive in the new lake. But that new lake supports a set of species that is just as diverse. Studies have shown that when humans introduce invasive plant species, native diversity sometimes suffers, but productivity — the cycling of nutrients through the ecosystem — frequently increases. Invasives can bring other benefits, too: Plants such as the Phragmites reed have been shown to perform better at reducing coastal erosion and storing carbon than native vegetation in some areas, like the Chesapeake.

And if biodiversity is the goal of extinction fearmongers, how do they regard South Florida, where about 140 new reptile species accidentally introduced by the wildlife trade are now breeding successfully? No extinctions of native species have been recorded, and, at least anecdotally, most natives are still thriving. The ones that are endangered, such as gopher tortoises and indigo snakes , are threatened mostly by habitat destruction. Even if all the native reptiles in the Everglades, about 50, went extinct, the region would still be gaining 90 new species — a biodiversity bounty. If they can adapt and flourish there, then evolution is promoting their success. If they outcompete the natives, extinction is doing its job.

There is no return to a pre-human Eden; the goals of species conservation have to be aligned with the acceptance that large numbers of animals will go extinct. Thirty to 40 percent of species may be threatened with extinction in the near future, and their loss may be inevitable. But both the planet and humanity can probably survive or even thrive in a world with fewer species. We don't depend on polar bears for our survival, and even if their eradication has a domino effect that eventually affects us, we will find a way to adapt. The species that we rely on for food and shelter are a tiny proportion of total biodiversity, and most humans live in — and rely on — areas of only moderate biodiversity, not the Amazon or the Congo Basin.

Developed human societies can exist and function in harmony with diverse natural communities, even if those communities are less diverse than they were before humanity. For instance, there is almost no original forest in the eastern United States. Nearly every square inch was clear-cut for timber by the turn of the 20th century. The verdant wilderness we see now in the Catskills, Shenandoah and the Great Smoky Mountains has all grown back in the past 100 years or so, with very few extinctions or permanent losses of biodiversity (14 total east of the Mississippi River, counting species recorded in history that are now apparently extinct), even as the population of our country has quadrupled. Japan is one of the most densely populated and densely forested nations in the world. A model like that can serve a large portion of the planet, while letting humanity grow and shape its own future.

If climate change and extinction present problems, the problems stem from the drastic effects they will have on us. A billion climate refugees, widespread famines, collapsed global industries, and the pain and suffering of our kin demand attention to ecology and imbue conservation with a moral imperative. A global temperature increase of two degrees Celsius will supposedly raise seas by 0.2 to 0.4 meters, with no effect on vast segments of the continents and most terrestrial biodiversity. But this is enough to flood most coastal cities, and that matters.

The solution is simple: moderation. While we should feel no remorse about altering our environment, there is no need to clear-cut forests for McMansions on 15-acre plots of crabgrass-blanketed land. We should save whatever species and habitats can be easily rescued (once-endangered creatures such as bald eagles and peregrine falcons now flourish), refrain from polluting waterways, limit consumption of fossil fuels and rely more on low-impact renewable-energy sources.

We should do this to create a stable, equitable future for the coming billions of people, not for the vanishing northern river shark. Conservation is needed for ourselves and only ourselves. All those future people deserve a happy, safe life on an ecologically robust planet, regardless of the state of the natural world compared with its pre-human condition. We cannot thrive without crops or pollinators, or along coastlines as sea levels rise and as storms and flooding intensify.

Yet that robust planet will still erase huge swaths of animal and plant life. Even if we live as sustainably as we can, many creatures will die off, and alien species will disrupt formerly "pristine" native ecosystems. The sixth extinction is ongoing and inevitable — and Earth's long-term recovery is guaranteed by history (though the process will be slow). Invasion and extinction are the regenerative and rejuvenating mechanisms of evolution, the engines of biodiversity.

If this means fewer dazzling species, fewer unspoiled forests, less untamed wilderness, so be it. They will return in time. The Tree of Life will continue branching, even if we prune it back. The question is: How will we live in the meantime?

FORMAT-CODED:

Near midnight, during an expedition to southwestern Ecuador in December 2013, I spotted a small green frog asleep on a leaf, near a stream by the side of the road. It was Atelopus balios , the Rio Pescado stubfoot toad. Although a lone male had been spotted in 2011, no populations had been found since 1995, and it was thought to be extinct. **But here it was, raised from the dead like Lazarus.** My colleagues and I found several more that night, males and females, and shipped them to an amphibian ark in Quito, where they are now breeding safely in captivity. **But they will go extinct one day, and the world will be none the poorer for it.** Eventually, they will be replaced by a dozen or a hundred new species that evolve later.

Mass extinctions periodically wipe out up to 95 percent of all species in one fell swoop; these come every 50 million to 100 million years, and scientists agree that we are now in the middle of the sixth such extinction, this one caused primarily by humans and our effects on animal habitats. It is an "immense and hidden" tragedy to see creatures pushed out of existence by humans, lamented the Harvard entomologist E.O. Wilson, who coined the term "biodiversity" in 1985. A joint paper by several prominent researchers published by the National Academy of Sciences called it a "biological annihilation." Pope Francis imbues the biodiversity crisis with a moral imperative ("Each creature has its own purpose," he said in 2015), and biologists often cite an ecological one (we must avert "a dramatic decay of biodiversity and the subsequent loss of ecosystem services," several wrote in a paper for Science Advances). "What is Conservation Biology?," a foundational text for the field, written by Michael Soulé of the University of California at Santa Cruz, says, "Diversity of organisms is good ... the untimely extinction of populations and species is bad ... [and] biotic diversity has intrinsic value." In her book "The Sixth Extinction ," journalist Elizabeth Kolbert captures the panic all this has induced: "Such is the pain the loss of a single species causes that we're willing to perform ultrasounds on rhinos and handjobs on crows."

But the impulse to conserve for conservation's sake has taken on an unthinking, unsupported, unnecessary urgency. Extinction is the engine of evolution, the mechanism by which natural selection prunes the poorly adapted and allows the hardiest to flourish. Species constantly go extinct, and every species that is alive today will one day follow suit. There is no such thing as an "endangered species," except for all species. The only reason we should conserve biodiversity is for ourselves, to create a stable future for human beings. Yes, we have altered the environment and, in doing so, hurt other species. This seems artificial because we, unlike other life forms, use sentience and agriculture and industry. **But we are**

a part of the biosphere just like every other creature, and our actions are just as volitional, their consequences just as natural. Conserving a species we have helped to kill off, but on which we are not directly dependent, serves to discharge our own guilt, but little else.

Climate scientists worry about how we've altered our planet, and they have good reasons for apprehension: Will we be able to feed ourselves? Will our water supplies dry up? Will our homes wash away? But unlike those concerns, extinction does not carry moral significance, even when we have caused it. And unless we somehow destroy every living cell on Earth, the sixth extinction will be followed by a recovery, and later a seventh extinction, and so on.

Yet we are obsessed with reviving the status quo ante. The Paris Accords aim to hold the temperature to under two degrees Celsius above preindustrial levels, even though the temperature has been at least eight degrees Celsius warmer within the past 65 million years. Twenty-one thousand years ago, Boston was under an ice sheet a kilometer thick. We are near all-time lows for temperature and sea level ; *whatever effort we make to maintain the current climate will eventually be overrun by the inexorable forces of space and geology. Our concern, in other words, should not be protecting the animal kingdom, which will be just fine. Within a few million years of the asteroid that killed the dinosaurs, the post-apocalyptic void had been filled by an explosion of diversity — modern mammals, birds and amphibians of all shapes and sizes.*

This is how evolution proceeds: through extinction. The inevitability of death is the only constant in life, and 99.9 percent of all species that have ever lived, as many as 50 billion, have already gone extinct. In 50 million years, Europe will collide with Africa and form a new supercontinent, destroying species (think of birds, fish and anything vulnerable to invasive life forms from another landmass) by irrevocably altering their habitats. Extinctions of individual species, entire lineages and even complete ecosystems are common occurrences in the history of life. The world is no better or worse for the absence of saber-toothed tigers and dodo birds and our Neanderthal cousins, who died off as Homo sapiens evolved. (According to some studies, it's not even clear that biodiversity is suffering. The authors of another recent National Academy of Sciences paper point out that species richness has shown no net decline among plants over 100 years across 16,000 sites examined around the world.)

Conserving biodiversity should not be an end in itself; diversity can even be hazardous to human health. Infectious diseases are most prevalent and virulent in the most diverse tropical areas. Nobody donates to campaigns to save HIV, Ebola, malaria, dengue and yellow fever, but these are key components of microbial biodiversity, as unique as pandas, elephants and orangutans, all of which are ostensibly endangered thanks to human interference.

Humans should feel less shame about molding their environment to suit their survival needs. When beavers make a dam, they cause the local extinction of numerous riverine species that cannot survive in the new lake. But that new lake supports a set of species that is just as diverse. Studies have shown that when humans introduce invasive plant species, native diversity sometimes suffers, but productivity — the cycling of nutrients through the ecosystem — frequently increases. Invasives can bring other benefits, too: Plants such as the Phragmites reed have been shown to perform better at reducing coastal erosion and storing carbon than native vegetation in some areas, like the Chesapeake.

And if biodiversity is the goal of extinction fearmongers, how do they regard South Florida, where about 140 new reptile species accidentally introduced by the wildlife trade are now breeding successfully? No extinctions of native species have been recorded, and, at least anecdotally, most natives are still thriving. The ones that are endangered, such as gopher tortoises and indigo snakes , are threatened mostly by habitat destruction. Even if all the native reptiles in the Everglades, about 50, went extinct, the region would still be gaining 90 new species — a biodiversity bounty. If they can adapt and flourish there, then evolution is promoting their success. If they outcompete the natives, extinction is doing its job.

There is no return to a pre-human Eden; the goals of species conservation have to be aligned with the acceptance that large numbers of animals will go extinct.

Thirty to 40 percent of species may be threatened with extinction in the near future, and their loss may be inevitable. But both the planet and humanity can probably survive or even thrive in a world with fewer species. We don't depend on polar bears for our survival, and even if their eradication has a domino effect that eventually affects us, we will find a way to adapt. The species that we rely on for food and shelter are a tiny proportion of total biodiversity, and most humans live in — and rely on — areas of only moderate biodiversity, not the Amazon or the Congo Basin.

Developed human societies can exist and function in harmony with diverse natural communities, even if those communities are less diverse than they were before humanity. For instance, there is almost no original forest in the eastern United States. Nearly every square inch was clear-cut for timber by the turn of the 20th century. The verdant wilderness we see now in the Catskills, Shenandoah and the Great Smoky Mountains has all grown back in the past 100 years or so, with very few extinctions or permanent losses of biodiversity (14 total east of the Mississippi River, counting species recorded in history that are now apparently extinct), even as the population of our country has quadrupled. Japan is one of the most densely populated and densely forested nations in the world. A model like that can serve a large portion of the planet, while letting humanity grow and shape its own future.

If climate change and extinction present problems, the problems stem from the drastic effects they will have on us. A billion climate refugees, widespread famines, collapsed global industries, and the pain and suffering of our kin demand attention to ecology and imbue conservation with a moral imperative. A global temperature increase of two degrees Celsius will supposedly raise seas by 0.2 to 0.4 meters, with no effect on vast segments of the continents and most terrestrial biodiversity. **But this is enough to flood most coastal cities, and that matters.**

The solution is simple: moderation. While we should feel no remorse about altering our environment, there is no need to clear-cut forests for McMansions on 15-acre plots of crabgrass-blanketed land. We should save whatever species and habitats can be easily rescued (once-endangered creatures such as bald eagles and peregrine falcons now flourish), refrain from polluting waterways, limit consumption of fossil fuels and rely more on low-impact renewable-energy sources.

We should do this to create a stable, equitable future for the coming billions of people, not for the vanishing northern river shark. Conservation is needed for ourselves and only ourselves. All those future people deserve a happy, safe life on an ecologically robust planet, regardless of the state of the natural world compared with its pre-human condition. We cannot thrive without crops or pollinators, or along coastlines as sea levels rise and as storms and flooding intensify.

Yet that robust planet will still erase huge swaths of animal and plant life. *Even if we live as sustainably as we can, many creatures will die off, and alien species will disrupt formerly "pristine" native ecosystems. The sixth extinction is ongoing and inevitable – and Earth's long-term recovery is guaranteed by history (though the process will be slow). Invasion and extinction are the regenerative and rejuvenating mechanisms of evolution, the engines of biodiversity.*

If this means fewer dazzling species, fewer unspoiled forests, less untamed wilderness, so be it. They will return in time. The Tree of Life will continue branching, even if we prune it back. **The question is: How will we live in the meantime?**

ABT REWRITE:

Not worth it.

COMMENTARY:

This was written by a young professor. It's such a mess I'm not bothering with the rewrite. His basic argument was that extinction doesn't matter. Or at least that's the message the conservation biology thought he was conveying, which enraged them.

But the author on his website said he was misunderstood and ended up posting a statement of clarification that was just as long and just as garbled. The net result was a case study in poor communication.

What was the source of all the confusion? Just look at the narrative structure revealed by the format-coding. There are at least 8 statements of contradiction, and probably more. It's a textbook example of DHY structure.

The only question worth asking is why in the world the Washington Post felt this was worth publishing and, didn't they have an editor look at it?

II. EXAMPLES OF STRONG NARRATIVE STRUCTURE

1) AGELESS ABT: Nursery Rhymes

Could there be a much simpler starting point? Most nursery rhymes fit the ABT mold. Here's five of the more popular ones. I've added the ABT words in parentheses to help reveal the structure.

Mary had a little lamb, it's fleece was white as snow.
(AND) everywhere that Mary went, the lamb was sure to go.
(AND) It followed her to school one day,
BUT that was against the rules.
(THEREFORE) it made the children laugh and play
to see a lamb at school.

Rock-a-bye, baby, in the tree top
(AND) When the wind blows the cradle will rock
(BUT) When the bough breaks the cradle will fall
(THEREFORE) Down will come baby, cradle and all

All around the mulberry bush,
The monkey chased the weasel.
(BUT) The monkey stopped to pull up his sock,

(THEREFORE) Pop! goes the weasel.

Peter, Peter pumpkin eater, had a wife,
BUT couldn't keep her.
*(THEREFORE) He put her in a pumpkin shell and there he kept her
very well.*

Little Miss Muffet
Sat on a tuffet,
Eating her curds and whey;
(BUT) Along came a spider[2]
Who sat down beside her
And (THEREFORE) frightened Miss Muffet away.

COMMENTARY:

Over and over again, the same basic pattern — set up, twist, consequence. It's eternal, and you were raised on it. Note that each one ends with an action that is the consequence of what happened.

Also think about how old these little ditties are. Some have been handed down for hundreds of years, retaining the same basic story over the ages. That is what hitting the ideal ABT form does — it retains fidelity.

2) PERFECT ABT : The Gettysburg Address

ORIGINAL:

Four score and seven years ago our fathers brought forth on this continent, a new nation, conceived in Liberty, and dedicated to the proposition that all men are created equal.

Now we are engaged in a great civil war, testing whether that nation, or any nation so conceived and so dedicated, can long endure. We are met on a great battle-field of that war. We have come to dedicate a portion of that field, as a final resting place for those who here gave their lives that that nation might live. It is altogether fitting and proper that we should do this.

But, in a larger sense, we can not dedicate—we can not consecrate—we can not hallow—this ground. The brave men, living and dead, who struggled here, have consecrated it, far above our poor power to add or detract. The world will little note, nor long remember what we say here, but it can never forget what they did here. It is for us the living, rather, to be dedicated here to the unfinished work which they who fought here have thus far so nobly advanced. It is rather for us to be here dedicated to the great task remaining before us—that from these honored dead we take increased devotion to that cause for which they gave the last full measure of devotion—that we here highly resolve that these dead shall not have died in vain—that this nation, under God, shall have a new birth of freedom—and that government of the people, by the people, for the people, shall not perish from the earth.

FORMAT-CODED:

Four score and seven years ago our fathers brought forth on this continent, a new nation, conceived in Liberty, and dedicated to the proposition that all men are created equal.

Now we are engaged in a great civil war, testing whether that nation, or any nation so conceived and so dedicated, can long endure. We are met on a great battle-field of that war. *(THEREFORE) We have come to dedicate a portion of that field, as a final resting place for those who here gave their lives that that* *nation might live. It is altogether fitting and proper that we should do this.*

But, in a larger sense, we can not dedicate—we can not consecrate—we can not hallow—this ground. The brave men, living and dead, who struggled here, have consecrated it, far above our poor power to add or detract. The world will little note, nor long remember what we say here, but it can never forget what they did here. *(THEREFORE) It is for us the living, rather, to be dedicated here to the unfinished work which they who fought here have thus far so nobly advanced. It is rather for us to be here dedicated to the great task remaining before us – that from these honored dead we take increased devotion to that cause for which they gave the last full measure of devotion – that we here highly resolve that these dead shall not have died in vain – that this nation, under God, shall have a new birth of freedom – and that government of the people, by the people, for the people, shall not perish from the earth.*

THE ABT REWRITE:

No, I'm not about to rewrite the Gettysburg Address. Sheesh. It's a masterpiece of ABT form.

3) PERFECT ABT OPENING: Martin Luther King, Jr. "I Have A Dream" speech

This is only the opening two paragraphs of the legendary speech.

ORIGINAL:

I am happy to join with you today in what will go down in history as the greatest demonstration for freedom in the history of our nation.

Five score years ago, a great American, in whose symbolic shadow we stand today, signed the Emancipation Proclamation. This momentous decree came as a great beacon light of hope to millions of Negro slaves who had been seared in the flames of withering injustice. It came as a joyous daybreak to end the long night of captivity.

But one hundred years later, the Negro still is not free. One hundred years later, the life of the Negro is still sadly crippled by the manacles of segregation and the chains of discrimination. One hundred years later, the Negro lives on a lonely island of poverty in the midst of a vast ocean of material prosperity. One hundred years later, the Negro is still languished in the corners of American society and finds himself in exile in his own land. So we have come here today to dramatize an shameful condition.

FORMAT-CODED:

I am happy to join with you today in what will go down in history as the greatest demonstration for freedom in the history of our nation.

Five score years ago, a great American, in whose symbolic shadow we stand today, signed the Emancipation Proclamation. This momentous decree came as a great beacon light of hope to millions of Negro slaves who had been seared in the flames of withering injustice. It came as a joyous daybreak to end the long night of captivity.

But one hundred years later, the Negro still is not free. One hundred years later, the life of the Negro is still sadly crippled by the manacles of segregation and the chains of

discrimination. One hundred years later, the Negro lives on a lonely island of poverty in the midst of a vast ocean of material prosperity. One hundred years later, the Negro is still languished in the corners of American society and finds himself in exile in his own land. *So we have come here today to dramatize a shameful condition.*

COMMENTARY:

This is another piece of text that needs no alteration. It's only the first 10.6% of the entire speech, but look what it provides — the synopsis statement right at the outset of why we are here. The rest of the speech was just the longer ABT version of this — "we were made a promise, BUT it has not yet been fulfilled, THEREFORE our work is not finished."

4) AN ABT OF ABT's: Oprah Winfrey's 2018 Golden Globes Speech

ORIGINAL:

Thank you, Reese. In 1964, I was a little girl sitting on the linoleum floor of my mother's house in Milwaukee watching Anne Bancroft present the Oscar for best actor at the 36th Academy Awards. She opened the envelope and said five words that literally made history:" The winner is Sidney Poitier." Up to the stage came the most elegant man I ever remembered. His tie was white, his skin was black — and he was being celebrated. I'd never seen a black man being celebrated like that. (BUT) I tried many, many times to explain what a moment like that means to a little girl, a kid watching from the cheap seats as my mom came through the door bone tired from cleaning other people's houses. But (THEREFORE) all I can do is quote and say that the explanation is in Sidney's performance in Lilies of the Field: "Amen, amen, amen, amen."

In 1982, Sidney received the Cecil B. DeMille award right here at the Golden Globes and it is not lost on me that at this moment, there are some little girls watching as I become the first black woman to be given this same award. It is an honor — it is an honor and it is a privilege to share the evening with all of them and also with the incredible men and women who have inspired me, who challenged me, who sustained me and made my journey to this stage possible. Dennis Swanson who took a chance on me for A.M. Chicago. Saw me on the show and said to Steven Spielberg, she's Sophia in 'The Color Purple.' Gayle who's been a friend and Stedman who's been my rock.

I want to thank the Hollywood Foreign Press Association. We know the press is under siege these days. We also know it's the insatiable dedication to uncovering the absolute truth that keeps us from turning a blind eye to corruption and to injustice. To — to tyrants and victims, and secrets and lies. I want to say that I value the press more than ever before as we try to navigate these complicated times, which brings me to this: what I know for sure is that speaking your truth is the most powerful tool we all have. And I'm especially proud and inspired by all the women who have felt strong enough and empowered enough to speak up and share their personal stories. Each of us in this room are celebrated because of the stories that we tell, and this year we became the story.

But it's not just a story affecting the entertainment industry. It's one that transcends any culture, geography, race, religion, politics, or workplace. So I want tonight to express gratitude to all the women who have endured years of abuse and assault because they, like my mother, had children to feed and bills to pay and dreams to pursue. They're the women whose names we'll never know. They are domestic workers and farm workers. They are working in factories and they work in restaurants and they're in academia, engineering, medicine, and science. They're part of the world of tech and politics and business. They're our athletes in the Olympics and they're our soldiers in the military.

And there's someone else, Recy Taylor, a name I know and I think you should know, too. In 1944, Recy Taylor was a young wife and mother walking home from a church service she'd attended in Abbeville, Alabama, when she was abducted by six armed white men, raped, and left blindfolded by the side of the road coming home from church. They threatened to kill her if she ever told anyone, but her story was reported to the NAACP where a young worker by the name of Rosa Parks became the lead investigator on her case and together they sought justice. But justice wasn't an option in the era of Jim Crow. The men who tried to destroy her were never persecuted. Recy Taylor died ten days ago, just shy of her 98th birthday. She lived as we all have lived, too many years in a culture broken by brutally powerful men. For too long, women have not been heard or believed if they dare speak the truth to the power of those men.But their time is up. Their time is up.

Their time is up. And I just hope—I just hope that (THEREFORE) Recy Taylor died knowing that her truth, like the truth of so many other women who were tormented in those years, and even now tormented, goes marching on. It was somewhere in Rosa Parks' heart almost 11 years later, when she made the decision to stay seated on that bus in Montgomery, and it's here with every woman who chooses to say, "Me too." And every man—every man who chooses to listen.

In my career, what I've always tried my best to do, whether on television or through film, is to say something about how men and women really behave. To say how we experience shame, how we love and how we rage, how we fail, how we retreat, persevere, and how we overcome. I've interviewed and portrayed people who've withstood some of the ugliest things life can throw at you, but the one quality all of them seem to share is an ability to maintain hope for a brighter morning, even during our darkest nights. So I want all the girls watching here, now, to know that a new day is on the horizon! And when that new day finally dawns, it will be because of a lot of magnificent women, many of whom are right here in this room tonight, and some pretty phenomenal men, fighting hard to make sure that they become the leaders who take us to the time when nobody ever has to say 'Me too' again."

FORMAT-CODED:

Thank you, Reese. In 1964, I was a little girl sitting on the linoleum floor of my mother's house in Milwaukee watching Anne Bancroft present the Oscar for best actor at the 36th Academy Awards. She opened the envelope and said five words that literally made history:" The winner is Sidney Poitier." Up to the stage came the most elegant man I ever remembered. His tie was white, his skin was black — and he was being celebrated. I'd never seen a black man being celebrated like that. **(BUT) I tried many, many times to explain what a moment like that means to a little girl, a kid watching from the cheap seats as my mom came through the door bone tired from cleaning other people's houses.** *But (THEREFORE) all I can do is quote and say that the explanation is in Sidney's performance in Lilies of the Field: "Amen, amen, amen, amen."*

In 1982, Sidney received the Cecil B. DeMille award right here at the Golden Globes and it is not lost on me that at this moment, there are some little girls watching as I become the first black woman to be given this same award. It is an honor — it is an honor and it is a privilege to share the evening with all of them and also with the incredible men and women who have inspired me, who challenged me, who sustained me and made my journey to this stage possible. Dennis Swanson who took a chance on me for A.M. Chicago. Saw me on the show and said to Steven Spielberg, she's Sophia in 'The Color Purple.' Gayle who's been a friend and Stedman who's been my rock.

I want to thank the Hollywood Foreign Press Association. **We know the press is under siege these days.** We also know it's the insatiable dedication to uncovering the absolute truth that keeps us from turning a blind eye to corruption and to injustice. To — to tyrants and victims, and secrets and lies. I want to say that I value the press more than ever before as we try to navigate these complicated times, which brings me to this: what I know for sure is that speaking your truth is the most powerful tool we all have. And I'm especially proud and inspired by all the women who have felt strong enough and empowered enough to speak up and share their personal stories. Each of us in this room are celebrated because of the stories that we tell, and this year we became the story.

But it's not just a story affecting the entertainment industry. It's one that transcends any culture, geography, race, religion, politics, or workplace. *So I want tonight to express gratitude to all the women who have endured years of abuse and assault because they, like my mother, had children to feed and bills to pay and dreams to pursue. They're the women whose names we'll never know. They are domestic workers and farm workers. They are working in factories and they work in restaurants and they're in academia, engineering, medicine, and science. They're part of the world of tech and politics and business. They're our athletes in the Olympics and they're our soldiers in the military.*

And there's someone else, Recy Taylor, a name I know and I think you should know, too. In 1944, Recy Taylor was a young wife and mother walking home from a church service she'd attended in Abbeville, Alabama, when she was abducted by six armed white men, raped, and left blindfolded by the side of the road coming home from church. They threatened to kill her if she ever told anyone, but her story was reported to the NAACP where a young worker by the name of Rosa Parks became the lead investigator on her case and together they sought justice. But justice wasn't an option in the era of Jim Crow. The men who tried to destroy her were never persecuted. Recy Taylor died ten days ago, just shy of her 98th birthday. She lived as we all have lived, too many years in a culture broken by brutally powerful men. For too long, women have not been heard or believed if they dare speak the truth to the power of those men. **But their time is up. Their time is up.**

Their time is up. *And I just hope—I just hope that (THEREFORE) Recy Taylor died knowing that her truth, like the truth of so many other women who were tormented in those years, and even now tormented, goes marching on.* It was somewhere in Rosa Parks' heart almost 11 years later, when she made the decision to stay seated on that bus in Montgomery, and it's here with every woman who chooses to say, "Me too." And every man—every man who chooses to listen.

In my career, what I've always tried my best to do, whether on television or through film, is to say something about how men and women really behave. To say how we experience shame, how we love and how we rage, how we fail, how we retreat, persevere, and how we overcome. I've interviewed and portrayed people who've withstood some of the ugliest things life can throw at you, **but the one quality all of them seem to share is an ability to maintain hope for a brighter morning,**

even during our darkest nights. *So I want all the girls watching here, now, to know that a new day is on the horizon! And when that new day finally dawns, it will be because of a lot of magnificent women, many of whom are right here in this room tonight, and some pretty phenomenal men, fighting hard to make sure that they become the leaders who take us to the time when nobody ever has to say 'Me too' again."*

COMMENTARY:

This was the powerful speech that the New York Times called, "A story about stories." She shows such a depth of narrative intuition, and given her enormous background in the entertainment industry, I have said all along she is the Democrat mostly likely to be able to handle The Toad if she were ever to want to take him on.

5) ABT OPENING: Richard Nixon's First Inauguration Speech

This may be my favorite ABT of all time.

ORIGINAL:

Senator Dirksen, Mr. Chief Justice, Mr. Vice President, President Johnson, Vice President Humphrey, my fellow Americans--and my fellow citizens of the world community:

I ask you to share with me today the majesty of this moment. In the orderly transfer of power, we celebrate the unity that keeps us free.

Each moment in history is a fleeting time, precious and

unique. But some stand out as moments of beginning, in which courses are set that shape decades or centuries.

This can be such a moment.

FORMAT-CODED:

Senator Dirksen, Mr. Chief Justice, Mr. Vice President, President Johnson, Vice President Humphrey, my fellow Americans--and my fellow citizens of the world community:

I ask you to share with me today the majesty of this moment. In the orderly transfer of power, we celebrate the unity that keeps us free.

Each moment in history is a fleeting time, precious and unique. **But some stand out as moments of beginning, in which courses are set that shape decades or centuries.**

This can be such a moment.

COMMENTARY:

Why do I love this ABT so much? It's Richard Nixon — the guy who got rejected in his 1960 bid for the presidency, but finally got his big shot in 1968. Has there ever been any more ominous, portentous and foreshadowing message from a president? He definitely shaped decades. It remains to be seen if he'll be remembered for centuries.

6) ABT OPENING: Obama speech to National Academy of Sciences

This is just the opening to a speech by President Barack Obama at the National Academy of Sciences in 2013.

ORIGINAL:

Thank you very much. Thank you so much. (Applause.) Please, everybody have a seat.

Well, it's good to be back. Good morning, everybody, and thank you, Dr. Cicerone, for the kind introduction and the great work that you do. The good doctor was reminding me that the first time I came here, apparently joking, I warned him and John Holdren not to age too much in their jobs. And it turns out I'm the guy who's aged. (Laughter.) They look great.

But, as always, it's an honor to join our nation's preeminent scholars, including my own Science Advisor, John Holdren, to celebrate the 150th anniversary of the National Academy of Sciences. And since I did not do well enough in chemistry or physics to impress you much on those topics, let me instead tell a story.

One hundred and fifty years ago, the nation, as all of you know, was in the midst of the Civil War, and the Union had recently suffered a devastating defeat at Fredericksburg. The road ahead seemed long and uncertain. Confederate advances in weapons technology cast a dark shadow on the Union.

The previous spring, in the waters outside of Hampton Roads, the ironclad Confederate battleship Virginia had sunk two wooden Union ships and advanced on a third, and this endangered the Union blockade of Virginia and threatening Union forces along the Potomac River. And then, overnight, the USS Monitor, an ironclad herself, arrived and fought the

Virginia to a draw in the world's first battle between iron-sided ships.

There was no victor, but the era of ironclad warfare had begun. And it brought unexpected challenges for President Lincoln and his Navy as they expanded this fleet in early 1863, because aboard their new iron-side battleships, sailors found that the iron siding made the ships' compasses unpredictable, so it skewed navigation, and they were bumping into things and going the wrong way. (Laughter.) So the basic physics of magnetism undermined the usefulness of the ironclad vessels, even as the Confederates were stocking up on them.

And that's where your predecessors came in. Because in March of 1983 -- 1863, rather -- President Lincoln and Congress established the National Academy of Sciences as an independent and nonprofit institution charged with the mission to provide the government with the scientific advice that it needed. And this was advice that was particularly useful in the thick of battle.

FORMAT-CODED:

Thank you very much. Thank you so much. (Applause.) Please, everybody have a seat.

Well, it's good to be back. Good morning, everybody, and thank you, Dr. Cicerone, for the kind introduction and the great work that you do. The good doctor was reminding me that the first time I came here, apparently joking, I warned him and John Holdren not to age too much in their jobs. And it turns out I'm the guy who's aged. (Laughter.) They look great.

But, as always, it's an honor to join our nation's preeminent scholars, including my own Science Advisor, John Holdren, to celebrate the 150th anniversary of the National Academy of Sciences. (BUT) And since I did not do well enough in chemistry or physics to impress you much on those topics, *(THEREFORE) let me instead tell a story.*

One hundred and fifty years ago, the nation, as all of you know, was in the midst of the Civil War, and the Union had recently suffered a devastating defeat at Fredericksburg. The road ahead seemed long and uncertain. Confederate advances in weapons technology cast a dark shadow on the Union.

The previous spring, in the waters outside of Hampton Roads, the ironclad Confederate battleship Virginia had sunk two wooden Union ships and advanced on a third, and this endangered the Union blockade of Virginia and threatening Union forces along the Potomac River. And then, overnight, the USS Monitor, an ironclad herself, arrived and fought the Virginia to a draw in the world's first battle between iron-sided ships.

There was no victor, **but the era of ironclad warfare had begun. And it brought unexpected challenges for President Lincoln and his Navy as they expanded this fleet in early 1863, because aboard their new iron-side battleships, sailors found that the iron siding made the ships' compasses unpredictable, so it skewed navigation, and they were bumping into things and going the wrong way. (Laughter.)** *So the basic physics of magnetism undermined the usefulness of the ironclad vessels, even as the Confederates were stocking up on them.*

And that's where your predecessors came in. Because in March of 1983 -- 1863, rather -- President Lincoln and Congress established the National Academy of Sciences as an independent and nonprofit institution charged with the mission to provide the government with

the scientific advice that it needed. And this was advice that was
particularly useful in the thick of battle.

ABT REWRITE:

None needed

COMMENTARY:

Look at what a nice job Obama did using good narrative structure to get the ball rolling. He used an ABT to segue into, "Let me tell you a story," then his story brought to life his main message.

Interestingly, when Obama was running for re-election in 2012, he was asked, "What was the biggest shortcoming of your first term?" which was the same question George W. Bush had been asked at the start of his second term.

Bush, of course, had answered pretty much "none," but Obama replied, "My failure to tell a story to the American people." The above speech was delivered shortly after his re-election. I wonder if his speechwriters had taken his words to heart and thus opened this speech by launching him right into storytelling mode.

Unfortunately, Obama was okay but never great with narrative (not like Martin Luther King, Jr. who lived and breathed it) and the rest of this speech reflects it. He ended up delivering pretty much of an "And, And, And" speech in which he just listed a ton of great things that science brings us, and eventually concluded by saying basically therefore ... we need more science.

There were more powerful overall ABT's he could have used. He could have talked about "Most countries do this with science, but in the US we do this …" or "Science brings us great things, but here's what happens when it gets curtailed …" or lots of other stronger themes than just the "Do more science!" message he delivered, but that's okay. He was a good communicator, not great.

7) FULL ABT : New York Times editorial on Miss America Pageant

This is an editorial in the New York Times published on December 23, 2017 detailing the debacle that the Miss America Pageant has become.

ORIGINAL:

During the summer nights in Provincetown, Mass., pedestrians and passers-by are treated to a show. As the sun sets, the queens come out. The heels are high; the hair is higher, the makeup expertly applied, turning the performers into amplified versions of Cher, or Barbie, or Lady Gaga, or creatures of their own invention.

They gamely pose for pictures with everyone from kids to straight couples from the suburbs to two-dad families pushing strollers.

The mood is exuberant and joyful. The traditional trappings of femininity are a pose, not a prison; a costume that you can slip in and out of, refashioning it until it suits you.

I thought about the queens of Provincetown, and the exuberance of their pageant, on Thursday. That's when Yashar

Ali of HuffPost broke the news that Sam Haskell, the chief executive of the Miss America Organization, wrote an email laughing along as Lewis Friedman, the televised pageant's head writer, referred to former crown-holders in the crudest, most derogatory, term for a woman's anatomy.

In this correspondence, the former Miss Americas are not winners. Not women. They're not even people; not even bodies. Just body parts.

Then it got worse.

HuffPost also reported that when Mary Ann Mobley, a former Miss America, died in 2014, Mr. Haskell was part of an email chain with the heading "It Should Have Been Kate Shindle." Ms. Shindle, Miss America 1998, has been an outspoken critic of some of the pageant's practices, as well as its decision to pay Mr. Haskell $500,000 when the organization was in debt.

Gretchen Carlson, the former Fox News anchor who was Miss America 1989, was shut out of pageant broadcasts after she refused to publicly criticize Ms. Shindle. Mallory Hagan, who won the Miss America title in 2013, was subject to fat-shaming (an email chain joked that she was "preparing for her new career ... as a blimp in the Macy's Thanksgiving Parade") and comments about her sex life.

In the #MeToo era, as a (highly conflicted) fan of the pageant, I've been bracing myself, waiting for this particular high-heeled shoe to drop. It's not surprising that a contest with objectification baked into its DNA has spawned this kind of talk, and behavior, from the men in charge.

For most of its life, the Miss America Pageant has been an odd hybrid. Born in 1921 as a bathing-beauty competition with the goal of extending Atlantic City's summer season, at first the pageant was, literally, about the use of women's bodies to sell a product — or a place. Even after sections for talent and interviews were added, even after the swimsuit competition was renamed to recognize "lifestyle and fitness" in swimwear, even after the organization swapped prizes of fur coats and screen tests for scholarships, the pageant has struggled to reconcile its search for brains with its obsession with beauty.

Miss America has soldiered on, though, even as it went from being one of the highest-rated broadcasts on television in the 1960s to a target of feminist ire in the 1970s to a relic and a curiosity in the 2000s. ABC stopped airing the contest in 2005. The pageant moved from Atlantic City to Las Vegas, from broadcast network to basic cable. Meanwhile, reality TV was eating its lunch, tempting young women with a bevy of options to win plummier prizes than the organization could offer, while competing pageants promised smaller swimsuits, higher heels, and fewer pesky questions about how to bring about world peace.

A 2014 segment on "Last Week Tonight With John Oliver" detailed how the organization that billed itself as the "largest provider of scholarship assistance to young women in the United States" was, in fact, handing out only a sliver of the $45 million it claimed was available, which didn't help the show's fortunes. Miss A. was on life support.

Mr. Haskell was instrumental in turning things around. He got the pageant back on ABC, hosted by Chris Harrison, dispenser of roses on the network's popular "Bachelor" franchise. Gingerly, Miss America began edging toward modernity.

In 2014, an Indian-American woman won the crown. The deposed Miss America Vanessa Williams got an on-air apology and was welcomed back into the fold. There have been winners with tattoos and piercings, and in 2016, the first contestant who identified as gay (hello, Miss Missouri!) Last year, the organization announced it plans to air the pageant on ABC through 2019.

Then came the bombshell HuffPost report. Ms. Carlson said she was "shocked and deeply saddened by the disgusting statements about women attributed to the leadership" of the Miss America Organization. On Friday, Kate Shindle wrote, "I almost don't have the words to respond to Yashar Ali's revelations about the current leadership of the Miss America Organization," adding, "it makes me physically ill."

Dick Clark Productions severed its relationships with the pageant. Mr. Friedman, the head writer, was fired, and the pageant announced that it was forming a committee and retaining independent legal counsel to investigate. By Friday afternoon, 49 former Miss Americas, including 87-year-old BeBe Shopp Waring, were pushing for more, calling on leadership to resign. Mr. Haskell was suspended on Friday.

It might not be enough. Nothing might be able to remove the stain of so much hateful, crude, sexist talk. It might be that we've seen our last weeping, rhinestone-crowned Miss A. making her way down the Atlantic City walkway.

So what's a pageant fan to do?

Maybe Mr. Haskell's emails hastened the process of a slow and natural death, an extinction by attrition, where eventually the pageant would ditch the swimsuits (as Miss Teen USA did in 2016), acknowledge that nobody, much less a 19-year-old college student, wears evenings gowns and admit — if we're all being honest — that drag queens are doing this better.

Maybe it's time to look to places like "RuPaul's Drag Race" for traditional femininity played as spectacle. There's still joy to be found in the transformation and performance, in watching someone with hair teased high and waist cinched tight competing for a prize. And if that joy comes from RuPaul's bevy of beauties and not the Atlantic City boardwalk?

We're surviving the presidency of a former pageant owner who called one of his beauty queens "Miss Piggy" when she gained weight after her win. Certainly we'll survive that, too.

FORMAT-CODED:

During the summer nights in Provincetown, Mass., pedestrians and passers-by are treated to a show. As the sun sets, the queens come out. The heels are high; the hair is higher, the makeup expertly applied, turning the performers into amplified versions of Cher, or Barbie, or Lady Gaga, or creatures of their own invention.

They gamely pose for pictures with everyone from kids to straight couples from the suburbs to two-dad families pushing strollers.

The mood is exuberant and joyful. The traditional trappings of femininity are a pose, not a prison; a costume that you can slip in and out of, refashioning it until it suits you.

I thought about the queens of Provincetown, and the exuberance of their pageant, on Thursday. (BUT) That's when Yashar Ali of HuffPost broke the news that Sam Haskell, the chief executive of the Miss America Organization, wrote an email laughing along as Lewis Friedman, the televised pageant's head writer, referred to former crown-holders in the crudest, most derogatory, term for a woman's anatomy.

In this correspondence, the former Miss Americas are not

winners. Not women. They're not even people; not even bodies. Just body parts.

(BUT) Then it got worse.

HuffPost also reported that when Mary Ann Mobley, a former Miss America, died in 2014, Mr. Haskell was part of an email chain with the heading "It Should Have Been Kate Shindle." Ms. Shindle, Miss America 1998, has been an outspoken critic of some of the pageant's practices, as well as its decision to pay Mr. Haskell $500,000 when the organization was in debt.

Gretchen Carlson, the former Fox News anchor who was Miss America 1989, was shut out of pageant broadcasts after she refused to publicly criticize Ms. Shindle. Mallory Hagan, who won the Miss America title in 2013, was subject to fat-shaming (an email chain joked that she was "preparing for her new career ... as a blimp in the Macy's Thanksgiving Parade") and comments about her sex life.

In the #MeToo era, as a (highly conflicted) fan of the pageant, I've been bracing myself, waiting for this particular high-heeled shoe to drop. It's not surprising that a contest with objectification baked into its DNA has spawned this kind of talk, and behavior, from the men in charge.

For most of its life, the Miss America Pageant has been an odd hybrid. Born in 1921 as a bathing-beauty competition with the goal of extending Atlantic City's summer season, at first the pageant was, literally, about the use of women's bodies to sell a product — or a place. (BUT) Even after sections for talent and interviews were added, even after the swimsuit competition was renamed to recognize "lifestyle and fitness" in swimwear, even after the organization swapped prizes of fur coats and screen tests for scholarships, the pageant has struggled to reconcile its search for brains with its obsession with beauty.

Miss America has soldiered on, though, even as it went from being one of the highest-rated broadcasts on television in the 1960s to a target of feminist ire in the 1970s to a relic and a curiosity in the 2000s. ABC stopped airing the contest in 2005. The pageant moved from Atlantic City to Las Vegas, from broadcast network to basic cable. (BUT) Meanwhile, reality TV was eating its lunch, tempting young women with a bevy of options to win plummier prizes than the organization could offer, while competing pageants promised smaller swimsuits, higher heels, and fewer pesky questions about how to bring about world peace.

A 2014 segment on "Last Week Tonight With John Oliver" detailed how the organization that billed itself as the "largest provider of scholarship assistance to young women in the United States" (BUT) was, in fact, handing out only a sliver of the $45 million it claimed was available, which didn't help the show's fortunes. Miss A. was on life support.

Mr. Haskell was instrumental in turning things around. He got the pageant back on ABC, hosted by Chris Harrison, dispenser of roses on the network's popular "Bachelor" franchise. Gingerly, Miss America began edging toward modernity.

In 2014, an Indian-American woman won the crown. The deposed Miss America Vanessa Williams got an on-air apology and was welcomed back into the fold. There have been winners with tattoos and piercings, and in 2016, the first contestant who identified as gay (hello, Miss Missouri!) Last year, the organization announced it plans to air the pageant on ABC through 2019.

(BUT) Then came the bombshell HuffPost report. Ms.

Carlson said she was "shocked and deeply saddened by the disgusting statements about women attributed to the leadership" of the Miss America Organization. On Friday, Kate Shindle wrote, "I almost don't have the words to respond to Yashar Ali's revelations about the current leadership of the Miss America Organization," adding, "it makes me physically ill."

Dick Clark Productions severed its relationships with the pageant. *(THEREFORE) Mr. Friedman, the head writer, was fired, and the pageant announced that it was forming a committee and retaining independent legal counsel to investigate. By Friday afternoon, 49 former Miss Americas, including 87-year-old BeBe Shopp Waring, were pushing for more, calling on leadership to resign. Mr. Haskell was suspended on Friday.*

(BUT) It might not be enough. Nothing might be able to remove the stain of so much hateful, crude, sexist talk. It might be that we've seen our last weeping, rhinestone-crowned Miss A. making her way down the Atlantic City walkway.

(THEREFORE) So what's a pageant fan to do?

Maybe Mr. Haskell's emails hastened the process of a slow and natural death, an extinction by attrition, where eventually the pageant would ditch the swimsuits (as Miss Teen USA did in 2016), acknowledge that nobody, much less a 19-year-old college student, wears evening gowns and admit — if we're all being honest — that drag queens are doing this better.

(BUT) Maybe it's time to look to places like "RuPaul's Drag Race" for traditional femininity played as spectacle.

(THEREFORE) There's still joy to be found in the transformation and performance, in watching someone with hair teased high and

waist cinched tight competing for a prize. And if that joy comes from RuPaul's bevy of beauties and not the Atlantic City boardwalk?

We're surviving the presidency of a former pageant owner who called one of his beauty queens "Miss Piggy" when she gained weight after her win. Certainly we'll survive that, too.

COMMENTARY:

This was a classic "journey" in its structure. It follows the form of theater described by the ancient Greeks that I detailed in "Houston, We Have A Narrative" (below is a figure from the book that illustrates it). It has a prologue setting up the problem (the decline of the Miss America Pageant), then sets off on the journey describing the decline that consists of a series of the repeated cycles that can be see with the blue/red combinations.

I've added the "(BUT)" which gives us a series of: but then, but even after, but meanwhile, but was in fact, but then, etc." You can see how he has episodically ratcheted up the tension with each agreement/contradiction pair until finally reaching his overall statement of consequence by saying, "So what's a pageant fan to do?"

The bottom line is that this is a well structured overall journey — posing a problem (the decline), offering up a solution (embrace the parody).

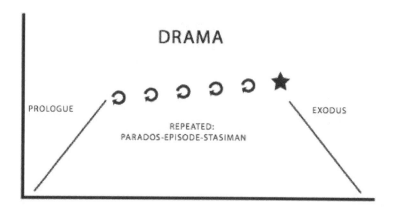

THE BASIC STRUCTURE OF A STORY AS DESCRIBED BY THE ANCIENT GREEKS. This is basic three act structure. The second act is the journey of repeated ABT cycles.

8) ABABT: Science summary of neuroscience research

ORIGINAL:

When a clinical trial of a pharmaceutical fails, participants usually move on by ceasing to take the drug. But it's not that simple for some people who took part in a trial of a bold, experimental treatment for people with severe depression. The BROADEN trial, which implanted metal electrodes deep in the brain in a region called area 25, failed early on to show a statistically significant effect on depression and was halted after just 90 participants were treated. Yet 44 of those patients want to keep their implants. Last month, researchers at a meeting at the National Institutes of Health in Bethesda, Maryland, discussed the ethical issues that such scenarios raise, such as who is responsible for overseeing—and paying for—long-term care when participants want to keep their implants?

FORMAT-CODED:

When a clinical trial of a pharmaceutical fails, participants usually move on by ceasing to take the drug. **But it's not that simple for some people who took part in a trial of a bold, experimental treatment for people with severe depression.** The BROADEN trial, which implanted metal electrodes deep in the brain in a region called area 25, failed early on to show a statistically significant effect on depression and was halted after just 90 participants were treated. **Yet 44 of those patients want to keep their implants.** *Last month, researchers at a meeting at the National Institutes of Health in Bethesda, Maryland, discussed the ethical issues that such scenarios raise, such as who is responsible for overseeing — and paying for — long-term care when participants want to keep their implants?*

COMMENTARY:

Look at the basic structure of this summary — it's ABABT. It presents two overall statements — the general first (AB) which sets up the general, big picture context of the research, followed by the specific project (ABT). This is a common and effective structure — much like the MLK, Jr. "I Have A Dream" speech in which the first paragraph lays out the overall narrative before going into detail with the speech.

9) EPIC ABT: HIPPOLYTA TELLS THE HISTORY OF THE AMAZONS IN "WONDER WOMAN"

This part of the screenplay begins with the directions, "Hippolyta slowly unfolds the large TRIPTYCH, revealing an elaborate PAINTING illustrating the history of the Amazons." It is followed by her narration.

ORIGINAL:

HIPPOLYTA: Long ago, when time was new, and all of history was still a dream... the gods ruled the Earth, Zeus king among them. Zeus created beings over which the gods would rule -- beings born in his image -- fair and good, strong and passionate. Zeus called his creation... man. And mankind was good.

But one grew envious of Zeus' love for mankind -- and sought to corrupt his creation. This was Ares. The God of War. Ares poisoned men's hearts with
jealousy and suspicion, vengeance and rage. He turned them against one another.

And war ravaged the Earth.

So the gods made us, the Amazons,
to influence men's hearts with love and to restore peace to the world.

For a brief time, there was peace, even a unity among the world, as the gods and man fought side-by- side against a great evil.

But it did not last.

Ares refused to give up his hold on mankind. Tightening his grip, he turned them against us.

When Zeus led the gods to our defense, Ares killed them, one-by- one... until only Zeus himself remained.

While Zeus used the last of his power to stop Ares... striking him such a blow, the God of War was forced to retreat. With Zeus' dying breath, he created this island to shield us from the outside world. Somewhere Ares could not find us.

But in the event he did, Zeus left us a weapon, one powerful enough to kill a God... to destroy Ares before he could destroy mankind... and us... with an endless war.

FORMAT-CODED:

HIPPOLYTA: Long ago, when time was new, and all of history was still a dream... the gods ruled the Earth, Zeus king among them. Zeus created beings over which the gods would rule -- beings born in his image -- fair and good, strong and passionate. Zeus called his creation... man. And mankind was good.

But one grew envious of Zeus' love for mankind -- and sought to corrupt his creation. This was Ares. The God of War. Ares poisoned men's hearts with
jealousy and suspicion, vengeance and rage. He turned them against one another.

And war ravaged the Earth.

So the gods made us, the Amazons,
to influence men's hearts with love and to restore peace to the world.

For a brief time, there was peace, even a unity among the world, as the gods and man fought side-by- side against a great evil.

But it did not last.

Ares refused to give up his hold on mankind. Tightening his

grip, he turned them against us.

When Zeus led the gods to our defense, Ares killed them, one-by- one… until only Zeus himself remained.

While Zeus used the last of his power to stop Ares… striking him such a blow, the God of War was forced to retreat. With Zeus' dying breath, he created this island to shield us from the outside world. Somewhere Ares could not find us.

But in the event he did, *Zeus left us a weapon, one powerful enough to kill a God… to destroy Ares before he could destroy mankind… and us… with an endless war.*

COMMENTARY:

You can see with this bit of classic storytelling how the ABT is the primal form. I first heard this narration in a movie theater. As everyone else was engaged in the movie I wanted to speak up — "Is everyone hearing how ABT all if this is?" Yeah, I know — the ushers would have escorted me out, saying, "Sir, please put down your Narrative Spectrum refrigerator magnet and return to just living life instead of analyzing everything for ABT structure." I'm hopeless. Therefore … a final example to close on …

10) POP ABT: Carlie Rae Jepson's "Call Me Maybe"

Come on. Could there be any better anthem for the entire ABT theme? Let's all go back to the summer of 2012 and close out this book by singing along together.

FORMAT-CODED:

I threw a wish in the well
Don't ask me I'll never tell
I looked at you as it fell
And now you're in my way

I trade my soul for a wish
Pennies and dimes for a kiss
I wasn't looking for this
But now you're in my way

Your stare was holding
Ripped jeans
Skin was showing
Hot night
Wind was blowing
Where you think you're going baby?

Hey I just met you
And this is crazy
But here's my number
So call me maybe

It's hard to look right at you baby
But here's my number
So call me maybe

Hey I just met you
And this is crazy
But here's my number
So call me maybe

And all the other boys,
try to chase me,
But here's my number
So call me maybe

COMMENTARY:

One billion Youtube viewers can't be wrong — ABT rules.

ACKNOWLEDGMENTS

In addition to all the folks I've thanked in my previous books this one owes a great deal to the growing crowd of fellow developers of our Story Circles Narrative Training program over the past five years. This includes the core group of Jayde Lovell, Mike Strauss, Liz Foote, Park Howell, Shirley Malcom, Rick Nelson, Steve Case and Cathleen Hapeman. Then, at the broader scale, there are lots more, including but not limited to Larry Perez, Heidi Koontz, Jeffrey Morisette, Katie Dubois, Anna Cummins, Bill Dennison and students, Marcus Eriksen, Chad Nelsen, Ayla Fox, Darcy Gentleman, Jennifer Jacquet, Jeremy Jackson, Nancy Knowlton, Andy Revkin, Peter Griffith, Kevin Kilbride, Bridgette Flanders, Jeff Davis, Sara ElShafie, Vivek Ramaswamy, Matt Brauer, Michael Bart, Lisa Thornhill, Michael Parrella, Greg Tillman, Aaron Huertas, Lucinda Johnson, Mark Brigham, Marcy Rockman, Kurt Fristrup, Mark Skinner, Colin Orians, Alan Thomas, Christie Henry, Brian Palermo, Dorie Barton, Dianna Padilla, Joe Newman, Rod Lamberts, Bec Susan Gil, Jane Muncke, Pete Myers, Tracy Ford, Scott Franklin, Matthew David, John Rael, and Michael Backes. Also thanks to Matthew David for production of the eBook, Dante Cervantes for help with cover design and Adina Yoffie for editing and proofreading (though any mistakes are due to me messing with things after she cleaned it all up). And lastly, to my friends Samantha and Shirley, you two "got" the ABT long before anyone else. You are both visionaries.

27580391R00194

Printed in Great Britain
by Amazon